EURODÉLICES

COLD
APPETIZERS

EURODÉLICES

COLD APPETIZERS

DINE WITH EUROPE'S MASTER CHEFS

KÖNEMANN

Acknowledgements

We would like to thank the following people, restaurants and companies for their valuable contributions to this book:

Ancienne Manufacture Royale, Aixe-sur-Vienne; Baccarat, Paris; Chomette Favor, Grigny; Christofle, Paris; Cristalleries de Saint-Louis, Paris; Grand Marnier, Paris; Groupe Cidelcem, Marne-la-Valée; Haviland, Limoges; Jean-Louis Coquet, Paris; Maître cuisiniers de France, Paris; Les maisons de Cartier, Paris; Philippe Deshoulières, Paris; Porcelaines Bernadaud, Paris; Porcelaine La Farge, Paris; Puiforcat Orfèfre, Paris; Robert Haviland et C. Parlon, Limoges; Société Caviar Petrossian, Paris; Villeroy & Boch, Garges-les-Gonesse; Wedgwood-Dexam International, Coye-la-Forêt.

A special thank you to: Lucien Barcon, Georges Laffon, Clément Lausecker, Michel Pasquet, Jean Pibourdin, Pierre Roche, Jacques Sylvestre, and Pierre Fonteyne.

Skill ratings of the recipes:

★   easy

★★   medium

★★★ difficult

Photos: Studio Lucien Loeb, Maren Detering
Copyright © Fabien Bellhasen and Daniel Rouche
Original title: Eurodélices – Entrées Froides

Copyright © 1998 for the English-language edition:
Könemann Verlagsgesellschaft mbH,
Bonner Str. 126, 50968 Cologne

Translation from German: Tobias Kommerell
English-language editor of this volume: Jana Martin
Coordinator for the English-language edition: Tammi Reichel
Typesetting: Goodfellow & Egan, Cambridge
Series project manager: Bettina Kaufmann
Assistant: Stephan Küffner
Production manager: Detlev Schaper
Assistant: Nicola Leurs
Reproduction: Reproservice Werner Pees, Essen
Printing and binding: Neue Stalling, Oldenburg

Printed in Germany

ISBN 3-8290-1128-8

10 9 8 7 6 5 4 3

Contents

Foreword

The Eurodélices series brings a selection of European haute cuisine right into your kitchen. Almost 100 professional chefs, many of them recipients of multiple awards and distinctions, associated with renowned restaurants in 17 countries throughout Europe, joined forces to create this unique series. Here they divulge their best and their favorite recipes for unsurpassed hot and cold appetizers, fish and meat entrees, desserts, and pastry specialties.

The series as a whole, consisting of six volumes with over 1,900 pages, is not only an essential collection for gourmet cooks, but also a fascinating document of European culture that goes far beyond short-lived culinary trends. In a fascinating way, Eurodélices explores the common roots of the different "arts of cooking" that have developed in various geographic locations, as well as their abundant variety.

For eating is much more than the fulfillment of a basic bodily need; cooking is often elevated to the level of an art, especially in association with parties and celebrations of all kinds, in private life and in the public sphere. Young couples plan their futures over a special dinner at an elegant restaurant, partners gather at table to launch new business ventures, heads of state are wined and dined. Every conceivable celebration involves food, from weddings to funerals, from intimacies shared over coffee and cake to Sunday dinners to Passover and Thanksgiving feasts.

We often have our first contact with the cultures of other lands, whether nearby or across an ocean, through their food. Precisely because the various contributing chefs are rooted in their distinct traditions, some flavors and combinations will be new to North American readers, and occasionally ingredients are called for that may be unfamiliar or even difficult to locate. The texts accompanying each recipe help elucidate and, wherever possible, suggest substitutes for ingredients that are not readily available in North America. A glossary is also included to explain terms that may not be obvious, listing some ingredients.

Because precision is often crucial to the success of recipes of this caliber, a few words regarding measurements and conversions are in order. In Europe, it is customary to use metric units of liquid volume or weight, that is, milliliters or grams. Every household has a kitchen scale and solid ingredients are weighed, rather than measured by volume. Converting milliliters to fluid cups and grams to ounces is straightforward, if not always neat. More problematic are ingredients given in grams that North Americans measure by volume, in tablespoons and cups. Throughout the Eurodélices series, the original metric measurement follows the North American equivalent. The conversions are painstakingly accurate up to 100 ml and 100 g (which necessitates some awkward-looking amounts). Thereafter, they are more neatly, and thus less accurately, rounded off. As with all recipes, measurements are approximate for many ingredients, and a wide variety of factors ranging from temperature and humidity to accuracy of kitchen implements to the way food is sold will affect the amount actually used. If the reader wants to recreate the recipes as given, however, the use of a kitchen scale is strongly recommended.

The unique collection of around 750 recipes contained in Eurodélices aims to excite its readers' curiosity. Classic dishes, which have been enjoyed for generations and thus form the foundations of modern cookery, are liberally presented. But there are also new and surprising pleasures, familiar foods prepared in novel ways, as well as culinary delights composed of ingredients from far away places that we experience for the first time. Allow yourself to be inspired by the European master chefs to try and, perhaps, try again.

Corn Ravioli

Preparation time: *1 hour*
Cooking time: *3 minutes*
Difficulty: ✲✲

Serves four

For the corn mousse:
1 cup / 250 g corn (boiled)
¹/₄ cup / 75 ml cream
1 sheet of gelatin
olive oil

For the dough:
2 eggs
⁷/₈ cup / 200 g flour
1 tsp olive oil

For the vanilla oil:
6 vanilla beans
¹/₄ cup / 50 ml sunflower oil

There are many conflicting theories about the provenance of corn. In fact, it originates from Latin America, where it was both the primary food and one of the sacred plants of pre-Columbian cultures. The Aztecs and Incas revered the corn plant, naming it "taiva," meaning "old." Cultivated on terraces cut into the mountains, it enjoyed the benevolence of the Aztec rain god "Tlaloc," who guaranteed its continual growth.

Corn belongs to the family of grass plants. It was introduced to Europe after the discovery of the New World, though some explorers are convinced that they have discovered traces of corn on the European continent that date back even further. Today, corn is cultivated the world over, and is used to make everything from pancakes (such as the famous Mexican tortillas), to mashes (the Italian polenta), to popcorn and alcoholic beverages.

In this recipe, our chef Fernando Adría, a longtime advocate of corn's value in haute cuisine, suggests a corn cream filling for the classic ravioli. According to tradition, the ravioli dough should be very thin – almost transparent – and only after cooking should it be filled with the cream. Furthermore, the filling should be extremely light (our chef insists on this point), which requires careful mixing of the ingredients.

The vanilla oil, made by marinating the vanilla beans in sunflower oil, adds that special touch. While a seemingly unlikely pair, corn and vanilla's harmony can be explained by their common provenance: introduced by the Spanish, vanilla, from Réunion Island just east of Madagascar, is the quintessential scent of the New World.

1. Soak the sheet of gelatin in cold water. Purée the corn in the blender. Put one tablespoon of corn purée into a casserole. Add the gelatin and melt over low heat. Add the remaining corn purée, let cool and then fold in the cream.

2. Either by hand or in a food processor, mix all ingredients for the dough. Let the dough sit for one hour. Roll out the dough as thinly as possible and cut into rectangles of about 1¹/₂ by 2¹/₂ inches (4 x 6 cm).

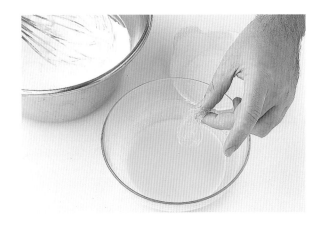

with Vanilla Oil

3. To make the vanilla oil, scrape the pulp from the halved vanilla beans and stir into the sunflower oil. Place the dough rectangles in a saucepan of boiling water, to which a drop of olive oil has been added, and simmer. Then rinse with cold water and leave to dry.

4. Place a teaspoonful of corn mousse in the center of each dough rectangle, moisten the edges of the rectangles with a brush, and then fold the dough into ravioli. Finally, pour the vanilla oil over the ravioli.

Cold Salad of Scallops

Preparation time: 10 minutes
Cooking time: 10 minutes
Difficulty: ★★

Serves four

For the salad:
12 scallops
12 cockles
1 large turnip
$^1/_2$ cup / 125 ml olive oil
1 bunch of chervil (only the leaves will be used)
salt, pepper to taste
half a bunch of parsley

For the parsley sauce:
a few parsley leaves
$^7/_8$ cup / 200 ml fish stock
$^1/_2$ tbsp butter
1 clove of garlic
$^1/_2$ cup / 125 ml vegetable oil

For the cauliflower cream:
1 cauliflower
$^3/_8$ cup / 100 g butter
$^3/_8$ cup / 100 ml crème fraîche

The area of Santiago de Compostela, in the northwestern Spanish province of La Coruña, inspired our chef to create this delicious recipe based on scallops. The Galician community is allegedly the site of the tomb of St. James (St. Jacques in French), and was a pilgrim's hospice in the sixteenth century. As a sign of their pilgrimage, pilgrims often carried a scallop shell; thus the ray-shaped shell pattern became the pilgrims' emblem in the Middle Ages.

Size and quality of scallops vary substantially. There are two types: the Mediterranean "pecten jacobeus" and the Atlantic fast-growing "pecten maximus." Both do nothing but sit peacefully (as if in meditation) on the ocean floor, devouring any passing prey and fleeing in a frenzy at the appearance of their archenemy, the starfish. Most molluscs of the Venus varieties share the same living habits.

For this salad only fairly heavy, medium-sized scallops should be used (roughly three per pound) and the scallops' shells must be intact and closed. Hilario Arbelaitz recommends the Galician scallops, which are high in vitamin B, calcium, and iodine, and make their home in the Bay of Biscay's rich waters. French scallops are also suitable, particularly from the Bay of Saint-Brieuc, and there particularly from Erquy, a region renowned for its scallop production.

Cauliflower combines very well with shellfish such as scallops and cockles. Those who manage to produce this entrée flawlessly could quite possibly be included in the "Ordre de la Coquille" (the "Order of St. Jacob," an honorary body whose name is a variation on the French: in France, scallops are "coquilles de St. Jacques"; one variation of Jacques is Jacob).

1. Open the scallops and remove the whiskers. Take out the meat and coral (roe) and rinse thoroughly in cold water. Let dry on a dishtowel or kitchen cloth.

2. Place the scallops on a plate and marinate for ten minutes in salt and olive oil. Heat the cockles in a casserole filled with fish stock, oil, and parsley over a high heat until they open up. Extract the meat and place on a plate; set aside. Retain the fish stock for the parsley sauce.

with Cauliflower Cream

3. Boil the cauliflower in salted water; let dry. In a blender or food processor, purée the cauliflower, the crème fraîche, and the butter together until smooth. Blanch the chervil, rinse briefly in cold water and set aside.

4. Heat the fish stock and the other ingredients for the parsley sauce in a saucepan. Into the center of a plate, drop a tablespoon of cauliflower cream. Set the scallops, cockles, and turnip slices around the cream, add the parsley sauce, and garnish with chervil leaves.

Cold soup

Preparation time: 20 minutes
Cooking time: 10 minutes
Difficulty: ✶

Serves four

For the soup:
¹/₂ lb to 1 lb / 250 g to 500 g salted cod
2 lbs / 1 kg potatoes
3 sprigs of thyme
half a bunch of parsley
5 cloves of garlic
2 cups / 500 ml olive oil

For the broth:
2 leeks
2 onions
half a bunch of parsley

For the garnish:
1 red pepper
1 green pepper
1 tomato

This soup is like a play for five actors taking very different roles – salted cod, potato, parsley, olive oil, and garlic – which, together, make an excellent soup that is delicious either hot or chilled. It can thus be enjoyed all year round, though our chef considers winter the most appropriate season for serving this particular fish.

Salted cod is a favorite among the Basque fishermen in Spain, who prepare the fish right on the boat by preserving it in salt brine before handing it over to their wives, who know hundreds of ways of preparing it. Salted cod is also regarded as a delicacy in other parts of Spain, as well as in Portugal, Norway, and France. For this soup, you need a salted cod that has been marinated in salt for at least six months, which is why it needs to be soaked in water for a few days before it can be used. Large fillets should be cut into strips first, which makes preparation much easier later on.

Garlic and olive oil, typical Basque ingredients, feature strongly in this recipe. Our chef always recommends the use of fresh garlic, though if its flavor seems too strong, you may substitute the lighter-flavored pickled garlic. Or, if for some reason you want to do without garlic completely, you can compensate by increasing the amount of olive oil you use.

1. Soak the salted cod in water for 36 hours before preparing it, changing the water every eight hours. Reserve the water for the broth, to which leeks, onions, and parsley are added.

2. Place the salted cod, potatoes, parsley, and thyme in a saucepan. Pour in the strained fish stock and simmer for about 15 minutes. Save an attractive-looking piece of cod for the garnish.

# of Salted Cod

3. Cut the garlic into strips. In a non-stick frying pan, fry until brown in a little olive oil and then add to the soup. Remove the seeds from the tomato, clean and dice the green and red peppers, then dice the tomato and the piece of fish saved for the garnish.

4. When the soup has been cooked, purée in a blender or food processor and season to taste. Place a tablespoon of the diced vegetables and cod garnish in the middle of a deep plate and pour the soup around it. This soup may be eaten hot, warm, or chilled.

Tuna Tartare

Preparation time: 45 minutes
Cooking time: 1 hour
Difficulty: ✶

Serves four
1/2 lb / 250 g red tuna
1 oyster
4 mild chilies
3 tomatoes
1 red pepper
1 shallot
juice of half a lemon
1/4 cup / 50 ml olive oil
1/2 tsp prepared mustard
salt, pepper to taste

For the vinaigrette:
1 tsp prepared mustard
3/8 cup / 100 ml olive oil
1/8 cup / 30 ml sherry vinegar
salt, pepper to taste

To garnish:
half a bunch of chervil
half a bunch of chives

It may seem unusual, but this refreshing summer dish is typically Basque. For centuries the red tuna has been caught off the Basque coast by a fleet of fishing boats from Saint-Jean-de-Luz. The famous mild chili from Espelette, with its unique and special aroma, is a delicious regional speciality.

Red tuna, the much-loved "ocean steak," is less bony and more nutritious (it contains more iodine, for instance) than white tuna. A popular ingredient in the Basque country as well as in other areas, red tuna can be grilled just like meat: it has the same color and firm texture as a good steak. For this recipe, which uses the tuna raw, for full nutritional value (and safety), only buy fish that is absolutely fresh. It should appear shiny. For easier dicing we suggest placing the tuna in the freezer for a couple of minutes before taking a knife to it.

The little town of Espelette, a picturesque village on the plateau between Saint-Jean-Pied-de-Port and Bayonne in the French Basque region, is proud of its production of both the mild chili, which is eaten fresh, and the dried chili, which is much stronger and should only be used in small quantities. Ideally, use mild chilies that measure between 4 and 6 inches (10 to 15 cm) long: these are cut into a fine julienne, so their flavor does not overpower that of the tomato.

If mild chilies are not available the tartare may also be served with arugula salad, which has a bitter aftertaste well-suited for this spicy appetizer.

1. Chop the tuna very finely. Brush the red pepper with olive oil and bake at a high setting in the oven for about fifteen minutes. Remove and let cool. Peel and very finely chop enough to yield a quarter-cup. Peel and finely chop the shallot and chives.

2. Mix the chopped tuna, shallot, red pepper, and chopped chives. Blanch, peel and quarter the tomatoes, remove the seeds and sprinkle with salt. After cutting the ends off the chilies, cut the chilies lengthwise, remove the seeds, and then slice into fine strips. Prepare the mustard vinaigrette.

with Mild Chilies

3. Add half a teaspoon of mustard, a few drops of lemon juice, salt and pepper to the tuna tartare. Purée the oyster flesh and add, with the oyster juices, to the tartare. Add the olive oil and mix thoroughly; chill.

4. For each serving, use two tablespoons to scoop three balls of tartare. On the plate, place the three scoops of tartare, alternating with three tomato quarters sprinkled with the julienne of chilies, in a star shape. Pour over the vinaigrette and garnish the center with some chervil and chives.

Salad of

Preparation time: 15 minutes
Difficulty: ☆

Serves four

For the salad:
half a bunch of basil
half a bunch of chervil
half a bunch of chives
half a bunch of garden cress
   (or, if unavailable, substitute watercress)
half a bunch of fennel
half a bunch of flat-leafed parsley
half a bunch of pimpernel (the leaves of a type
   of primrose)

half a bunch of cilantro
half a bunch of spinach
half a bunch of arugula
a few borage flowers (if available, or substitute
   nasturtiums or violets)

For the dressing:
⁷/₈ cup / 220 ml extra virgin olive oil
1 clove of garlic
half a bunch of basil
salt to taste

Most aromatic herbs are Mediterranean in origin. Their therapeutic properties have been well known since antiquity, and during Roman times they made the transition from medicine to cuisine. Even today we can enjoy their variety and full flavor without any further ingredients, as chef Jean Bardet proves with this herbal feast.

We have spicy and aromatic parsley and garden cress, whose sharp flavor becomes surprisingly mild when chopped, and chervil with its complex scent, which quickly evaporates. You will substantially enhance this dish's visual impact if you use the freshest herbs available; your palate will be all the more pleased as well. You can, of course, add seasonal herbs according to taste. The edible flowers are an interesting addition, brightening up the dish with their luminous colors. Borage, a

European flower that blooms from May to September, sometimes at altitudes of more than five thousand feet, has lovely blue, white, and red flowers, of which the best should be picked for this recipe. But if these are unavailable, you might substitute the hotter-colored nasturtiums, or violets.

In order to underline the marvelous spicy flavor of the fresh herbs and complement the vivid green of this salad, only extra virgin olive oil, with its lovely green color, should be used. "Extra vergine" olive oil (as it is known in France), which is less than one year old, has a distinctive flavor that melds extremely well in this Provençal recipe.

1. Clean one garlic clove and the basil and chop finely, mix into the olive oil.

2. Strip the leaves off the remaining herbs and toss in cold water. Let drip-dry before putting them into the salad spinner to get rid of any remaining water.

Fresh Herbs

3. If necessary, dry the herbs even further on kitchen towelling. Mix with part of the dressing.

4. Place a ring of borage flowers on a plate. Place a portion of salad in the middle and garnish with a few more borage flowers. Sprinkle with dressing.

Terrine of beans

Preparation time: 30 minutes
Cooking time: 2 hours
Soaking time: 12 hours (optional)
Cooling time: 2 hours (at least)
Difficulty: ★★

Serves ten

1¼ cups white beans
scant ¼ lb / 125 g bacon
3 tbsp duck fat
2 lbs / 1 kg goose fat
half the liver of a duck
2 leeks
1 onion

3 cloves of garlic
1 small bouquet garni
3 sheets of gelatin
1⅛ cups / 280 ml cream
1 tbsp coarse sea salt
salt, pepper to taste

For the garlic sauce:
(see basic recipes)

For serving:
¼ cup / 60 ml walnut oil
sprinkling of coarse sea salt

In Europe, beans are available at market stands from June through September, and exist in both round and long forms. As, in general, the long bean has a superior aroma, our chef prefers it for this recipe.

Chef Bardet recommends buying beans that are still in the pod, if they can be found, to ensure that they are unblemished and firm. After being shelled, the beans are then cooked for quite a while – first brought to a boil, then left to simmer for about an hour. If you use dry beans, remember to soak them in water for at least 12 hours before cooking, and to boil them for a little longer than you would fresh beans. To lend them a stronger flavor, place chunks of smoked bacon or bacon rind in the stockpot: the beans will absorb the sharp, hearty flavor. Making the terrine itself will present no problem. Just make sure not to mix it too vigorously once the cream has been added, as its consistency at that point is very delicate, and it will only retain its airiness if it is mixed gently.

As is usually the case with terrines, we recommend that you make it the day before you plan to serve it, as storing it overnight improves its flavor and consistency. To slice the terrine, use a very flat and pointed knife. Just before serving, brush the terrine with some walnut oil to give it a gloss, and sprinkle a few grains of coarse sea salt over it as well.

1. Blanch the two leeks, rinse briefly with cold water and set aside to dry. Line the terrine form first with plastic wrap, then with the leek leaves. Cut the smoked bacon into large chunks and slice the onion thinly. Peel and crush the cloves of garlic. Soak the gelatin in cold water and set aside.

2. Blanch the fresh beans, drain and set aside to dry. Put the duck's fat into a saucepan and add the beans, bacon, and onion. Cover with cold water, bring to a boil, skim off some of the foam and add the garlic. Cook for about one and a half hours, then taste, adding coarse sea salt if necessary, and then add the bouquet garni. Pour into the blender and mix, adding the soaked gelatin.

and Duck's Liver

3. Pour the lukewarm purée into a salad bowl and add the 1$\frac{1}{8}$ cups / 280 ml of whipped cream. Add salt and pepper, and set aside. Cut the duck's liver into two equal pieces and remove the tendons. Add salt and pepper, place on a piece of aluminum foil and roll into a "sausage"; place in a deep plate and cover with hot goose fat; leave to cool.

4. Prepare the garlic sauce (see basic recipes). Distribute half of the bean purée over the bottom of the terrine pan, place the liver pieces on top, and finally cover with the remaining purée. Cover with the overlapping leeks and then with the plastic wrap. Leave to chill for at least two hours, if not overnight.

Baccalà

Preparation time: 15 minutes
Cooking time: 7 minutes
Difficulty: ✶

Serves four
1¼ lbs / 600 g Baccalà (fresh cod)
scant ¾ lb / 350 g potatoes
4 plum tomatoes
4 sundried tomatoes
4 basil leaves
¾ cup / 180 ml extra virgin olive oil
¼ cup / 60 ml lemon juice
1 tbsp tapenade (olive paste)
3–4 black olives
salt, pepper to taste

The Provençal writer Alphonse Daudet caught the spirit of the cod's popularity and its numerous styles of preparation by coining the phrase "cod evenings," referring to regular events held at a famous Parisian café. Many contemporary chefs continue to use cod in their creations and thus help to maintain the gastronomic importance of this fish, which lives in the Atlantic Ocean, the English Channel, and the North Sea.

Like their German colleagues, French fishermen distinguish between fresh and dried cod. Cod is particularly easy to catch when the fish converge toward the open sea for reproduction. In Italy, cod dried gently in the air is referred to as "baccalà," based on the Spanish term for it, "bacalao." This salad, created by Giuseppina Beglia, should be eaten at once as it can not be stored. The salad can also be prepared with extremely fresh

monkfish or with sliced freshwater trout, providing these fish have been pre-boiled a little to make their flesh tender.

"Tapenade" is a typical Provençal accompaniment, which conveys close links to neighboring Italy. First-class, tangy ingredients are needed to produce a fine tapenade: olive oil, capers, black olives, and anchovies are pressed according to traditional methods in an olive wood press. Sundried tomatoes are prepared in a very simple manner: they are exposed to the summer sun for a few weeks. They can, of course, also be bought in the shops already dried, and as a last resort you can dry them yourself in the oven. To soften them for eating, they are soaked in a bowl full of hot water and olive oil for a half an hour, then drained.

1. Skin the cod and remove the bones. Wash and quarter the potatoes. Place the potatoes in boiling salted water and add the cod two or three minutes later. Simmer for five minutes.

2. Place the fish on a plate and carefully cut into chunks with a tablespoon. Finely chop the sundried tomatoes and basil leaves.

Salad

3. Put a tablespoon of tapenade into a bowl, then add four tablespoons of lemon juice. Add salt and pepper, then stir in the olive oil. Blanch and skin the plum tomatoes and set them aside.

4. On a plate, place the potato pieces in a star shape. Place the cod slices in the center of the plate, on top of the inside of the star, and garnish with the chopped tomatoes and basil. Pour over a little sauce, sprinkle with freshly ground pepper and decorate with plum tomato strips and black olive pieces.

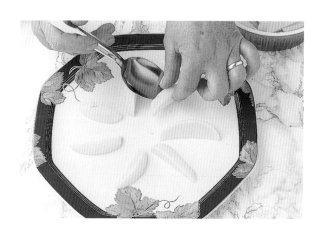

Artichoke and Lobster

Preparation time: 30 minutes
Cooking time: 30 minutes
Difficulty: ★★

Serves four

2 lobsters, either European blue or Northern,
   1¼ lbs / 600 g each
8 artichokes
fish stock
juice of 1 lemon
2 tbsp flour
2 cups / 500 g cream

½ cup / 125 ml mustard vinaigrette
   (see p. 14 for recipe)
2 tsp peanut oil
2 sheets of gelatin
salt, pepper to taste

For the green sauce:
1 cup mayonnaise (see basic recipes)
half a bunch of tarragon
half a bunch of chervil
half a bunch of flat-leafed parsley
half a bunch of basil
half a bunch of spinach

The inhabitants of coastal areas, lobsters can grow up to 30 inches / 76 cm long. Nature has equipped them with two large claws for good reason: one claw is used to pulverize, the other to catch prey. Both also represent a danger for the cook, so they must be tied with string, or plugged with small pieces of wood and tied with rubber bands, before being cooked. For this recipe, it is not so crucial whether you use a male or female lobster since it will only be boiled for a short time, and coral (roe) is not called for.

In centuries past, the artichoke (originally from Sicily) was believed to have not only therapeutic, but also aphrodisiac proporties – which often resulted in women being forbidden from consuming it. But the French Queen Catherine of Medici, who favored them for just that reason, wholeheartedly encouraged the cultivation of this vegetable. Thanks to her, the artichoke eventually enjoyed substantial popularity at the

royal court by the end of the sixteenth century, and became increasingly popular in France.

Most artichoke varieties reach full maturity in May and June. Choose large, fleshy artichokes with rough, green leaves that sit heavily in your hand. They should be boiled in water to which a little lemon juice has been added; add a little flour to the water as well to prevent the artichokes from oxidizing and losing their color. Once out of the pot, the latter is, alas, unavoidable unless they are eaten almost immediately.

The artichoke hearts are prepared with olive oil and herbs, ingredients that provide a link to the green sauce – an ideal sauce for shellfish whose color may be intensified by adding more spinach. The aromatic herbs should all be very fresh, otherwise one may overpower the others. Mix them in the order they're listed in the recipe.

1. Ahead of time, soak the gelatin in cold water. Separate the artichoke hearts from the globes by twisting them; rub with lemon. Put about two inches of water into a glass and add the peanut oil and flour; mix. Add lemon juice and a pinch of salt; transfer to a saucepan; add enough water to cover the artichoke hearts, and boil for ten minutes. Leave the hearts to cool in the liquid. Using a very sharp knife, cut four hearts into twelve slices.

2. Finely dice two of the remaining hearts (yielding approximately ¾ cup / 150 g). In a food processor, chop the remaining hearts and the top leaves, then pass through a fine-meshed sieve. Thicken the resulting purée with the gelatin, which has previously been soaked in cold water. Whip the cream until stiff and fold into the mixture. Season to taste; let chill.

Layers in a Green Sauce

3. Drop the lobsters into boling fish stock; boil for five minutes and simmer for another ten minutes. Drain, then plunge lobsters into cold water. When cool, extract the lobster meat, discarding the stomach, internal vein, coral (roe) and tomalley or liver. Cut one tail into medallions and dice the other. Retain some of the chervil for the garnish, and blanch all the herbs. Rinse with cold water and work into a purée; mix the mayonnaise into the purée.

4. Mix together the diced lobster and diced artichokes. Pour green sauce onto the plates. Place one artichoke base in the center, and then cover it with a ring of artichoke purée piped through a pastry bag. Add the diced lobster and artichoke. Repeat this procedure five or six times, finishing with an artichoke base on top. Add a few drops of mustard vinaigrette. Decorate with lobster medallions, a small section of the claw, and chervil leaves.

Terrine of Lentils and

Preparation time: 50 minutes
Cooking time: 40 minutes
Difficulty: ★★

Serves four

16 langoustines
1/2 cup / 100 g green lentils
3/8 cup / 40 g celeriac
1 onion
4 carrots
2 cloves of garlic
fish stock for cooking
1 cup white wine (if desired)
1 bouquet garni

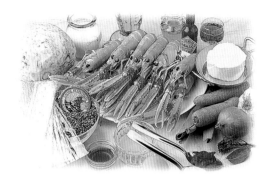

2 sheets of gelatin
1/2 lb / 100 g unsalted butter
1 tsp Tabasco sauce
1/4 cup / 60 ml vinegar
salt, pepper to taste

For the caviar cream:
1 oz / 35 g caviar, such as Sevruga or Ossetra
1/2 cup / 100 ml mayonnaise (see basic
    recipes)
7/8 cup / 200 ml whipping cream
1/2 cup / 100 ml sherry vinegar
salt, pepper to taste

The lentil is one of the oldest pulses and was already known by the time of the ancient Egyptians; it is also mentioned in the Bible. Initially exclusively consumed by the affluent, this basic food was soon to be abandoned by them to become a staple for the poor. Thanks to intensified cultivation, lentils have regained their excellent culinary reputation and found their way back into domestic cuisine and on to the menus of many restaurants. The green lentil, from Le Puy, France, is the queen of all lentils. France, to control its production and maintain its superior quality, has given it the distinguishing hallmark, "Appellation d'Origine Contrôlée." Le Puy lentils are carefully selected and require only a very short cooking time before they release their excellent flavor. They should never be brought to a boil, however, as this may cause them to burst.

Langoustines, a small saltwater shellfish that scientists refer to as *Nephrops norvegicus*, are also known as prawns, a term that can cause much confusion. Langoustines are best purchased alive or at least extremely fresh. For cooking they should be tied with string and plunged into boiling fish stock laced with vinegar. Their flesh is so tender that they should be boiled-depending on their size – for no more than two to eight minutes.

As is the case with terrines, prepare this one a day ahead so it is easier to slice. It need not necessarily be lined with carrot strips; blanched spinach or endive leaves will work just as well.

1. Soak the gelatin in cold water ahead of time. Blanch the lentils and simmer with half of the bouquet garni for 30 minutes. Remove the langoustines' heads, tie the bodies with string, and simmer for three minutes in the fish stock. Rinse with cold water, extract the meat, and leave to cool. Choose four langoustine heads for decoration, and make a broth from the remaining heads. To line the terrine, cut some of the carrots into long strips and boil in salt water.

2. Chop the remaining carrots, celeriac, and onion and sauté in butter until brown. Set aside. Take crushed garlic and lentils, sauté in butter. Pour in 2 cups / 500 ml of langoustine broth. Cook slowly, then add the previously soaked gelatin and the remaining bouquet garni. Adjust seasoning with vinegar, Tabasco sauce, and salt. Line the terrine pan with the cooked carrot strips (or blanched spinach or endive leaves).

Langoustines with Caviar Cream

3. Place a layer of lentils in the terrine pan. Place the langoustines end-to-end along the long sides of the dish. Repeat the layers until the dish is filled. Fold over the carrot, spinach or endive strips to close the terrine; chill.

4. To make the caviar cream, stir mayonnaise into the whipped cream and vinegar mixture, season, and add the caviar. On to a plate pooled with a light layer of caviar cream, place a slice of terrine; decorate with chervil and a langoustine head. Serve chilled.

Turbot and Lobster Pâté

Preparation time: *1 hour, 30 minutes*
Cooking time: *1 hour, 10 minutes*
Difficulty: ★★★

Serves twelve

3 European lobsters from Scotland or Brittany, or, if unavailable, Northern lobsters from the U.S. 1 lb / 500 g each
2¹/₂ lbs / 1¹/₂ kg each turbot fillets
2 oz / 60 g Périgord truffles
10 anchovy fillets, in strips
2 tbsp / 15 g pistachio kernels
¹/₂ lb / 250 g raw spinach
2 carrots
1 large leek

1 large celeriac
whites of 3 eggs
2 tbsp herbs, dried and ground (your choice)
1¹/₈ cups / 300 ml cream
3 tbsp / 25 g butter (1 tbsp is for the julienne)
3 sheets of gelatin

For the sauce:
⁷/₈ cup / 200 ml spicy mustard mayonnaise (see basic recipes)
4 tomatoes or 1 cup tomato juice
juice of 1 lemon
¹/₄ cup / 50 ml crème fraîche
salt, pepper to taste

This pâté, which our chef continues to improve year after year, has become something of a masterpiece. It should ideally be prepared the day before in a terrine pan lined with fresh spinach leaves that have been tossed in melted butter.

Turbot, renowned for its delicious flavor, is readily available in April. Choose a very fresh fish with healthy-looking, shiny skin. The lobster (bought live), whose unique taste will dominate the flavor of the aspic, should also be extremely fresh, with a shiny shell. If you can find blue lobster from Brittany or Scotland, these are ideal, but Northern lobster will also work. The successful making of the lobster cream is crucial to the outcome of this dish, and a certain amount of skill and technique is required for its preparation. The cream, ideally made

directly on ice, should not be too fluffy, or the egg white will not sink into it. If you can't find suitable lobster, you may try substituting it with freshwater trout or pike.

Checking the quality of the truffles can only be done by tasting them: though they are ripe in January and February, you should still make sure they are absolutely fresh. You can use whatever dried herbs you prefer, but the aromatic ones should only be used sparingly.

The dish's delicate, refined sauce was created by our chef, Michel Bourdin, who served it with cold fish terrines at Maxims in Paris during the 1960s. The sauce, which features tomato juice, is mixed with crème fraîche until it turns pink.

1. Cut the turbot fillets open for the filling and season with herbs. Julienne the carrot, celeriac and leeks; cook by lightly sautéing in butter; place in the middle of the fillets. Add the anchovy strips, close the fillets, and set aside for the fish to absorb the flavors. Drop the live lobsters into a rolling boil; cook for eight minutes. To end the boiling process, add ice water, and retain the boiling liquid. Drain lobsters and extract the meat; slice the lobster tails into long strips and retain.

2. Soak the gelatin in cold water. In a food processor, purée the remaining turbot and lobster meat. Add egg whites and cream; season, and strain. Place the lobster shell into the cooking liquid retained earlier and cook well; remove the shell. Bind the liquid with the gelatin. Slice the truffles into small strips. Quickly boil the spinach leaves in salted water, rinse with cold water, chop, fry in butter very briefly, then line the terrine pan with them.

with a Delicate Sauce

3. To fill the terrine pan: start with a layer of cream filling, follow with a layer of filled turbot fillets, then add another layer of cream with lobster tails, truffles, and pistachios. Repeat and finish with a layer of filling. Cook for one hour in an oven at 250 °F / 120 °C. When done, discard the cooking liquid; replace with the liquid lobster aspic.

4. After letting the pâté cool for 24 hours, remove it from the form, slice, and glaze each slice with the lobster aspic. To prepare the sauce, blend spicy mustard mayonnaise, tomato juice, crème fraîche and lemon juice. Season to taste. Serve the terrine slices with a pool of the sauce, garnished with diced lobster jelly.

Connaught

Preparation time: 3 hours
Cooking time: 1 hour, 15 minutes
Marinating time: 24 hours
Cooking time: 24 hours
Difficulty: ★★★

Serves twelve

2 wild ducks (of the light-fleshed variety
    or, if unavailable, 2 pheasants)
2 lbs / 1 kg pork shoulder
scant 1 lb / 400 g fatty belly of pork
    (use pancetta)
³/₈ cup / 75 ml port

2 tbsp Cognac
1 tbsp / 10 ml rum
¹/₄ lb / 100 g goose liver (foie gras)
4 button mushrooms
2 cups / 500 ml duck stock
1 tbsp salt
fresh-ground black pepper to taste
1 tsp mixture of four herbs
1 tsp baking soda
¹/₄ cup / 50 g sliced truffles
3 sheets of gelatin
2 tbsp / 30 g pistachios
half a bunch of thyme
1 bay leaf

Wild duck, such as canvasback or mallard, is rich in potassium and phosphorus and is highly prized by gourmets and hunters alike. It has also been the symbol of Chinese cooking for four thousand years.

This terrine is particularly suitable for ducks with very white flesh, such as the ducks from Nantes in France. Pheasants, another popular game bird, can be used instead, but, as the meat is a bit drier, it needs to be mixed with pork. In the case of this dish, whether one is using duck or pheasant, the choicer parts of pork, for example the shoulder, should be used.

According to chef Michel Bourdin's directions, making this terrine will take the better part of three days, and baking can only begin on the third day. Ten minutes before baking is complete, the lid of the terrine should be removed to allow a

thin and aromatic crust to develop. Once the terrine has been removed from the oven, a small glass (about ¹/₂ / 125 ml) of rum should be poured over it. Or, if pheasant has been used, pour over an herbal liqueur. Then the most difficult part begins: slowly pressing the terrine as it cools, in order to build up the natural aspic it contains.

This dish develops its full flavor after sitting for a week, but it should never be kept for longer than three weeks, as the quality of the aspic will deteriorate. The original version of this terrine can be found on the menu of the eminent Connaught in London, an undisputed highlight amongst the restaurants of the British capital.

1. Soak the gelatin in cold water ahead of time. Remove the bones and tendons from the ducks, then slice the meat into ³/₈ in / 1 cm strips wide. Marinate the meat for 24 hours in a mixture of port, Cognac, salt, and pepper. Separate the pork meat from the bone, put ⁷/₈ lb / 450 g of lean pork aside, and make a stock with the duck bones, pork bones, and spices. Strain through a fine-meshed sieve. Place the bones in fresh water and cook until reduced to half a cup of aspic.

2. Run the lean pork and the pork belly through the meat grinder using a coarse blade; do the same with the marinated duck meat on a medium blade. Mix the soaked gelatin with the duck stock. Soak the four-herb mixture in alcohol; add salt, pepper, and baking soda. Prepare a stuffing with the duck stock, the aspic, the sliced truffles, and the ground meat. Chill and let the flavors blend for 24 hours.

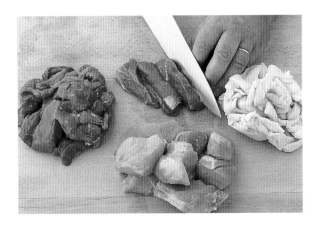

Terrine

3. Cut the goose liver and mushrooms into ³/₈ in / 1 cm strips wide. At the bottom of the terrine form, place a layer of meat stuffing, then alternate strips of duck meat, liver, and mushrooms. Place a second layer of stuffing on this, then sprinkle with the pistachios. Cover with the remaining stuffing. Add thyme and bay leaf; cover.

4. In a bain-marie, bake for 50 minutes at 375 °F / 175 °C. Remove cover and increase heat to 400 °F / 200 °C; bake for 10 to 15 minutes without cover. Remove from the oven, pour a little rum over it, and set aside to cool. Cover with an adequately sized board and place on top a weight heavy enough to apply pressure without breaking the terrine. Store. Serve sliced, garnished with diced aspic.

Fillet of Goatfish with Coriander

Preparation time: 45 minutes
Cooking time: 15 minutes
Difficulty: ★★

Serves four

4 goatfish, approximately 5 oz / 150 g each
a pinch of saffron threads

For the oriental sauce:
2 leeks
2 tomatoes
2 small onions
2 cloves of garlic
$^3/_4$ cup / 200 ml white wine
$1^2/_3$ cup / 400 ml fish stock
$^3/_4$ cup / 200 ml olive oil
1 tbsp / 15 g coriander seeds

half a bunch of thyme
1 bay leaf
1 tbsp / 15 g peppercorns
1 tbsp / 15 g salt

For the vegetable tartare:
2 small fennel bulbs
2 celery stalks
4 tomatoes
2 carrots
4 gherkins
2 tbsp / 30 g capers
2 eggs
$^1/_4$ cup / 60 ml red wine vinegar
$^1/_4$ cup / 60 ml olive oil
1 bunch of chivessalt, pepper to taste

For cooks, the versatility of the goatfish, with its tangy flavor and strong color, is famous. A type of fish often sold only on the East coast, from Maine to Florida, goatfish is often available in the form of red mullet, which is not actually a true mullet at all. Goatfish dwells in deep, rocky waters, where it is not easily caught. Unlike its large-bellied cousins, the striped and silver mullets, its profile is a straight line. In southern France it is called *bécasse de mer*, and apparently featured prominently in the cuisine of the ancient Greeks and Romans. It should not to be confused with the gurnard (known in North America as the sea robin), which is fabulous for fish soups but belongs to an altogether different family of fish.

That Christian Bouvarel has included goatfish on his menu of the restaurant Paul Bocuse reveals his preference for it. The fish for this recipe should be very fresh and quickly prepared

after purchase, as it will deteriorate if it's stored for too long. The broth that is poured over the fish should be very hot but not boiling. In case the meat becomes a little stiff from the heat of the broth, it can be left for a few moments to soak, which will increase its tenderness.

Christian Bouvarel is determined to bring about the "rehabilitation" of this oriental sauce, a concoction that is increasingly rare. The choice of spices here is crucial: coriander and saffron are indispensable and must be dosed in adequate proportions.

The vegetable tartare is another indispensable aspect of this dish, adding variety and freshness. If desired, young zucchini can be added.

1. Gut and fillet the goatfish and remove the whiskers; cut into eight fillets. Then the rest: skeleton, tails, etc., may be used to make the stock. For the oriental sauce, cut the leeks into short strips, chop the onions and garlic, and briefly fry all in olive oil. Add a quarter of a bay leaf, chop and add the tomatoes, add the thyme, half the coriander seeds, and pepper and salt to taste. Pour in the wine and fish stock, salt, and boil for approximately eight minutes.

2. Place the fish fillets close together in a roasting or baking pan, sprinkle with saffron threads. Pour the oriental sauce over; shake the dish slightly. For the vegetable tartare, prepare a vinaigrette with wine vinegar and 4 tbsp / 60 ml of olive oil, adding salt and pepper to taste. Chop the fennel bulbs, celery stalks, and carrots; fry briefly in olive oil.

and Vegetable Tartare

3. Chop and hard-boil the eggs; chop two tomatoes. Mix the briefly fried vegetables with the gherkins, capers, chopped hard-boiled eggs, and tomatoes. Season the mixture with the vinaigrette and chives. Cut the remaining tomatoes into eight parts; fry briefly and gently in a olive oil.

4. Place two goatfish fillets sprinkled with coriander seeds on a plate. Add the vegetable tartare in the shape of a half-sphere and garnish with tomato pieces; pour a small amount of the goatfish's cooking broth onto the plate.

Preparation time: 30 minutes
Difficulty: ☆

Serves four

2 freshwater perch fillets
1 salmon trout fillet
1¼ cups / 300 ml virgin olive oil
½ oz / 15 g caviar, such as Sevruga, Ossetra,
  or Beluga
2 tsp / 10 g salt
1 tsp / 5 g black pepper
1 tbsp / 15 g pink peppercorns

Two generations of chefs have worked on the creation on this recipe. It was initially rather problematic to use freshwater fish for food because preservation presented a major problem. The first generation of chefs concentrated on salmon trout, the second on perch. Then Chef Carlo Brovelli came along and suggested serving both fish together in wafer-thin slices. Simple freshwater fish are turned into a delicacy when served as fillets with olive oil and herbs.

Salmon trout, a large variety of rainbow trout, are especially good in Europe when caught in Lago Maggiore, northern Italy; in North America they are available on all coasts. When fresh, this firm-bodied fish is tender and delicious. The perch provides firmer fillets and is thus easy to handle; for this recipe, choose perch of medium size, a little under three-quarters of a pound. Since perch lives in clean waters and avoids sand and mud, its aroma is unimpaired by any organic or other pollutants.

The fillets are first rolled together in plastic wrap and pressed well. They are then put in the freezer to firm up so they can be cut into wafer-thin slices without disintegrating. Because the fish is cut so thin, this dish is called a *carpaccio*, named after the classic Italian *carpaccio*, which is, of course, made with beef. In the nineteenth century, the chef of Harry's Bar in Venice (not to be confused with the Harry's Bar in Paris) invented the dish as a culinary homage to the Venetian painter Vittore Carpaccio. The occasion was a retrospective exhibition of the painter's work. Incidentally, the pink peppercorns Chef Brovelli lists in this recipe are not actually true peppercorns, but dried berries from Madagascar; they can be found in high-quality food stores. And if preferred, you may gently heat this dish in the oven before serving.

1. Salt and pepper the fish fillets; place the trout fillet on top of the perch fillet and roll up both together.

2. Wrap the rolled-up fish in plastic wrap and place in the freezer for 12 minutes.

Trout and Perch

3. In a blender, mix the olive oil, a tablespoon of pink peppercorns, and a pinch of salt.

4. After removing the fish from the freezer, take off the plastic wrap. Cut the fish roll into wafer-thin slices with a sharp knife-either with a smooth or serrated edge will work. Place the fish slices on the plate, brush with the pepper-oil, and place a dollop of caviar in the middle.

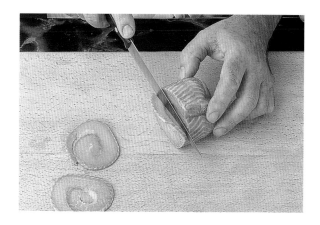

Carpaccio of Langoustines

Preparation time: 20 minutes
Difficulty: ✶✶

Serves four

16 langoustines
1/2 cup / 125 ml cup olive oil
salt, pepper to taste

For the sauce:
1 cup / 250 ml mayonnaise (see basic recipes)
2 oz / 65 g Sevruga caviar
1/4 cup / 55 g horseradish root (to yield 31/2
     tbsp / 50 g grated and 1 tbsp / 5 g chopped)
salt, pepper to taste

For the herb broth:
2 cups / 500 ml water
11/4 cups / 300 ml white wine
1 carrot
1 celery stalk
1 shallot
1 clove of garlic
zest of half a lemon
half a bunch of parsley
half a bunch of thyme
1 bay leaf

For the garnish:
1/2 oz / 12 g Ossetra caviar
4 sprigs fresh dill

The differing shapes and consistencies of langoustines lend this small shellfish a great deal of versatility; it can be prepared in a wide variety of highly original ways. Closely related to the lobster – they look like a slimmer, miniature version – langoustines are readily available throughout the year. Certain markets may sell them under the name "prawn." When very fresh, they have dark, shiny eyes and a pink shell; if you can't get live ones, make sure they have been out of the water for only a short time as their quality soon deteriorates.

The delicate meat of the langoustine is ideal for making that classic Italian dish, *carpaccio*, which is normally made with beef (see preceding recipe for the origin of the dish). In this version, the langoustine's tail has to be pressed flat but not crushed: for this purpose, plastic wrap is placed between each layer of langoustine meat.

Horseradish and langoustines are an ideal combination. The pulp of this root vegetable is very popular in eastern and northern Europe, where it is frequently used to strengthen the taste of a variety of sauces. It is available in grated form in jars, or can be bought as a root that is then peeled and grated fresh, just as needed.

As far as the caviar is concerned, our chef Jean-Pierre Bruneau recommends – if available – a mixture of tiny Sevruga for the sauce and the slightly larger-grained Ossetra for the decoration. Both varieties are ideally suited to their respective functions in this recipe. A few basic tips: always store the caviar chilled and in a tightly closed container, and stir into the sauce only at the very last moment.

1. Make the herb broth the day before: put all the herbs and the finely chopped zest of half a lemon into two cups of water; add white wine. Boil with the carrot, celery stalk, shallot, and clove of garlic and leave to infuse for three hours. Purée in a blender; set aside to cool. Extract the langoustine meat from the shells, cut and discard the intestinal veins, and reserve the tails.

2. Make a traditional mayonnaise and stretch it with the herb broth. Add the grated horseradish root and Sevruga caviar. Adjust seasoning to taste with salt and pepper.

with Caviar Cream

3. Very carefully and gently flatten the langoustines with a flat mallet, placing a plastic wrap between each layer, until they are flat and large enough to cover the interior of a plate.

4. Pour the sauce in a ring around the flattened langoustines, place half a tablespoon of Ossetra caviar in the center of each plate on top of the langoustines, and garnish the caviar with a sprig of dill. Just before serving, sprinkle with freshly ground pepper and coarse salt.

Lobster Salad

Preparation time: 45 minutes
Cooking time: 25 minutes
Difficulty: ☆

Serves four

4 European lobsters, or, if unavailable,
  Northern lobsters, a bit over $^3/_4$ lb each, and
  female if possible
4 Granny Smith apples
1 head radicchio
1 head green frisée lettuce
1 head red frisée lettuce
$^1/_4$ / 50 g cup roasted pine nuts

$^3/_4$ cup / 200 ml peanut oil
$^1/_2$ cup / 125 ml red wine vinegar
2 cups / 500 ml white wine
1 gallon plus one cup / 4 l water
a pinch of curry powder
half a bunch of thyme
1 bay leaf
salt, pepper to taste

For the mustard mayonnaise:
yolks of 4 eggs
$^1/_2$ cup / 100 ml wine vinegar
1 cup / 250 ml peanut oil
1 tsp / 5 g prepared Dijon mustard
salt, pepper to taste

Usually, two lobster varieties are considered for cooking: the European or blue lobster from Brittany or Norway, and the Northern lobster from Canada and northern New England. The European lobster is more popular in France as it is considered to have a more delicate flavor. Buying more small live lobsters as opposed to a couple of large ones is recommended, as the larger the lobster, the tougher, usually, the meat.

The lobsters can be prepared a few hours in advance. They need to boil in the broth for only a few minutes. Once they have been removed from the pot, let the cooking liquid cool off and put the lobsters back to keep them moist and juicy. When the meat is extracted, the roe, or coral, of the female lobster should be taken out, dried, and then retained, as it is an invaluable ingredient for many kinds of sauces.

The lobster tail, which should be very crisp, is an ideal partner for the tangy, slightly acidic apple slices. Granny Smith apples were first grown in Australia and are now widely cultivated in France; they are in season from October to April and have white flesh underneath characteristically shiny, light-green skin.

The mayonnaise called for here will be modified by adding to it a bit of the lobsters' cooking broth, some mustard, and a pinch of curry, which needs to be carefully measured and added at the very last moment.

For a slightly less expensive version of this dish, use crab or langoustines instead of lobsters.

1. In a stockpot, prepare a broth of white wine, water, herbs, salt and pepper. Bring to a rolling boil and cook the lobsters for fifteen minutes in the broth. When done, add cold water to slow the cooking process, and leave the lobsters to cool in the broth. For the mayonnaise: add salt and pepper to the egg yolks; add mustard. Whisk vigorously, adding the vinegar and, bit by bit, the oil. Set aside for later.

2. Roast the pine nuts in a pre-heated oven at between 375 and 400 °F / 190 and 200 °C until light brown, or in a frying pan on a high heat on the stovetop for between three and four minutes. Wash the salad greens and dry thoroughly; season with salt, pepper, vinegar, and oil, and add the pine nuts. Place the salad decoratively in the center of the plate.

with Green Apples

3. Take the lobsters out of the broth, halve, and set aside the legs and shells for decoration. Cut the tails lengthwise into thin slices. Reserve the roe for future uses (see, for instance, the recipe on page 40). Quarter the apples and cut these as well into thin slices.

4. Stir two tablespoons of cooking broth into just under five-eights of a cup of mayonnaise. Taste, then add a pinch of curry. Dip each lobster slice into the mayonnaise and place on a plate, always alternating with an apple slice. Decorate with the shell and legs.

Marinated

Preparation time: 20 minutes
Cooling time: 24 hours
Difficulty: ✶

Serves four

1 lb / 500 g sardines
8 young leek stalks
1 large Granny Smith, Melrose, or Cameo
    apple
1 lemon
$^1/_4$ cup / 50 ml heavy cream
$^1/_3$ cup / 80 ml whole milk
$1^1/_3$ tbsp / 20 ml olive oil
salt, pepper to taste

For the garnish:
4 sprigs of dill
2 tbsp / 30 g poppy seeds
1 tsp / 5 g paprika
salt, pepper to taste

Normandy has natural treasures, lively fishing villages and large agricultural farms aplenty, and our chef, Michel Bruneau, takes special interest in creating recipes that use the ingredients from this area. We all know and love the famous Normandy butter and cream, but the region also produces fabulous cheeses and apples in an endless range of flavors and colors.

This refreshing appetizer is prepared with fillets of sardines (or anchovies), if possible bought straight from the fishing boat. The marinated sardines, however, should be eaten a day after being prepared, for the ingredients will need twenty-four hours' chilling to meld and deliver their unique flavor, and only then will the dish have developed its finesse. The sardines should be small, firm, and have shiny eyes, and their flesh should be a bit fatty. The way their innards are arranged makes gutting very easy. The choice of apples is more difficult: should one opt for the very aromatic, originally American (now cultivated in New Zealand) Melrose or similar Cameo, or the more acidic, originally Australian (now also American) Granny Smith? In any case, whatever kind of apple is chosen, it must be very fresh and crisp.

If you have trouble inverting the marinade right onto a plate, you can try to separate it from the container by very carefully running a knife around the rim, making sure not to break its contents. The completed dish is then graced with sprigs of fresh dill or other seasonal herbs, small leeks, olive oil, poppy seeds, lemon zest, and paprika.

1. Gut, fillet and wash the sardines. Peel a lemon and squeeze the juice into a glass. Cut the lemon peel into fine strips; blanch. Peel the apples and cut into thin round slices; with a serrated-edged, circular cutter, cut out disks that are 2$^1/_2$ inches / 65 mm in diameter from the apple slices. Spice and sprinkle with lemon juice.

2. Marinade the sardine fillets in salt, pepper, and half of the lemon juice for about 15 minutes. Whisk the double or heavy cream and whole milk into a light whipped cream; add the rest of the lemon juice.

Fresh Sardines

3. Trim the young leeks and wash. Blanch briefly and set aside. Take four circular forms of around 2¹/₂ inches / 65 mm in diameter and one-and-a-half inches high. Place an apple disc at the bottom of each form, then line the sides of the form with a marinated sardine fillet.

4. Continue to fill the forms with layers of cream, then apple, then cream, and finally, sardine. Chill for about 24 hours. Invert each one carefully onto a plate, place two leeks on the side, sprinkle with olive oil. Garnish with lemon zest, dill, poppy seeds, and paprika.

Aïoli of Plaice

Preparation time: 1 hour, 30 minutes
Cooking time: 25 minutes
Difficulty: ★★

Serves four

2 plaice, a bit over ³/₄ lb / 400 g each
8 potatoes
4 onions
4 cloves of garlic
2 egg yolks
generous 1¹/₂ cups / 500 ml fish stock

2 sheets of gelatin
2 tsp / 10 g truffles
pinch of saffron threads
1 tsp / 3 g dried lobster coral
1 tsp / 3 g 4 star anise

For the pastis-vinaigrette:
¹/₂ cup / 125 g oil
¹/₂ cup / 125 g vinegar
2 tbs / 30 g pastis
salt

Plaice has two varieties, one European and one North American: both flatfish of the flounder family, they are similar sweet-tasting and differ mainly in coloration. A good size plaice can make a light and appetizing first course. It goes without saying that extremely fresh plaice is needed for this recipe; one way to determine freshness is to cut the skin near the tail: it should resist just a bit, a sign that removing skin from flesh would involve a certain amount of effort.

If plaice is not available, you can substitute sea bass, monkfish, or sea bream instead. Preparation of this appetizer is relatively easy: waxy potatoes should be used as they slice easily. The

garlic mayonnaise, which makes this dish lighter, is cooked the same way as custard: in the end, the sauce should coat the wooden spoon with a film. We must note that our version of aïoli is a modified one: the original is essentially a simple emulsion of oil and garlic.

The addition of a little chopped truffle, whose aromatic flavor wonderfully complements the garlic, gives the dish that extra touch. The lobster coral provides another welcome addition in color and flavor. In keeping with the oceanic theme, the dish can be garnished with seaweed (such as kombu, hijiki, or wakame), or, as shown here, with star anise.

1. Soak the gelatin ahead of time in cold water. Fillet the plaice and press flat. Cut into long thin strands, weave into braids and boil in 2 cups / 500 ml of fish stock for four minutes. Gently heat the finely chopped onions in a little oil.

2. Peel the potatoes and cut into thin, even slices. Make a classic vinaigrette, adding a little pastis for a different taste.

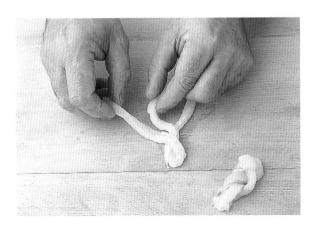

with Potatoes

3. Chop and add the garlic, and add soaked gelatin and egg yolks to the onions. Cook as if cooking custard, constantly whisking until it becomes a purée; set aside to cool. Place the plaice fillet strands in small, greased glass forms, pour aïoli over the fish.

4. Boil the potatoes for 20 minutes in the fish stock seasoned with saffron and star anise. Leave to cool. Invert the plaice-aïoli onto a plate and surround with a decorative border of potatoes and a pool of the vinaigrette. Sprinkle with the mixture of finely chopped truffle and lobster coral.

Crayfish and Caviar

Preparation time: 45 minutes
Cooking time: 45 minutes
Difficulty: ★

Serves four

24 crayfish
2½ oz / 75 g Ossetra caviar
20 green asparagus stalks
1 leek
1 onion
1 potato
scant 1 quart-chicken stock

1 cup / 250 ml whipping cream
scant ½ cup / 100 g butter
¼ tsp / 1 g ground nutmeg
salt, pepper to taste

It could be called a crayfish revolution: initially caught exclusively in rivers, from where they have all but disappeared, these freshwater crustaceans are today farmed on a large scale, with excellent results. Crayfish farms can be found in Australia and, in the U.S., in Louisiana, where the variety *procambarus clarki*, better known simply as red crayfish, is farmed. Before preparation you must remove the intestinal vein that runs down a crayfish's back, as its bitter taste would impair the crustacean's otherwise fine flavor. The stomach, which is attached to the vein, should be removed at this point as well.

Today, sturgeons are found almost exclusively in the Caspian Sea, which severely limits the number of countries that can produce caviar. These wonderful "pearls of the sea" were mentioned as early as the sixteenth century by the French writer François Rabelais. For this recipe, chef Jan Buytaert recom-

mends Ossetra caviar, which many people prefer to Beluga. Its coarse grains will mix well with the cream.

The asparagus tips should be steamed *al dente*, so that their firmness provides a nice contrast to the smooth cream; the asparagus stalks, however, should be poached. To achieve good results buy only very firm, green asparagus.

This cold appetizer is the ideal opener for a summer dinner. If you prefer, you may substitute thin strips of lobster for the crayfish.

1. Coarsely chop the leek and onion, and peel the potato. Peel the asparagus and halve into tips and stalks. Set aside the tips and sauté the stalks with the leek and onion in butter. Add the chicken stock and the whole potato; simmer for 45 minutes.

2. Steam the asparagus tips in a steamer. In a blender or food processor, blend two-thirds of the cream with the leek, onion, potato, and asparagus stalks to make the asparagus cream. Adjust its flavor with salt and pepper. Reserve the stock for the crayfish, adding some nutmeg to the liquid and then letting it cool before cooking again.

in Asparagus Cream

3. Boil the crayfish in the nutmeg-infused stock for four to five minutes, depending on size, let cool, and then remove the shells. Mix two-thirds of the asparagus cream with the remaining third of the cream and blend in the caviar.

4. Distribute the caviar-asparagus cream on the plates. Place a few tepid asparagus tips on each plate, and set the crayfish on top. Garnish with a crayfish head. Serve immediately.

Preparation time: 45 minutes
Cooking time: 45 minutes
Difficulty: ★★

Serves four

2¼ lbs / 1 kg zucchini
2 lbs / 850 g tomatoes
3 onions
6 cloves garlic
1 bunch of watercress
1½ lbs / 675 g eggplant
4 green peppers

4 red peppers
12 eggs
salt, pepper to taste

If desired, for an alternative garnish:
¼ lb / 125 g mixed lettuces, such as mesclun
    and arugula
2 tbsp / 30 ml red wine vinegar
3 tbsp / 45 ml virgin olive oil
salt, pepper to taste

The word "piper," (pronounced "peeper"), from which the name of this dish is derived, is the term for peppers used by the inhabitants of the Béarn region in southwestern France. The many different versions of this Basque dish vary from region to region, and, depending on how hearty the ingredients added are, it can be served as an appetizer or a main course. In this recipe, the color red predominates, but our inventive chef Jacques Cagnas adds even more colors, extending the palette with the green watercress purée and a yellow omelette. To achieve an intensive red for this dish, use only very ripe and fleshy tomatoes, ideally Mediterranean varieties. The red-green-yellow color aspect of the dish is reminiscent of the flags of many French-speaking African countries.

In Europe, watercress has always been credited with having blood-cleansing properties. Due to its tangy and sharp flavor, it has developed widespread popularity. It grows in water and will wither as soon as it is taken out of its natural habitat. The most successful watercress breeders can be found in the Essonne area just outside Paris, where growers trade their precious goods at large cress markets every Easter.

Nature should determine the choice of what other vegetables are used: according to season, choose either medium-sized eggplants or red and green peppers.

1. In a blender, purée the watercress and set aside; then do the same with enough tomatoes (probably four) to make about ½ cup / 125 ml of purée. Dice and strain the remaining tomatoes. Into three separate bowls, beat four eggs apiece. Blend the puréed cress into one, and the puréed tomato into the second. The eggs in the third bowl should be left plain. Season with salt and pepper and then prepare three flat omelettes.

2. Once the omelettes have cooled, use a circular cutting tool to cut out four slices of about 3 in / 75 mm in diameter from each omelette. Place each slice on a separate plate and set aside.

Piperade

3. Dice the garlic and remaining vegetables; sauté each vegetable separately for about 15 minutes or until brown; mix together and set aside to cool.

4. In the bottom of a 3 in / 75 mm (about 1¹/₂ in / 40 mm in height) circular form, place one cut-out omelette slice. On it place about a tablespoon of the diced and cooked vegetables, then lay down another slice of omelette in a different color, top with another layer of vegetables, and finish with an omelette of the third color. Invert onto the center of a plate. Decorate with the watercress purée, the diced vegetables, and the tomato purée. Or, garnish with dressed lettuces.

Duck's Heart Sausage

Preparation time: 1 hour
Cooking time: 2 hours
Marinating time: 8 hours
Difficulty: ★★

Serves four

For the sausage filling:
$^1/_2$ lb / 250 g duck hearts
$^1/_2$ lb / 250 g duck meat
$2^1/_2$ oz / 75 g pickled pig's skin
generous $^1/_4$ lb / 125 g bacon
scant $^1/_4$ lb / 100 g pork lard
generous $^1/_4$ lb / 125 g veal
scant $^1/_4$ lb / 100 g sheep's or pig's intestine
3 tbsp / 40 g bread crumbs
2 pickled shallots

1 onion
4 cloves
herb and spice mixture
salt, pepper to taste

For the potato salad:
$1^1/_4$ lbs / 600 g potatoes
2 tbsp / 20 g shallots
1 cup / 250 g chopped herbs (such as parsley, dill, thyme)
scant $^3/_4$ cup / 150 g mixed lettuce
1 bunch of chervil

For the vinaigrette:
$^1/_2$ cup / 100 ml orange juice
1 tbsp / 10 ml sherry vinegar
1 tbsp / 10 ml white wine vinegar
generous $1^1/_2$ cups / 400 ml olive oil
salt, pepper to taste

The Chinese have bred ducks for thousands of years, and a large part of their cuisine is dedicated to this bird. In time, grilled duck covered in oil became the staple diet of most people in the Far East. Today, duck remains one of the main attractions of Asian cooking.

Far removed from classic combinations, our chef Jacques Cagnas presents a dish that combines duck heart and meat with veal. He recommends, if available, ducks from Challans. Whichever type of duck you get, it should be extremely fresh. As for the veal, find milk-fed veal, as it will be easier to cut.

As with all sausages, the strength of the intestine casing is very important: one should buy only intestines suitable for sausage-making, for example a piece of thin pig's intestine, or sheep's. You may have to pickle it yourself; check with the butcher on

the best methods. The choice you make also depends on the filling: the firmer the filling, the firmer the casing has to be. It must, above all, survive cooking without bursting. This can be achieved by carefully controlling the water temperature so it never reaches a boiling point.

This sausage, lettuce, and potato salad appetizer is fairly substantial. Its rich flavors will combine well with the vinaigrette of two vinegars.

1. Overnight, marinate the duck hearts. Stick the onion with cloves; set aside. Mix the duck meat, pickled pig's skin, lard, veal, bread crumbs, bacon, pickled shallots and the herb-and-spice mixture in a bowl. Season with salt and pepper. Grind in the meat grinder on a fine blade.

2. Add the marinated duck hearts. Taste, and fill the intestine casing. For the potato salad: boil the potatoes (still with their peel on), then peel and then slice into even rounds. In a bowl, blend with the chopped shallots and herbs; keep warm.

with Potato Salad

3. In a large saucepan of water, simmer the sausage with the onion, avoiding a boil. Let simmer for one hour at approximately 155 °F / 70 °C. Prepare the vinaigrette.

4. To serve, place a small heap of salad in the center of the plate, and ring it with alternating slices of potato and sausage. Spread the vinaigrette around the entire plate. Garnish with chervil leaves.

Scottish Salmon

Preparation time: 30 minutes
Cooking time: 5 minutes
Difficulty: ☆

Serves four

$^5/_8$ lb / 300 g smoked salmon
1 lemon
4 sprigs of dill

For the lemon cream sauce:
$^1/_2$ cup / 100 ml heavy cream
juice of 1 lemon
salt, pepper to taste

For the oat cakes:
$^1/_4$ cup / 50 g ground oats
$^1/_4$ cup / 50 g oats
$1^1/_2$ tbsp / 115 g lard
water to moisten
1 tsp / 3 g dry yeast
pinch of salt

Our chef Stewart Cameron devised this recipe on a trip to Japan. The rose is a symbol of England, the oat cake is symbolic for Scotland, and the simple presentation is Japanese in flavor.

Scottish salmon usually comes from the River Tay, where it can be caught all year round, as opposed to most other rivers where catching salmon is a seasonal affair. For this recipe, a chef might choose a large salmon (about 10 lb / 5 kg), then marinate it overnight in sea salt to make it tender, and then smoke it. Everybody has their own private trick for curing salmon: Cameron, for example, uses salmon rubbed down with wood chips from the whisky barrels that originally stored sherry imported from Spain. In other words, the recipe can be as complicated or simplified as you want. For the private cook it is best to just buy a large piece of smoked salmon, about $^5/_8$ lb / 300 g. Making the "roses" may appear a little difficult at first: before you fold the first triangle, you must wrap several triangles around its base and make them stick together. It is all made easier because salmon is, of course, rather oily.

The oat cake dough should not be too moist before it is put in the oven. Or, if you don't like the taste or consistency of oat cakes, you can substitute brioche, toasted bread, or brown bread.

1. With a very sharp knife, cut the salmon into very thin slices.

2. Halve each slice lengthwise to get strips of around 2 in / 5 cm in width. Cut each strip into relatively even-sided triangles.

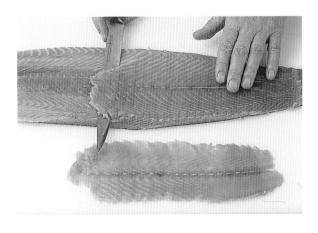

Rose on Oat Cake

3. Form the triangles into "roses," beginning in the middle and working your way out. To prepare the lemon cream sauce, carefully stir the lemon juice into the cream. Taste and, if necessary, add more lemon, then set aside to chill. Peel the other lemon, quarter, and remove any remaining pith or skin.

4. To make the oat cakes, mix all the oat cake ingredients in a bowl with enough tepid water to lightly moisten; roll out the dough very thinly on a pastry board or a cold marble slab and cut with a circular cutter. Place the dough discs on a baking tray and bake for five minutes at 355 °F / 180 °C. To serve, place an oat cake on each plate, place a salmon rose on top, and garnish with sprigs of dill, lemon pieces, and a dollop of lemon cream.

Blue Fish Pâté with

Preparation time: 45 minutes
Cooking time: 10 minutes
Marinating time: 3 hours
Difficulty: ✫

Serves four

scant $^1/_2$ lb / 200 g sardines
$^5/_8$ lb / 300 g anchovies, or, if preferred,
    mackerel or mullet
2 tbsp / 30 g capers
1 onion
1 bunch of parsley
1 cup / 250 ml dry white wine
1 tbsp / 15 ml extra virgin olive oil
salt

For the green sauce:
$^1/_4$ cup / 50 g capers
2 tbsp / 30 g anchovies
1 egg
1 bunch of parsley
juice of 1 lemon
1 shallot
$^1/_2$ cup / 125 ml extra virgin olive oil
salt

Here, the term "blue" refers not to the large and tenacious bluefish found along the Atlantic and Gulf coasts, but to the blue shimmer that marks the skin of much smaller fare. There are many kinds of blue fish in the Adriatic sea: anchovies, sardines, mullet and mackerel – all highly suitable for this original and delicious pâté. Their flesh is light, tender, and rich in iodine, with a low fat content and a delicate flavor that should not be overpowered by too many spices.

One begins this dish by choosing small mackerels, whose blue skin is scattered with black spots (or, if preferred, anchovies or mullet). As their fillets tend to disintegrate rather easily, mackerels are difficult fish to prepare, and should be carefully poached. The Italians have established a previously disputed etymological link between sardines and the island of Sardinia. Granted, sardines are certainly prominent in the Mediterra-

nean, but they also appear in the Atlantic. In this recipe, they serve as an ingredient for the paté as well as the decoration. True gourmets prefer their sardines raw and marinated, though, for this dish, the sardines are cooked.

Every region in Italy has its own way of preserving anchovies, be it by immersing them in salt, oil, lemon juice, or any other method. Here, the anchovies' particular flavor combines well with the spicy pâté, which is dominated by the taste of capers and herbs.

The tangy green sauce, which also uses capers, is a typical accompaniment for this dish. Try dunking some roasted hazelnut bread (or any toasted bread) into the sauce for yet another dimension of flavor.

1. Chop the parsley and cut the onions into rings. Wash, gut, and fillet the sardines, sprinkle with salt and put them in a deep oven dish with the chopped parsley, the onion rings and the capers; add white wine and bake in a pre-heated oven at 350 °F / 180 °C for approximately three minutes.

2. Wash, gut and fillet the other fish; steam in a covered pan for ten minutes. Place the sardines and their cooking liquid as well as the steamed fish and its cooking liquid in a deep oven dish; sprinkle with olive oil, and marinate at room temperature for three hours.

Green Shallot Sauce

3. Hard-boil the egg. Halve the shallot and set aside one half. To prepare the green sauce, place all ingredients in the blender and chop for a few seconds. Adjust to taste with lemon juice, olive oil, and salt.

4. To make the pâté, remove the sardines and the other fish from the marinade. Take half the sardines and curl into rolls; set aside. Finely chop half of the sardines and all of the fish, season with the marinade, strain, and mix well. Form the mass into rounds of around 4 in / 10 cm in diameter, and about 1¹/₂ in / 4 cm in height. To serve, decorate the plates with the green sauce, place the paté on the plate and top with green sauce. Garnish with marinated sardine rolls.

Grilled Tuna

Preparation time: 50 minutes
Cooking time: 30 minutes
Marinating time: 1 hour, 30 minutes
Cooling time: 2 hours
Difficulty: ★★

Serves four

$^7/_8$ lb fresh tuna (bonito if available)
4 medium-sized eggplants, or
6 Italian or baby eggplants
2 tomatoes
1 lemon
1 small cucumber
1 red pepper
1 green pepper
4 zucchini flowers

1 clove garlic
1 dozen shelled or blanched almonds
4 basil leaves
2 sprigs flat-leafed parsley

2 sprigs thyme
1 dozen red olives
$^1/_2$ cup / 125 ml cold-pressed olive oil
salt, pepper to taste

For the gazpacho:
1 clove garlic
1 onion
1 cucumber
1 red pepper
1 green pepper
6 tomatoes
6 sprigs flat-leafed parsley
6 mint leaves
$^1/_2$ cup / 125 ml cold-pressed olive oil
2 tbsp / 30 ml sherry vinegar
salt, fresh-ground pepper to taste

This delicious recipe, which combines marinated tuna and chilled gazpacho, is typically Spanish. An ideal variety of tuna for the dish is the small, flavorful bonito. The flavor of the grilled and marinated eggplant complements the fish perfectly and makes this dish a feast for the palate.

The whole tuna should be a fine, fresh specimen with striped skin, weighing about 6–8 lb / 3–4 kg. The tender and flavorful meat will be cut into twelve medallions. When preparing and grilling these, care must be taken not to let them dry out, as the flesh will fray. Marinating the tuna in olive oil beforehand will ensure that the fish remains moist, making it easier to grill.

The eggplants are the perfect side vegetable, particularly if they are of the smaller Italian or baby variety, which retain most of their juices when grilled. Grilled and then cut into strips, the eggplant will retain its flavor and firmness.

The gazpacho that chef Francis Chauveau presents here should be left to infuse in olive oil for at least an hour so that its flavor can develop fully. This chilled soup can also be sprinkled with lightly crushed star anise, and served with socca, or chickpea pancakes, an old Niçoise recipe (see the following pages).

1. Finely chop the garlic. Grill the eggplants whole and unpeeled. After letting them cool, halve lengthwise, carefully separate the flesh from the skin, and cut into thin strips. Marinate the strips with the garlic in olive oil for one and a half hours.

2. For the gazpacho, wash the peppers, halve, and discard the seeds. Cut the peppers, tomato, onion and cucumber into large chunks, finely chop the garlic and add mint and parsley. Season with vinegar, olive oil, salt and pepper; refrigerate for two hours. Stir well and then strain. Peel the almonds; briefly sauté the basil leaves and zucchini flowers over low heat, just until they wilt.

with Gazpacho

3. Cut the tuna into twelve medallions. Marinate these in olive oil, thyme, and lemon juice for half an hour. Grill each medallion for a minute on each side. Grill the remaining peppers, peel under cold running water, and discard the seeds. Peel the second tomato and, if desired, cut the peel into the form of flower petals. Cut the olives into slivers. Trim the leaves off the parsley sprigs.

4. To serve, place the eggplant strips in the center of the plate. Place the tuna medallions on top, along with zucchini flowers and basil leaves and, if you made them, the petals of tomato skin. Pour a little gazpacho around the eggplant and tuna; garnish with vegetable chunks, almonds, olive slivers, and parsley leaves. Serve the remaining chilled gazpacho in an accompanying bowl.

Langoustines with Chickpea

Preparation time: *45 minutes*
Cooking time: *20 minutes*
Difficulty: ★★

Serves four

4 red langoustines, about ³/₄ lb / 350 g each
2 lbs / 1 kg viola asparagus
generous ¹/₄ lb / 150 g mixed lettuce
¹/₈ lb / 50 g Parmesan cheese
²/₃ cup / 160 g chickpea flour
¹/₄ cup / 60 ml olive oil
2 cups / 500 ml cold water
broth
salt, fresh-ground pepper to taste

For the vinaigrette:
¹/₄ cup / 60 ml balsamic vinegar
¹/₂ cup / 125 ml olive oil
salt, fresh-ground pepper to taste

Fresh herbs:
8 sprigs of chervil
8 sprigs of chives
2 sprigs of flat-leafed parsley
2 sprigs of tarragon
2 sprigs of dill

This Mediterranean recipe combines the fine aroma of langoustines with fresh herbs and the traditional flavor of chickpea cakes, also known as socca, which are still relatively unknown even in gastronomical circles. The "Royal" red langoustine variety, though rare in the Mediterranean, is the perfect variety for this recipe. It is primarily caught off the coast of Brittany, though it can also be found in Morocco. The other varieties of langoustine, not as valued by the experts, are pink, green or brown. They will all turn red immediately upon hitting boiling water. Buying live langoustines is recommended. A good way to determine if the langoustines are alive or not is to check their tail movements, as they wiggle their tails vigorously when alive.

Viola asparagus is really white asparagus whose tip has broken through the soil surface and been exposed to the sun for a few hours, giving it both a violet hue and an intense, fruity flavor.

The famed white asparagus of Provence is grown completely under the ground's surface; the purple variety is equally outstanding in flavor. Combined with the fresh herbs, the asparagus lends this dish a refreshing touch.

The chickpea cakes are also typically Provençal. The chickpea flour must be free of lumps, which is why it is laced with water. The small cakes "à la Niçoise" must be fried for quite a while if they are to develop their flavor. If you want them to be a little firmer, chef Francis Chauveau recommends chilling the dough before using it.

1. In a saucepan, stir chickpea flour constantly while adding cold water and a ¹/₄ cup / 60 ml olive oil. Season with salt and pepper. Bring to a rapid boil, still constantly stirring, and let boil for approximately ten minutes. Pour into an oiled, square form (a small terrine pan will also work) and chill.

2. When the dough is completely cooled, cut into slices; fry in olive oil until crisp. Make a vinaigrette from the balsamic vinegar, salt, pepper, and olive oil. Bring the cooking broth to a boil; drop the langoustines in one by one and cook for six minutes. Set aside to cool, then shell the langoustines.

Cakes and Asparagus

3. Peel the asparagus and wash. Set in boiling water and reduce heat; simmer so that the tips don't disintegrate. Set twelve good tips aside and chop up the rest, seasoning with vinaigrette. Place the chopped asparagus in the center of each plate, in a circular form of about 4 in / 10 cm in diameter.

4. Cut the langoustine meat into medallions. While the circular form is still on the plate, arrange the medallions into a rosette on top of the chopped asparagus, then place three asparagus tips in the middle. Carefully lift off the form. Dribble vinaigrette around the rosette; decorate with herb leaves. Around the plate place three bunches of the mixed lettuce, alternating with three small piles of chickpea cakes; cover the lettuce with shavings of Parmesan cheese.

Fresh Oysters with

Preparation time: 20 minutes
Cooking time: 1 5 minutes
Difficulty: ★★

Serves four

2 dozen French oysters (Bouzique, Belon, or
    Marennes) or
2 dozen Atlantic oysters (such as Bluepoint)
scant $^1/_2$ lb / 200 g celeriac
3 tbsp / 40 g celeriac leaves
scant $^1/_2$ lb / 200 g zucchini
scant $^3/_8$ lb / 150 g lamb's lettuce
quarter bunch of chervil

1 sheet of gelatin
$^1/_2$ cup / 125 ml whipping cream
1 cup / 250 ml milk
$^5/_8$ cup / 150 ml olive oil
$1^1/_2$ tsp / 7 g paprika
celery salt
1 cup / 250 ml mineral water
salt, pepper to taste
1 tbsp / 15 ml balsamic vinegar

For the dressing:
$^1/_4$ cup / 60 ml olive oil
juice of half a lemon
salt, pepper to taste

The Bouzique oysters from the breeding banks of the Thau Basin in the Languedoc, France, are rated as a particular delicacy amongst gourmets; of these, the small variety with the rough shell, also known as Mediterranean oysters, are favored. Though not as well-known and expensive as the Marennes oysters from Marennes-Oléron, they have an intense and long-lasting iodine taste favored by experts. These oysters used to be offered in huge amounts, though today they are sold only by the dozens. Another French oyster often available in North American markets, Belon, is from northern Brittany, and also has a rich, iodine taste. If none of these are available, choose Atlantic oysters, particularly the outstanding and popular bluepoint variety.

The oysters are briefly cooked at a temperature of around 120 °F / 50 °C before being combined with the celeriac, which

should be very fresh and have strong green leaves. The celeriac should be firm and heavy, ensuring an even puree, which will be enhanced with paprika.

Celery salt is simply salt enriched with celery powder, which enhances the character of the dish.

Lamb's lettuce, which may originally hail from southern Italy, but in any case was first cultivated in Europe, comes in two varieties: one has rounder leaves and is more tender; both contain a great deal of chlorophyll. Its aroma suits oysters perfectly. This lettuce must be washed very thoroughly, and its single leaves picked off, so each serving plate will end up ringed with little "flowers."

1. Ahead of time, soak the gelatin in cold water. Open the oysters, shell, and pour both the water contained in the oyster shell and the oysters into a saucepan. Add the mineral water. Heat very gently, add soaked gelatin and glaze the oysters.

2. Cook the celeriac in milk, then blend with a little milk, the cooking liquid, celery salt, pepper and celery leaves into a very smooth puree. Leave to cool and add the whipped cream, a few drops of lemon juice and $^1/_4$ cup / 60 ml olive oil.

Celeriac Mousse

3. Wash and pat dry the lamb's lettuce. Prepare a vinaigrette with $^1/_2$ cup / 120 ml olive oil, the juice of half a lemon, salt, and pepper. Cut the zucchini into very thin, flat strips 3 in / 7.5 cm long. Cook al dente in salted water, rinse with cold water, let dry and then season with salt, pepper, and the vinaigrette.

4. To serve, form a ring of lamb's lettuce leaves on each plate. Set a circular form 4 in / 10 cm diameter in the center, layering lamb's lettuce leaves, zucchini strips, and celeriac puree inside it. Place the oysters on top, moistening with a few drops of dressing and balsamic vinegar. Garnish with chervil leaves and sprinkle with paprika.

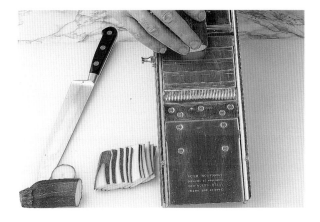

Sea Bass with Fresh

Preparation time: 15 minutes
Cooking time: 2 minutes
Difficulty: ★

Serves four

2 lbs / 1 kg sea bass (or, if unavailable,
  monkfish or turbot)
⁵/₈ lb / 300 g tomatoes
scant ¹/₄ lb / 100 g zucchini
1 red pepper
1 yellow pepper
¹/₈ lb / 50 g fennel

¹/₁₆ lb / 30 g turnip
¹/₂ lb / 200 g mesclun
1 tbsp / 10 g black olives
1 tbsp / 10 ml Noilly-Prat vermouth
1 sprig fresh tarragon
3 sprigs dill
2 sprigs basil
salt, pepper to taste

For the lemon dressing
1 lemon
1 cup / 250 ml olive oil
salt, pepper to taste

Etymologically, basil is an herb fit for royalty: the ancient Greeks called it a "royal herb," and only kings could enjoy the privilege of cutting off a few stems for themselves with a gold knife. The herb has since lost none of its noble character. It stars in many Provençal recipes, such as the famous pesto. The dish we present here calls for a particularly aromatic variety of basil with the large leaves; it will combine well with the fish.

Sea bass is considered the king of the Mediterranean, where this predatory fish has been known since antiquity. Its flesh has a delicate and fine flavor, but it must not be cooked for too long or it will become watery and flaky. If you prefer, you can have the fishmonger fillet it for you. In keeping with Mediterranean tradition, this appetizer is accompanied by tomatoes. The best kind for this recipe are round, meaty, ripe tomatoes that come into their own with the fresh dill and tarragon. We recommend

you take advantage of the seasons and preserve such tomatoes for the winter months, perhaps in the form of a puree enriched with olive oil.

Mesclun, as mixed lettuce is now known (the term originated in Provence), consists of small, young leaves of several different lettuces. If you prefer to mix a mesclun yourself, use raddichio, oakleaf, and portulaca. The mesclun should be dressed quickly, and on no account should it be seasoned too strongly.

If sea bass is unavailable, you may substituted another white-fleshed fish, such as monkfish or turbot. But no matter the other substitutions, for this dish basil is indispensable.

1. Peel the tomatoes, discard the seeds and cut into ³/₈ in / 1 cm chunks. Pit the olives; slice thin; simmer with the tomatoes in water for five minutes. Drain and set aside to dry. Finely chop the remaining vegetables and briefly simmer each one separately in salted water.

2. Prepare a lemon vinaigrette. Mix the cooked vegetables, add the vermouth, chopped tarragon and basil, and olives; work into some of the lemon vinaigrette. Add salt and pepper. Wash and dry the mesclun. In a salad bowl, dress with ¹/₄ cup / 60 ml of the vinaigrette, adding salt and pepper to taste.

Herbs and Mesclun

3. Fillet the fish, skin, and divide into four equal portions. Season with salt and pepper and briefly fry in ¼ cup / 60 ml of olive oil.

4. To serve: place the mesclun in the center of each plate; place the fried fish on top. Sprinkle with the vegetable-dressing mixture and garnish with dill sprigs.

Mackerel Strips

Preparation time: 30 minutes
Marinating time: 24 hours
Difficulty: ✶

Serves four

4 large mackerels
1 red pepper
1 lemon
herb and spice mixture
1 bay leaf
half a bunch of chives
half a bunch of tarragon

half a bunch of parsley
$^{1}/_{2}$ cup / 125 ml olive oil
coarse sea salt
fresh-ground pepper
4 basil leaves

The mackerel, a distant cousin of the tuna, is a fast-swimming, spindle-shaped fish with an instantly recognizable steel-blue back. It does not like to be lonely, always appearing in large groups. This schooling instinct makes it easy for fishermen to catch them, even without bait, in rather small nets. Occasionally, when a huge school of mackerel has been caught in the nets, it has been known to drag the fishing boats along for a ride. Its firm, medium-fat flesh is suitable for all kinds of preparations.

To check a mackerel's freshness, look for bright red gills and luminous colors along the skin. This is particularly important since this recipe requires mackerels that have just been caught: they are served raw after having marinated for twenty-four hours. Cutting them into thin strips may present the only difficult part of preparation, but this task can be made easier by chilling the fish for a few hours in the freezer to firm up the flesh.

1. Gut each mackerel, separating the back from the belly and removing the bones with pincers. Marinate in sea salt in the refrigerator for 24 hours.

2. The following morning, wipe the fillets clean, making sure to remove all traces of salt; cut into even strips 4 in / 10 cm long; chill.

à la Sète

3. Cut the chilled fillets into even smaller pieces, about 2 in / 5 cm long. Crush the chives, tarragon, and parsley with a mortar and pestle. Finely chop the red pepper.

4. In a large metal bowl mix the fresh herbs, herb and spice mix, bay leaf, pepper, and chopped peppers; add olive oil and lemon juice. To serve, place the mackerel strips on the plate in a fan shape, covering the entire surface. Dress with the herbs and vegetable sauce; garnish with basil leaves.

Terrine of Rabbit and

Preparation time: 35 minutes
Cooking time: 2 hours
Marinating time: 8 hours
Cooling time: 8 hours
Difficulty: ★

Serves four

2 lbs / 1 kg rabbit
$^1/_4$ cup / 50 ml Chardonnay de Champagne
1 bunch of parsley
1 bunch of tarragon
1 bunch of chives
salt, pepper to taste

For the garnish:
$^1/_2$ lb / 250 g mesclun
$^1/_4$ cup / 60 ml olive oil
$^1/_2$ cup / 125 ml red wine vinegar
salt and pepper to taste

There are endless recipes for rabbit, an animal that originated in North America and has been around at least since the tertiary period. Rabbit meat has a very high protein content and is therefore well suited for low-calorie cuisine.

For this recipe we recommend you use a fairly large, young domestic rabbit, as the smaller ones tend to overcook too quickly and therefore produce tough meat. In general, rabbit meat is light and slightly pink, with a very shiny liver. Since this type of rabbit lives on clover, barley, and wheat, its meat and muscles are much better developed than those of the stronger-flavored breeding rabbits from large farms.

A cold dish quickly loses its spicy flavor. One should, therefore, spice and season generously, keeping in mind that about a quarter of the strength of spices and seasoning will be absorbed by the cold. This is particularly true for the herbs used in this terrine. The meat should marinate overnight. And, as per usual for terrines, this terrine should be made the day before. Line the terrine form with plastic wrap to make inverting it easier on serving day.

1. Cut the rabbit into chunks and completely remove the legs. Retain the liver and kidneys. For this dish, all the meat should be used.

2. Cut the rabbit meat into walnut-sized chunks. Quarter the kidneys, and cut the liver and belly into thin strips.

Parsley with Chardonnay

3. Finely chop all the herbs, place in a bowl along with the meat, salt, pepper and Chardonnay; mix well.

4. Let sit overnight so all the flavors are absorbed and blended. In a bain-marie, bake in the oven for two hours at 260 °F / 140 °C. After baking, remove from the oven and set aside to rest for two hours. Then cover the terrine pan with a weighted lid and store in a cool place overnight. To serve, slice with a sharp knife and invert carefully; garnish with a small salad.

Fried Duck Liver

Preparation time: 30 minutes
Cooking time: 15 minutes
Difficulty: ★★

Serves four

1¼ lbs / 600 g duck liver
1 bunch of white asparagus
1 bunch of green asparagus
a few chervil leaves
3 tbsp / 45 g lard
½ cup / 250 g fresh cranberries
half a bunch of chives (optional)

For the vinaigrette:
1 cup / 250 ml olive oil
generous 1½ cups / 400 ml vinegar
salt, pepper to taste

In antiquity, the Gauls introduced the Romans to the concept of foie gras. According to the Gaul recipe, ducks and geese destined for the delicacy were force-fed succulent figs; their livers would then be preserved in a mixture of honey and milk, which caused the organs to bloat and develop a delicate, oily film.

Whether from a goose or a duck, the liver should be very fresh, smooth and well-lobed, with an even color ranging somewhere between yellow and white. Too thick a liver may lose all its fat when frying. It is increasingly common these days to find raw livers available in markets, but note that these will last only a week in the refrigerator before the gall seeps out and renders the entire organ bitter.

Since scallops of consistent width and shape are called for here, the chefs Bernard and Jean Couseau recommend using a very thin knife. For easier cutting, warm the blade in hot water just before use.

You may experiment with the two different asparagus colors, choosing, for example, violet and white stalks instead of green and white, but the bottom line should always be quality. The stalks should be rough and stiff, the tips very straight; they should be cooked, appropriately, in an asparagus cooker or a similarly tall saucepan, and steamed or boiled in an upright position with the tips up. Since the top half of the spears will be used for decoration, it is essential that the tips in particular retain their color.

Serve this dish warm – not hot – to better feature the delicate flavor of the duck liver.

1. Cut the duck liver into even slices, ³⁄₈ in / 1 cm thick.

2. Peel the asparagus; boil each bunch separately in salted water for ten minutes. Rinse with cold water and set aside.

with Asparagus Tips

3. Sprinkle the duck liver scallops with salt and fry in lard, browning each side for about three minutes; set aside. Prepare the vinaigrette.

4. To serve, arrange the asparagus tips in a fan-shape on half of each plate, alternating colors. Brush with vinaigrette. On the other half of the plate, arrange the duck liver. Garnish with chervil, cranberries, and, if desired, chive sprigs.

Lobster Salad with

Preparation time: 45 minutes
Cooking time: 30 minutes
Difficulty: ★★

Serves four

2 1 lb / 450 g lobsters
2 tomatoes
3 Chinese potatoes
4 egg yolks
2 tbsp / 30 ml balsamic vinegar
1 cup / 250 ml vegetable oil
half a bunch of chervil

For the broth:
2 carrots
1 onion
1 bouquet garni
black peppercorns
$^1/_4$ lb / 100 g salt

Contrary to the generally accepted notion, the military pharmacist Antoine Parmentier did not discover the potato, nor did he introduce it to France. The "tartoufle" or "cartoufle" was known only as cattle feed and considered to be unhealthy as well as a pest carrier. Parmentier did, to his credit, suggest the cultivation of the potato on a large scale as a basic food stuff, and he was supported in this mission by King Louis XVI, on whose fields near Neuilly the French cultivation of potatoes began. Every potato variety has its own characteristics; the Chinese, or blue potato, does not change its consistency during cooking. It has a violet skin that should be smooth and without any green spots or seedlings. Rich in starch and vitamin C, the potato is a nutritious foodstuff that is best cooked without any addition of fat. The Chinese potatoes can also be replaced with salad potatoes, such as new potatoes, if you prefer.

For this recipe, the blue lobsters from Brittany should be used, whose shell turns red when cooked, but whose flesh remains white. The female lobsters are bigger and longer and have more flavor and coral (roe) – choose female lobsters, if you can, weighing between 1–1$^1/_4$ lb / 450–565 g. Do not boil them for longer than five to six minutes or the flesh will begin to toughen.

Balsamic vinegar is a versatile and delicate product and has such an intense aroma that it should be used sparingly to give the dish that special note. In order to benefit fully from the balsamic vinegar's aroma, the sauce should have a syrup-like consistency, which is particularly suitable for use with lobsters.

1. Prepare a broth with 9 pints / 4$^1/_2$ l of water, salt, the onion, thin carrot slices, bouquet garni and peppercorns. Bring to the boil and cook for 20 minutes. Insert the live lobsters and cook for seven to eight minutes; take them out and leave to cool. Scrape out the lobster heads.

2. Mix the flesh from the lobster heads with balsamic vinegar and two tablespoons of the now-cold broth. Puree with the four egg yolks and stir in some oil, as you would if making a mayonnaise. If the sauce becomes too thick, stir in some broth drop by drop until the desired consistency is achieved.

Chinese Potatoes

3. Boil the potatoes for about 15 minutes in salted water. Leave to cool. Peel the potatoes and slice. Peel the tomatoes, discard the seeds and chop into small chunks. Extract the lobster meat from the shell.

4. Cut the lobster tails into thin slices and halve the claws. Trim the heads for decoration. Pour a little sauce on the plate, place lobster and potatoes on the plate and garnish with the chopped tomato. Sprinkle with chervil leaves.

Carpaccio of Monkfish

Preparation time:	30 minutes, with some preparations made in advance
Smoking time:	36 hours
Marinating time:	3 hours
Difficulty:	☆

Serves four

1 lb / 450 g monkfish tail, filleted
¹/₂ lb / 250 g sea snails
1 tomato
1 shallot

1 lemon
4 lbs / 2 kg sea salt
scant ¹/₂ cup / 100 ml olive oil
2 tbsp / 30 g green peppercorns
2 tbsp / 30 g pink peppercorns
1 bouquet garni
half a bunch of fresh tarragon
half a bunch of fresh chervil
half a bunch of fresh chives
salt, pepper to taste

Originally made with beef (see page 32 for a fuller explanation), the nineteenth-century innovation known as *carpaccio* has many imitators, and this *carpaccio* of monkfish created by Richard Coutanceau is definitely one of the best.

Though the recipe calls for monkfish – a fish increasingly used in a variety of dishes – it is not always readily available. If this is the case, you can substitute monkfish with sea bass, which is another fish well-suited for *carpaccio*. In any case, the fish must be marinated in sea salt for a few hours to firm up the flesh without impairing its tenderness. As preparation takes quite a while, it is advisable to start a few days in advance. The biggest challenge for this dish, however, will be cutting the monkfish into very thin slices and then gently flattening them in order to conform to the definition of a *carpaccio*.

The snails, with their very crisp flesh, provide a good contrast for the monkfish. After being cooked in an aromatic, salted broth, they must be extracted from their shells with a needle, a task that requires some patience and a calm hand. Their soft ends are their most delicious part, earning this section praise from culinary experts, who like to call it the snail's own foie gras.

1. If it has not been skinned already, skin the monkfish fillet. Dab it with olive oil to moisten, and marinate in sea salt for one hour. Rinse with water; let rest for 12 hours. Then place in a smoking oven for 36 hours (a procedure known as hot-smoking).

2. Scrub the snails, removing their opercula, and soak for three hours in frequently changed, salted water. Rinse several times. To cook, blanch in a broth seasoned with salt, a few peppercorns, and the bouquet garni for three to four minutes. Let drip dry, then use a needle to scoop them out of their shells.

with Snail Salad

3. Peel the tomato, discard the seeds, and dice; crush the peppercorns; chop the chervil and shallot. Prepare a dressing for the snails made of lemon juice and olive oil, adding chopped tarragon, crushed pink and green peppercorns, some of the diced tomatoes, chopped chervil, and a pinch of salt, and finally, the chives and chopped shallot. Set aside some of the dressing.

4. To serve, slice the monkfish fillet into extremely fine, even slices and arrange on the plate like the petals of a flower. Season with the same dressing used for the snails. In the center of this "flower," place a small heap of the snail salad. Garnish with chervil leaves and chopped tomato.

Langoustine Tartare in

Preparation time: 35 minutes
Difficulty: ★★

Serves four

5/8 lb / 300 g langoustines
1 dozen large oysters, such as Bluepoint or
   Belon
1 tomato
1/2 sheet of gelatin
6 pink peppercorns
1 bunch of chervil
1 bunch of tarragon

1/2 cup / 125 g lamb's lettuce
salt, pepper to taste

For the sherry vinegar sauce:
1/4 cup / 50 g mayonnaise (see basic recipes)
2 tsp / 10 ml sherry vinegar
1 1/4 cups / 300 ml whipping cream
salt
green peppercorns

Today, dishes "à la tartare" usually connotes a dish of raw meat, often spicily seasoned. Here, Richard Countanceau uses langoustines, whose delicious meat is ideally suited for this highly original recipe.

Both the langoustines and the oysters must be very fresh indeed. In France, one would choose No. 3 Special oysters, which are bigger and fleshier than other varieties. Not far from Richard Coutanceau's restaurant, between La Rochelle and Fouras, is an oyster farm where the shellfish are bred in salt swamps. In two to four months, excellent oysters are produced that are low in calories and rich in vitamins and minerals. In North America, however, it might be easier to look for bluepoint oysters, or the increasingly popular Belon, which originated in France.

Since the action of a blender would begin heating the langoustine meat, thus getting the cooking process off to a premature

start, the raw langoustines should be chopped with a knife. The oysters are made into an aspic, which, to make it completely translucent, is passed through a muslin cloth. If necessary, the jelly may be stretched with a little langoustine broth. The flavor of the chopped langoustines should be allowed to determine the overall flavor of the dish, so when adding the herbs to season, take care to do so in moderation. No flavor but that of the langoustines should be allowed to dominate.

Sherry vinegar, on the other hand, has a more delicate flavor that will underscore the finesse of the langoustines. The same applies to the pink pepper (its color is really a sort of rosy red), which has a subtle, slightly sweet aniseed flavor.

Finally, both the oyster juice (about 1/2 cup / 120 ml) and the broth made from the langoustine shells are reserved to be used for flavor.

1. Prepare a classic mayonnaise and add to it 2 tsp / 10 ml of sherry vinegar. Fold in the whipped cream, salt, and green peppercorns. Wash the lamb's lettuce thoroughly. Shell the langoustines and prepare a broth with the shells. When the broth is finished, skim and strain it until it is clear.

2. Open the oysters, saving the water inside their shells. Place the shelled oysters on absorbent paper towels. To make the oyster aspic, soak the sheet of gelatin in water for a few minutes, drip dry, and add to the oyster juice and the strained langoustine broth. Chill. With a sharp knife, chop the langoustine meat.

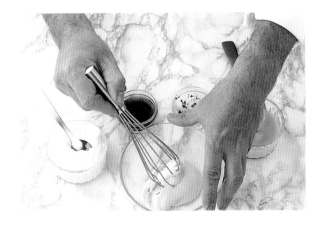

a Delicate Oyster Aspic

3. Chop a teaspoon of tarragon; crush the pink peppercorns. Mix into the chopped langoustine meat, then add 2 tbsp / 10 ml of the sherry vinegar sauce. Adjust seasoning to taste. Peel the tomato, discard the seeds and dice.

4. To serve, fill a circular form in the center of a plate with the langoustine tartare. Remove the form and surround the tartare with an arrangement of three oysters, three small bunches of lamb's lettuce and a ring of oyster aspic. Garnish with chervil and tomato.

Asparagus Charlotte

Preparation time: 1 hour
Cooking time: 15 minutes
Difficulty: ✶✶

Serves four

2 dozen stalks green asparagus
4 oz / 120 g caviar
4 leeks
3 cups / 800 ml whipping cream
salt, pepper to taste

This appetizer combines caviar with green asparagus stalks that wrap decoratively around the charlotte, complemented by a light pool of cream.

Our chef, Jean Crotet, recommends medium-sized green asparagus, the color and flavor of which combine well with the caviar. Select extremely fresh and strong spears without any dry patches, and with firm tips. Though many people practice the unfortunate habit of scraping the asparagus, it should, as Crotet points out, be peeled instead for this recipe.

Forming the charlotte can prove a little tricky for beginners. The halved asparagus spears surrounding it should be arranged vertically, with the cut surface facing out. When tying the whole bundle with the strips of leek or chive, one really needs four hands.

Caviar's consistency provides an intriguing contrast to the smooth charlotte. The most suitable caviar for this recipe is, of course, Sevruga, which comes from small sturgeons producing very tender roe. This caviar is soft and has a strong aroma, making it a popular choice among gourmets. Ossetra caviar, on the other hand, is coarse and golden in color, and its flavor is much fruitier. The small caviar mounds should be carefully formed in a spoon so that the eggs are not crushed.

If the ingredients for this recipe are not available, it can also be made with broccoli and salmon roe. But though a far less expensive option, the flavor will not match that of the original recipe.

1. Peel the asparagus, trim the tips at about 3¹/₂ in / 8 cm in length, and reserve the stalks. Cook the tips in salted water for about three minutes. Rinse with cold water and leave to dry on paper towels.

2. Blanch the asparagus stalks in salted water for about three to four minutes, letting them drip dry. Boil them once more in the cream for three minutes, seasoning gently. After cooking, mix the asparagus and the cream in the blender; set aside to chill.

with Caviar

3. To create the charlottes, place a circular metal form (3 in / 7.5 cm in diameter and 1 in / 2.5 cm high) in the middle of each of four plates. Trim half the asparagus tips to 2 in / 5 cm, and cut the rest into small chunks. Halve the intact tips lengthwise, placing them vertically against the inside wall of the metal form with their cut surface facing outwards. Fill the form with the asparagus chunks; pour the asparagus cream over them; the cream will leak out to form a pool on the surface of the plate.

4. Lightly steam the leeks to soften their green leaves enough to render them malleable. Carefully lift the form off the plate. Tie up the charlotte with the leek leaves. Shortly before serving, place dollops of caviar in the bed of cream around the plate.

Hot and Cold

Preparation time: 30 minutes
Cooking time: 15 minutes
Difficulty: ✷✷

Serves four

3 dozen large oysters
$^1/_4$ cup / 50 ml cream, whipped
$^1/_4$ lb / 100 g spinach
$^1/_4$ lb / 100 g leeks
$^1/_8$ lb / 50 g carrots
6 shallots
1$^1/_2$ cups / 370 ml dry white wine

$^3/_4$ cup / 200 ml wine vinegar
$^1/_4$ cup / 50 ml olive oil
$^1/_2$ cup / 125 ml crème fraîche
$^1/_4$ lb / 100 g butter
pinch of saffron thread
coarse sea salt
salt, pepper to taste

For the dressing:
$^1/_2$ cup / 125 ml olive oil
salt, pepper to taste

Chef Jean Crotet had the idea of using the small portions of different sauces that were left over; thus was this oyster recipe conceived. A delectable appetizer, it consists of a delicate mixture of vegetables with warm and cold oysters.

The recipe requires fresh oysters with a wavy shell, as thick and fleshy as possible. Oysters from Normandy, with their strong iodine taste, are perfect, especially the heavy "special" oysters with their excellent aroma; if these are unavailable, look for any curly-shelled variety of the flavorful Atlantic oyster. These high-quality molluscs should be carefully simmered at a maximum of 100 °F / 40 °C, otherwise their flavor will literally evaporate. Some fine oysters will simply not survive any cooking; they are eaten raw.

The vegetables, including the shallots, need to be as fresh as possible. They will be mixed with an olive oil-based dressing and dry white wine to make a smooth cream. Instead of white wine, champagne may also be used: its flavor will further the link between vegetables and oysters.

A little trick for the presentation: generously sprinkle the plates with coarse sea salt first and place the oysters on the salt. This way the shells will not wobble, making it easier not to spill the sauce when you pour it in. On no account should this dish be reheated as the taste of the oysters will be irrevocably altered. Instead, this dish should be eaten immediately upon serving.

1. Open the oysters and carefully shell them; save the sea water inside the shell. Wash well and place in a casserole with the sea water; infuse at a gentle simmer over low heat for three minutes; set aside.

2. Cook a quarter of the shallots in vinegar; set aside half of those and let cool, then mix them with whipped cream, salt and pepper. To the other half of the cooked shallots add olive oil, salt, and pepper to make what is in fact a warm dressing. Cook the remaining shallots in wine. Divide this batch in half as well, adding crème fraîche and saffron to one half and bringing it to a boil; season. To the other half, add butter and whisk constantly.

Oyster Platter

3. Wash the spinach, discard the stalks and quickly blanch the leaves until they wilt. Julienne the leeks and carrots and blanch for five minutes.

4. To serve, sprinkle each plate with a ring or a bed of coarse sea salt. Place nine oyster shells on each. Fill as follows: three shells with spinach under saffron sauce, three with leeks under butter sauce, three with julienned carrots in the warm dressing. Heat the oysters briefly in the oven and place them in the shells as well.

Gazpacho

Preparation time: 20 minutes
Cooking time: 2 hours
Difficulty: ☆

Serves four

10 tomatoes
1 cucumber
1 bunch of celery
1 zucchini
1 red pepper
1/2 green pepper
1 shallot

1 egg yolk
generous 4 tbsp / 60 g black olive tapenade
5/8 lb / 300 g fromage frais (from sheep's milk)
2 tbsp / 30 ml heavy cream
2 tbsp / 30 ml olive oil
1 drop of Tabasco
4 good basil leaves
half a bunch of chives
salt, pepper to taste
1 cup / 250 g ice cubes

Elegantly served with a bit of stuffing, this dish features a slightly modified version of the traditional gazpacho in order to provide an appetizer suitable for a more substantial meal. Chef Michel Del Burgo has created this recipe in his kitchen at the Hôtel de l'Europe in Avignon, France, which makes it, therefore, an ideal participant in a collection of European delicacies.

Although gazpacho is a simple dish in Spain, where it originated, it can nonetheless be prepared with special ingredients. Our chef includes, for example, French fromage frais (or unripened cheese) made from sheep's milk, which blends well with the tomatoes. There are many varieties of this kind of fromage frais available, including brousse, cachat, and tomme fraîche. If sheep's milk fromage frais is not available, fromage frais made from cow's or goat's milk may be used. Del Burgo also

prefers small, very aromatic, sun-ripened tomatoes, since they lend the necessarily full-bodied flavor to the soup. Select firm, full tomatoes that are a deep, vibrant red.

Preparing gazpacho presents one basic problem: binding the liquid, which rarely forms a smooth emulsion with the tomato pulp alone. Furthermore, the amount of juices the tomatoes release can render the gazpacho too thin. In order to achieve an even emulsion, Michel Del Burgo recommends binding the sauce with egg yolk.

The other vegetables featured here underscore the tomato flavor: the cucumber, for example, is marinated in salt to make it more digestible. The olive tapenade gives the gazpacho a tangy touch.

1. To prepare the gazpacho, dice half the red pepper and chop the shallot; in a blender or food processor mix them with the olive oil and egg yolk. Chop five tomatoes; add them to the mixture. Add Tabasco to taste; blend with enough ice cubes to make a fine puree and continue blending until the liquid has emulsifies.

2. Peel and seed one of the remaining tomatoes. Cut them, as well as the remaining red pepper, the cucumber, green pepper, zucchini, and celery into small chunks. Briefly blanch the green peppers, zucchini and celery. Peel the other four tomatoes, cut off their tops, hollow them out, and bake in the oven for 15 minutes at 250 °F / 120 °C.

with Tapenade

3. Drain any excess liquid from the fromage frais and mix with the cream into a creamy, rich emulsion. Chop the chives; add with salt and pepper to the mixture. Pour four-fifths of it into a bowl, add the olive tapenade, and whisk into a smooth paste.

4. Thoroughly mix the chopped vegetables together. Finely chop the basil. Season the vegetables with salt, pepper and the basil; stuff the tomatoes with this mixture. To serve, place one stuffed tomato in the center of each shallow bowl; replace the top of each tomato. Surround this centerpiece with the creamy gazpacho, and garnish with basil leaves and a small mound of leftover vegtables.

Stuffed Garden

Preparation time: 1 hour
Cooking time: 5 minutes
Difficulty: ★★

Serves four

4 each of the following baby vegetables: small
   round zucchini, small tomatoes, violet
   artichokes, zucchini flowers, small onions
6 tomatoes
juice of 1 lemon
2 tbsp / 30 g tapenade
6 small olives
1 cup / 250 ml olive oil
half a bunch of basil
salt, pepper to taste

For the tomato aspic:
2 lbs / 1 kg green tomatoes
1 bunch of thyme
1 sheet of gelatin

For the chopped vegetables:
4 tomatoes
4 onions
1 bouquet garni

For the stuffing:
4 lbs / 2 kg zucchini
4 onions
6 tomatoes
2 oz / 50 g Parmesan (to yield 1/4 cup / 75 g
   grated)
1/2 cup / 125 ml olive oil
half a bunch of basil
salt, pepper to taste

For the garnish:
half a bunch of chervil
half a bunch of chives
half a bunch of rosemary

Chef Michel Del Burgo is particularly fond of this recipe, which brings together all the best vegetables from the gardens of the Roussillon, Languedoc and Provence. Incidentally, this is the appetizer that our chef first brought to notice. Del Burgo was still working for Alain Ducasse at the Byblos in Courchevel when Jean-Michel Signoles, owner of the Barbacane, was so taken by this appetizer that he promptly asked Del Burgo to become his head chef.

Certainly appropriate to the coming of warm weather, this dish should be prepared when these vegetables are in season, from May to the end of August. You will need very young vegetables, such as those grown by the farmers in the Languedoc, for example; in the United States, the increasing vogue for such baby produce should make them easy to find. The zucchini

flowers are either blanched first and then stuffed or the other way round, depending on your preference. But if you do blanch them first, take extra care, as the flower is very delicate and closes quickly. To be on the safe side, Del Burgo recommends you remove the flower's stamen, stuff the flower and then steam it.

The small violet artichokes are prepared raw, and sometimes also eaten raw. Every small vegetable is filled with its own special stuffing, which together constitute a veritable palette of colors – the only source of green is the zucchini. If you wish, you can also serve stuffed puff pastry with this dish to add a hearty touch. Finally, the tomato aspic adds an agreeable tartness.

1. To prepare the baby vegetables, chop the tops off the tomatoes and take out their pulp; do the same with the round zucchini. Peel the onions and hollow them out. Remove the leaves from the artichokes and cook until glazed. Cook the zucchini and onions al dente; very briefly blanch the zucchini flowers.

2. To make the aspic: chop the tomatoes, simmer with the thyme, purée in a blender; add the soaked gelatin sheet, and chill. For the chopped vegetables: peel and seed the tomatoes; chop. Sweat the onions in olive oil, add the chopped tomatoes and the bouquet garni, season, and reduce. For the puree: peel and seed six tomatoes, puree; let drain in a fine colander or sieve.

Vegetables

3. To prepare the stuffing; dice four onions and marinate in olive oil. Peel the zucchini, gently and briefly fry the peel. Peel and seed the tomatoes and work into a pulp. After letting dry, put into a blender and mix with the marinated onions, three tablespoons of tomato pulp, the grated Parmesan, salt, pepper, and chopped basil. Whisk the aspic thoroughly.

4. Cook the artichokes and then hollow out; stuff with tapenade. Stuff the other vegetables with their appropriate fillings. Slice the olives and chop the basil; add to the rest of the tomato pulp and use to decorate the tomatoes. Mix the prepared tomato puree with olive oil, lemon juice and basil. Garnish with the tomato aspic and sprigs of fresh herbs.

Salad Cocktail with

Preparation time: 30 minutes
Cooking time: 3 minutes
Difficulty: ★

Serves four
20 scallops
16 tomatoes
1 bunch of dill
1 cup / 250 ml olive oil

For the salad:
choose any of the following:
1 head bibb or boston lettuce
1 bunch of lollo rosso
1 bunch of lamb's lettuce
1 head radicchio

4 endives
1 bunch of frisée
1 bunch of oak leaf lettuce

For the cream vinaigrette:
1/2 cup / 125 ml red wine vinegar
1 cup / 250 ml olive oil
3/4 cup / 200 ml cream
salt, fresh-ground pepper to taste

For the sherry vinaigrette:
1/4 cup / 60 ml sherry vinegar
1/2 cup / 125 ml peanut oil
3/4 cup / 175 ml cold-pressed olive oil
salt, fresh-ground pepper to taste

In France, lettuce comes in endless varieties, with nicknames like "Queen of May," "Pride of Nantes," or "Capucin beard." Originally regarded as an appetizer and served without any other ingredients, green salads have advanced to become the diverse and tasty dishes they are today, served with a seemingly endless variety of sauces and seasonings. They need to be well mixed with their dressing for the flavors to be fully expressed.

Here, the salad bed for the scallops includes lettuce, lamb's lettuce, and frisée, as well as some other distinctive varieties: as going to the market with such a diverse shopping list may not be everyone's cup of tea, there are alternatives. For instance

one can purchase ready-mixed salads at the market that will include at least some of the lettuces listed above.

The scallops add finesse to this appetizer. The best scallops for this purpose, ideally, are very fresh and medium-sized, with tightly closed shells – in other words, still alive. The scallops and their coral (roe) are washed and then carefully fried. Scallops are, incidentally, the symbol of the pilgrims of Santiago de Compostela (see page 10 for a brief history). Correctly preparing the scallops will ensure that their iodine-rich taste will harmonize wonderfully with the crispy salad and the two vinaigrettes.

1. Shell the scallops. Remove the whiskers; wash the scallops and the coral (roe) quickly and thoroughly. Leave to dry on kitchen towels. Marinate in olive oil sprinkled with dill for at least 15 minutes.

2. To prepare the cream vinaigrette, in a bowl mix olive oil and red wine vinegar and add a pinch of salt. Fold in the cream; adjust seasoning to taste. To prepare the sherry vinaigrette; mix the sherry vinegar, peanut oil, olive oil, salt, and pepper.

Warm Scallops and Dill

3. *Dress the lettuces with the cream vinaigrette. Into a hot frying pan, sprinkle a pinch of salt; fry the scallops and the coral for a maximum of one minute on each side.*

4. *Score the tomatoes in a cross; submerge in boiling water for one to two minutes. As soon as the skin begins to peel off, rinse with cold water, then peel. Quarter, cut into strips, then dice. Place the diced tomatoes in the sherry vinaigrette and whisk to coat thoroughly. To serve, heap the salad cocktail in the middle of a plate; ring with an alternating arrangement of scallops and scoops of chopped tomato; decorate with a generous sprinkling of dill sprigs.*

Oysters in

Preparation time: 15 minutes
Cooking time: 45 minutes
Difficulty: ★

Serves four
2 dozen oysters, such as bluepoint
1¹/₂ oz / 40 g Sevruga caviar
7 sheets of gelatin
1 bunch of chervil

Some historians claim that caviar first became popular in the fifteenth century: it is mentioned in a work by Rabelais as a coveted *hors d'oeuvre*. The name for this noble and rare delicacy appears to have come from the obscure Turkish term *kawjâr*, adapted by the Italians into the word *caviale*. Only the roe of a particular species of sturgeon, still found in the Black Sea and predominantly in the Caspian Sea, may be called caviar.

The roe's color and flavor vary according to season and age of the sturgeons, which explains why there are three different qualities of caviar: Beluga, Ossetra, and Sevruga. Our chef prefers the latter, which comes from small sturgeons with a funnel-shaped mouth. The quality of any caviar is determined by the density of the roe and the intensity of its aroma. Most gourmets consider Sevruga to be the most sublime.

Caviar, which is always consumed raw, has a fine jelly that underscores its freshness and suits the maritime flavor of the oysters. Rich in protein, there are countless varieties: in Europe, according to taste and availability, they include those from Brittany or Normandy, or from Marennes-Oléron and Arcachon. Along with the oysters bred in the Mediterranean, France can claim fourth place among oyster producers worldwide. In the U. S., other varieties may be more readily available, such as Bluepoint, or Belon, which originally was only farmed in France. It is important to choose large or very large oysters, as they contain a lot of sea water. If the aspic tends to be too thin, just add another sheet of gelatin. With this dish, the oysters are arranged on the plate in the gelatin in advance, so they set in place before the caviar is added.

1. Open the oysters over a saucepan to retain the sea water for the aspic. Arrange the oysters around a plate. Put the plate in the refrigerator.

2. Add the gelatin and the required amount of water to the sea water in the saucepan (2 cups / 500 ml water per ¹/₄ oz / 10 g sheet of gelatin); heat over low heat until the gelatin has dissolved.

Aspic with Caviar

3. Pass the mixture through a muslin cloth. Pour the mass over the oysters and put back into the refrigerator to chill for half an hour.

4. When the jelly has set, take the oysters out of the refrigerator. Into the center of the plate, set a rounded tablespoon of caviar. Garnish with chervil leaves and serve chilled.

Tuna Carpaccio

Preparation time: 25 minutes
Cooking time: 10 minutes
Difficulty: ☆

Serves four

generous ³/₄ lb / 400 g red tuna
3 tbsp / 40 g truffles
3 tbsp / 40 g celeriac
2 tbsp / 20 g garlic
3 tbsp / 40 g chives
1 bunch of basil
3 sprigs chervil

¹/₈ lb / 40 g Parmesan
¹/₂ cup / 125 ml milk
2 tbsp / 40 ml olive oil
¹/₄ cup / 60 g coarse sea salt
1 tbsp / 4 g celery salt
pepper to taste

It seems unlikely that chef Philippe Dorange would never have discovered tuna for his kitchen at Fouquet's in Paris. The gourmet and poet Jean de la Fontaine dedicated a poem to the magnificent fish, and our chef has done his best to create a worthy recipe.

Tuna, of the mackerel family, is a large fish (bluefins can weigh over a 1000 lb / 500 kg) at home in all seas: the Pacific (where the Japanese discovered it and first included it in their cuisine), the Atlantic, and the Mediterranean. Philippe Dorange prefers adult bluefin, as it has a firm, red flesh that is more suitable for cutting into the thin slices that are necessary for *carpaccio*. The result is also more colorful than if yellow-fleshed tuna is used.

Garlic has been cultivated in the Mediterranean region since antiquity. In Rome, it was a fixed component of the legionnaires' diet, and its beneficial properties as an antiseptic and tonic were soon well known. But it can not be denied that, for some, the scent of garlic can be overwhelming, in which case the garlic slices should be blanched twice in water and once in milk or cream, then stored in a cool place. It is only deep-fried at the last moment, once the *carpaccio* has been arranged on the plate. Chopped truffles and celeriac are added at the end as well. Together with the olive oil, they emphasize this dish's Mediterranean character. If you prefer, Dorange proposes an alternative *carpaccio* made of beef, or of a mixture of scallops and salmon with melon on the side.

1. Finely chop the celeriac – its tiny pieces are intrinsic to the decoration of this dish. Shave a few pieces from the Parmesan; dice the green part of the chives. Finely chop the truffles.

2. Peel the garlic. Use a slicer or an extremely sharp knife to cut into thin slivers. Blanch in water twice, then once in milk or cream, leave to drip dry.

with Deep-fried Garlic

3. Cut the tuna into wafer-thin slices, flatten; arrange on a plate brushed with olive oil and pepper. Brush the tuna as well with oil and season with pepper and sea salt. In oil heated to 355 °F / 180 °C, deep-fry the garlic; season with celery salt.

4. Sprinkle the chopped celeriac, chives and chopped truffles over the entire plate. Garnish with a few shavings of Parmesan, chervil leaves, basil leaves, and the fried garlic slices.

Velouté of Asparagus

Preparation time: 40 minutes
Cooking time: 25 minutes
Difficulty: ★★

Serves four

$^3/_4$ lb / 340 g white asparagus
1 cup / 250 ml whipping cream
$^1/_4$ oz / 4 g caviar (Sevruga or Ossetra)
1 large onion
$^1/_4$ cup / 50 g all-purpose flour
$^3/_8$ cup / 90 ml chicken stock (see basic recipes)
salt, fresh-ground white pepper to taste

The cream sauce we are using here is a "velouté," so named for its velvety consistency. It is rarely used today. But chef Philippe Dorange, who trained with the masters Roger Vergé and Jacques Maximin, refuses to accept velouté's disappearance. Instead he has taken a lovely bunch of asparagus to prove that there are still plenty of ways to incorporate this classic, traditional sauce.

If you prefer, you might use green asparagus for this recipe instead of white, which would add a dash of color. Harvested towards the end of winter, green asparagus is certainly worthy of attention, and not only for its outstanding flavor. If you want to buy the asparagus well ahead of time, store it your refrigerator's bottom shelf, with the stalks immersed in water and standing upright. For this recipe the asparagus, whether white or green, should not be peeled but rather scraped care-

fully to avoid breaking it. The velouté can be prepared the day before you are going to serve the dish. Always cook the two parts of the asparagus, the tips and stems, separately before you puree them.

As our chef stresses, work with only high-quality chicken stock, made from only the freshest ingredients (though this could also apply as a general rule). The same applies to the whipping cream, which here is, unusually, seasoned with salt. The combination of cream and caviar results in contrasting black-and-white scoops of the most delicate consistency; a sublime combination, to be sure.

The recipe can also be adapted for poultry or veal velouté, which is more traditional, but which will not taste as exquisite.

1. Cut off the asparagus tips, peel the asparagus stems and cook a portion of them – a bit over 1 cup / 250 ml – in the chicken stock, to which should be added $^1/_2$ cup / 125 ml of cream.

2. Once the asparagus is cooked, chop into small pieces; pass through a fine-meshed sieve.

with Caviar-chantilly

3. Cook the asparagus tips, rinse with cold water, and set aside.

4. Whip the remaining cream, adding salt and pepper to taste. Blend in the caviar. Chill, so the cream can set, then use spoons to form into scoops. To serve, in the center of each plate set a small mound of caviar; surround it with an arrangement of five scoops of the cream alternating with asparagus tips. Serve the asparagus velouté separately in a bowl.

Remoulade with Scallops

Preparation time:	*40 minutes*
Cooking time:	*2 minutes, plus 3 hours for oven-drying the tomatoes*
Difficulty:	✶

Serves four

generous ¹/₂ lb / 280 g shelled scallops
1 lb / 450 g goatfish (red mullet)
generous ¹/₂ lb / 280 g celeriac root
2 tomatoes
¹/₂ cup / 125 ml lemon juice
3 tbsp / 40 g mayonnaise
1 tbsp / 15 ml cream

1 tbsp / 15 ml vinegar
¹/₂ cup / 125 ml olive oil
3 cloves garlic
half a bunch of chervil
half a bunch of basil
half a bunch of chives
1 cup / 250 g celeriac leaves
pinch of sea salt
¹/₄ cup / 60 g sugar

For the dressing
¹/₃ cup / 80 ml olive oil
3 lemons
salt, pepper to taste

To change the usual chronology, let us concentrate on the vegetables first, normally confined to the status of side order. The celeriac should be heavy, completely round and unblemished. After peeling it should be coated with lemon juice immediately to prevent oxidization and keep it fresh and crisp.

The tomatoes should be fresh, ripe and full. In the winter, making this dish may be problematic, as most of the tomatoes available in markets are of poor quality, with mealy flesh that becomes bitter when it is dried. Instead, opt for imported tomatoes, such as the Marmane or Rio Grande varieties from Provence or the succulent Dutch tomatoes, or take advantage of the summer bounty. For this dish the tomatoes are dried in the oven on low heat and seasoned with thyme, salt, and sugar, which neutralizes the fruit's natural acidity. The addition of balsamic vinegar (which should have a syrupy consistency) and olive oil make this appetizer one of the most delicious of the Mediterranean dishes.

The composition of taste and texture is enhanced by the goatfish (or red mullet, as it is commonly called in the United States; see page 30 for more information) and by scallops. To preserve the scallops' tenderness, fry them only very briefly on each side. Sprinkled with sea salt and heated quickly once more on the grill, these shellfish will win over the most demanding gourmet.

1. In advance, wash and slice the tomatoes into even, half-inch rounds. Baste lightly with olive oil and balsamic vinegar and place on a rack in an oven at 150 °F / 60 °C; leave for three hours. To make the remoulade, peel the celeriac root, coat with lemon juice, and run through a grater on the julienne side to make thin strips. Gently mix together the mayonnaise and cream and dress the celeriac slices; set aside.

2. Wash and clean the scallops; slice thinly.

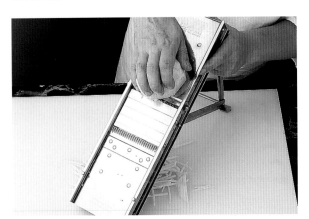

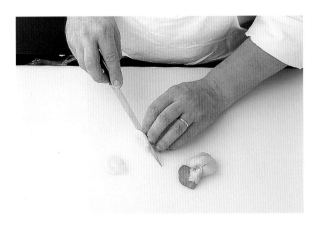

and Grilled Goatfish

3. Prepare a dressing with the olive oil, lemon juice, salt and pepper; brush on the scallops; set the shellfish aside. Slice the garlic cloves and toast for a minute or so until light brown.

4. Remove the scales and fillet the fish. Fry briefly skin side down in olive oil. Immediately before serving, sprinkle coarse sea salt over the scallops; chop herbs and sprinkle over the dried tomato slices. To serve, place a broad ring of tomato slices in the center of each plate. Use a circular form of 4 in / 10 cm in diameter on top to add the remoulade. Remove the form and arrange the scallops on top in a star shape. Add the fish fillets. Garnish with celeriac leaves and toasted garlic slices.

Salmon and Sea Bass

Preparation time: 30 minutes
Marinating time: 24 hours
Difficulty: ★★

Serves four

generous 1 lb / 500 g fresh salmon
generous 1 lb / 500 g sea bass
2¹/₂ oz / 80 g Ossetra caviar
2 tbsp / 25 ml peanut oil
2 tbsp / 25 ml olive oil
2 tomatoes
1 bunch of dill
1 lime
salt, pepper to taste

For the ginger marinade:
generous ¹/₄ lb / 150 g fresh ginger root
5 tbsp / 75 g sugar
¹/₂ cup / 100 ml water
2¹/₂ tbsp / 40 ml red wine vinegar

For the dressing:
³/₈ cup / 90 ml mayonnaise (see basic recipes)
¹/₄ cup / 60 ml water
¹/₄ cup / 60 ml broth

The creation of this raw fish remoulade was inspired by Japanese cuisine. Marinating fish is very common in Japan, and it provides the chef with seeimgly endless culinary possibilities.

Whether you really have a sea bass in your shopping basket can sometimes be difficult to ascertain, as it is known by many names. It has almost disappeared from the English Channel and most of the northern waters. Determining its freshness is also difficult because it has practically no scent. As far as the salmon is concerned, our chef Claude Dupont prefers Scottish salmon, which has superior flavor and appearance. However, if there is no good salmon available, instead try another firm-fleshed fish, such as John Dory or pike perch. While the vinaigrette does not have to be bound with an egg yolk, doing so will make the consistency more suitable for this dish. The olive

and peanut oils should be mixed before the paper and fillets are brushed with it. The mixture of these two oils determines the overall flavor of this appetizer.

In referring to Asia, we must give ginger a mention as well. It has been around since the first century AD, when Greeks and Persians used to barter with it. It continued to be popular through the Middle Ages, when it entered the world of cooking, baking, and even beer brewing. You can season jams with ginger, but it should be used sparingly. The best ginger root is a young root that is both knotty and feels rough and hard to the touch, but without an overly strong scent.

1. In a small saucepan, simmer a mixture of water, vinegar, and sugar for the ginger root's marinade. Wash and fillet the salmon, taking care to remove all the bones. With a sharp knife, cut the fillets into wafer-thin slices. Do the same with the sea bass. Peel the ginger root and marinate for at least one hour in the water, vinegar, and sugar mixture.

2. Let the ginger drip dry; finely chop. Mix together the olive and peanut oils. Place the salmon strips on a piece of paper greased with the oils. Salt and pepper the fish; brush with the mixed oils, sprinkle with chopped ginger and lime juice. Prepare the sea bass in the same way.

with Caviar Cream

3. Layer the two fillets, without the paper, one on top of one another; roll up to form a long cylinder. Wrap in plastic wrap, close the ends tightly, and chill for 24 hours. Prepare the dressing and pass it through a fine-meshed sieve to make it completely smooth.

4. Cut the marinated fish into slices with an electric kitchen knife (or an extremely sharp one, since it's crucial not to destroy the fish's round shape). Cut the tomatoes into slivers. To serve, place three slices on each plate, pool dressing over them, and top with three tablespoons of caviar. Garnish with a few slivers of tomato and sprigs of dill.

Lobster with Apple

Preparation time: 25 minutes
Cooking time: 10 minutes
Difficulty: ✴

Serves four

2 1½ lb / 700 g lobsters
2 Golden Delicious apples
2 tomatoes
¼ lb / 100 g fine green beans
¾ lb / 400 g mixed lettuce
¼ lb / 100 g lamb's lettuce
½ cup / 100 ml olive oil
½ cup / 100 ml red wine vinegar
salt, pepper to taste

For the curry vinaigrette:
3 tbsp / 40 g curry powder
1 cup / 250 g tomato puree
¼ of an apple
2 egg yolks
2 tsp / 10 g mustard
scant 1 cup oil
scant 1 cup crème fraîche
2 tbsp / 200 ml lemon juice
2 tbsp / 200 ml vinegar
salt, pepper to taste

Claude Dupont describes this starter as a "méli-mélo," which translates roughly as a hodge-podge with a little bit of everything. But with its harmonious mix of colors, tastes, and textures, the dish does not resemble anything so unplanned. Dupont is probably also referring to the freestyle method with which he created this refreshing composition of shellfish, fruit, and vegetables.

Choose fresh, healthy, live lobsters. When extracting the meat in a fresh lobster, it will be well attached to the shell. Lobster meat is lean, tender and spicy – and in this dish, those qualities are well underscored. If at all possible, seek out blue lobsters from Brittany, or a North American variety such as the Maine lobster. To cook, peg and bind the claws and bring a large stockpot of broth to a rolling boil before immersing the lob-

sters head-first. Boil for eight minutes and then leave in the broth to cool off, a process that ensures that the meat will remain tender.

The balance of flavors in this recipe depends on the correct dosage of curry powder; its exotic perfume is the leading flavor in the vinaigrette. There are many different varieties of curry powder, which is really a mixture of many individual spices: ginger, cumin, coriander, turmeric, and other ingredients. They may be mixed to form a powder, or at times can be found as a paste. Too much curry powder would most certainly kill the delicate flavor of the lobster, whose subtle taste is easily drowned out. That is why for this recipe – as in all recipes, really – careful application of spices takes top priority.

1. Prepare the vinaigrette: grate the apple quarter and pass the tomato purée through a sieve; whisk two egg yolks with the mustard, oil, vinegar, salt, and pepper. Add the curry powder, the grated apple and the sieved tomato purée. Fold in the crème fraîche and lemon juice. Set aside to rest for 15 minutes, then pass through a sieve.

2. Cook the lobsters briefly in broth and leave immersed in the liquid to cool. Halve the lobsters and extract the flesh (tails, claws, and legs) from the shell. Set aside any coral (roe) for later use. Dress the mixed lettuces with salt, pepper, olive oil, and vinegar.

and a Light Curry Sauce

3. Peel tomato strips for decoration; blanch the green beans. Garnish the plate with an arching ring of these tomato strips and the green beans. Arrange a rosette of lamb's lettuce, and press it down to stay within a circular form. Chop one and a half Golden Delicious apples and dress with a little of the curry vinaigrette.

4. Dress the lamb's lettuce. Fill the circular form with chopped apple, then a layer of mixed lettuce, and finally place a few slices of lobster meat and one or two claws on top. Dress with the curry vinaigrette; garnish with a sprig of herb.

Venison Tartlets with Goose Liver,

Preparation time: 1 hour, 30 minutes
Cooking time: 8 minutes
Cooling time: 2 hours
Difficulty: ★★

Serves four

For the tartlets:
1/2 lb / 240 g saddle of venison
generous 1/4 lb / 150 g goose liver
1 sheet of gelatin
1 carrot
1/2 bulb celeriac
1 tbsp / 10 ml Sauternes
1 tbsp Cognac
1/2 cup / 125 ml meat juice (to be retained from the venison)
1/2 cup / 125 ml whipping cream

salt, fresh-ground pepper to taste

For the jelly:
1 cup / 250 ml venison broth
1 1/2 sheets of gelatin

For the marinated white cabbage:
1/2 lb / 200 g white cabbage
1/2 cup / 100 ml grapeseed oil
1/2 cup / 100 ml white wine vinegar
1/2 tsp / 10 g sugar
a pinch of ground cumin
salt, pepper to taste

For the sauce:
1/4 lb / 250 g chanterelles
1 shallot
1 cup / 250 ml meat juice (to be retained)
1/4 cup / 60 ml raspberry vinegar
half a bunch of chervil

In the heart of the dark forests of Württemberg in southwest Germany is an elegant hotel and restaurant. Located in an old hunting lodge on grounds belonging to the Prince of Hohenlohe-Öhringen, it is home for our talented chef, Lothar Eiermann. As he puts it, to be a chef there is to be in the center of "game heaven": the forests are so plentiful with deer and other forest animals that the preparation of game has become his speciality. This recipe is Eiermann's homage to Prince Kraft-Alexander, the present proprietor of the hotel.

Chef Eiermann has an ideal delivery system: animals are delivered whole to his kitchen almost directly from the forest. Provided with every part, he can let his creativity run free to conceive unforgettable recipes. The end of summer is the only time the supply is slightly less plentiful: then, Eiermann has to make do with deer that have fed entirely on fresh herbs, which requires him to wait a few days before preparing the meat. But

this seems like a minor detraction from a veritable cornucopia of game.

This appetizer is based on a boneless saddle of venison from which the tendons have also been removed. The most difficult aspect of the preparation involves the jelly, which is made by first blanching the chopped bones, then cooking them until they reduce down to a thick aspic.

The venison tartlets are accompanied by cabbage, the result of the chef's frequent experiments with both red and white varieties – eventually, he opted for the white. This is the same unassuming white cabbage used in the Alsatian speciality, sauerkraut. The raspberry vinegar, which the chef settled on after some unsuccessful tries with sherry vinegar, provides an ideal link between venison and goose liver pâté.

1. To make the goose liver mousse, reduce the venison gravy by half, cool, and then puree with the washed goose liver in the blender. Soak the gelatin in the Sauternes, then fold into the puree. Mix a third of the whipping cream with the liver puree; fold in the rest with a spatula. Adjust seasoning to taste and add the cognac.

2. Separate the venison from the bones; briefly fry on all sides; set aside to cool. Peel the carrot and celeriac, cut into strips of approximately 2 in / 5 cm high and 1/4 in / 1 cm thick; blanch in salted water. Rinse with cold water; set aside to drip dry. Take four circular forms and vertically line their inside walls with alternating strips of carrot and celeriac. Chop the white cabbage; marinate in the ingredients listed above.

White Cabbage, and Chanterelles

3. Fill the circular forms up to a $^1/_4$ in / 1 cm from the top with the goose liver mousse. For the sauce, fry the chopped shallot until brown, add some raspberry vinegar, then add venison gravy; reduce over low heat.

4. Cut the saddle of venison into thin slices. Lay in a rosette shape on top of the goose liver mousse still in the forms. Mix the game broth with the gelatin and pour over the tartlets; set the tartlets to chill. Drip-dry the cabbage and lightly fry until brown. Sweat the chanterelles. Garnish the plate with the cabbage and chanterelles. Add the sauce at the last moment, and decorate with chervil leaves.

Salad of Smoked

Preparation time: 1 hour
Soaking time: 8 hours
Smoking time: 10 minutes
Cooking time: 20 minutes
Difficulty: ✷✷

Serves four

1 dozen cod cheeks
2 cloves garlic
2 bay leaves
2 cloves
2 juniper berries
half a bunch of thyme
half a bunch of rosemary
1 tbsp / 15 ml vegetable oil
2 cups / 500 ml sawdust (for smoking)

For the potato and leek fritters:
2 small potatoes
1 leek

For the lentil salad:
1/8 lb / 50 g green lentils
1/8 lb / 50 g red lentils
1 tbs / 15 g vegetable brunoise
1/4 bunch of chives
1 tsp / 5 ml balsamic vinegar
1 tbsp / 15 ml olive oil
1 tbsp / 15 ml grape seed oil
1 tbsp / 15 ml lemon juice
1 tbsp / 15 ml sugar
salt, pepper to taste

For the decoration:
1 cup mesclun or frisée and lamb's lettuce

Culinary history is full of stories of masterpieces created accidentally. Such is the case with this recipe. Chef Eiermann and his kitchen staff have always served smoked cod for Friday lunch. But, as fate would have it, a young trainee chef in charge of smoking the cod did so without adding enough spices, and thus created – unintentionally – a sensational dish. Once the amazing result had been adequately celebrated, the search was on for a suitable accompaniment.

How they finally stumbled upon potato and leek fritters is, unfortunately, one of the secrets Lothar Eiermann's kitchen will never share. But we do know that a trip to Egypt brought our chef to lentils, which are Eiermann's proposed, if unusual, garnish. The mixture of red and green lentils should be cooked *al dente* and served warm; the red lentils lose a bit of their color during the cooking process, which is a shame, but does not affect their fantastic flavor. Finally, a salad completes the dish.

Cod is a very inexpensive fish, but, usually, you will have to buy the whole fish to obtain the cheeks, and you should try to get fishes of the same size, so the cheeks are as well, enabling them to cook evenly. If cod is unavailable, monkfish may be used instead. In view of the previous kitchen "mishap," the spices used during smoking are limited to juniper berries and cloves. The process is relatively simple, even if you have no experience with smoking food. The maximum smoking temperature is 495 °F / 250 °C. Just marinate the fish in oil, lay on a grill in a roasting pan that has a layer of sawdust, juniper berries, and cloves in the bottom, cover, and then insert it into a smoky oven for no more than ten minutes.

1. The night before, soak the lentils. The next day, wash the cod cheeks; infuse with garlic and thyme for an hour. Grate the remaining herbs and spices and mix with the sawdust. Put the mixture into a container, such as a baking tray, that fits into the base of the oven. Lay the cheeks on an oven rack above that is covered in aluminum foil perforated with a fork. Set the oven on high heat for up to ten minutes; remove; keep warm.

2. To prepare the fritters, peel the potatoes and slice thin; wash the leek, chop finely and blanch. Reduce the cream by half, add the chopped leek, and simmer for a short while (about five to eight minutes). Remove from the heat and set aside to cool. Use a slotted spoon to lift out the leek; place a small heap on a potato slice. Brush the rim of the potato slice with a water and flour, place a second potato slice on top, and press around the edges to form a sandwich.

Cod Cheeks

3. Deep-fry the fritters; set aside to dry on paper towels. Cook the lentils for around 20 minutes in a stockpot of lightly salted water. Do not rinse with cold water when done, as the lentils should be served warm. Prepare the vinaigrette.

4. To serve, mix the warm lentils with the vinaigrette and arrange on the plate. Place the cod cheeks in the middle, and surround with an arrangement of fritters. Garnish with salad leaves of different colors, and, if you prefer, a few sprigs of chives.

Young Herring

Preparation time: 20 minutes
Cooking time: 30 minutes
Difficulty: ✷

Serves four

4 young marinated herrings
4 round potatoes
1 onion
1 tsp / 5 g mustard
1 cup / 250 ml dry white wine
1 cup / 250 ml soy oil
sea salt, pepper to taste

In the Netherlands, the arrival of young herrings at the beginning of May is a similar event to the arrival of the Beaujolais nouveau in France. In the eighteenth century, the season was marked by a traditional fishing race, involving scores of fishermen – numbering in the thousands. The aim of the race was to be the first to present Her Majesty with the "Queen's herring." The young herrings, caught by the netloads, would be cured while still on the boat: according to the method developed by a certain Willem Benkleszoon, the fish would promptly be put into barrels to marinate in salt. The commodity was considered a veritable treasure: the barrels of pressed and salted herrings fetched high prices. At one public auction, a barrel reportedly fetched some 35,000 gilders (approximately US$18,000).

Normally, herring is served with sliced onion, cucumber, and white bread (particularly in Amsterdam), and eaten with the fingers. In this recipe, created specially for Eurodélices, the herring is served with potatoes instead. If at all possible, seek out the Dutch variety of potato known as Opperdoezer Ronde, a unique and completely round variety that grows in sulphur-rich soil, is harvested by hand, ripens in a mere nine weeks, and remains very firm during cooking. However, the variety is somewhat rare outside the Netherlands, and may take some serious sleuthing. If not, some suitable alternatives might be new potatoes or Katahdin round whites.

Unfortunately, there are few substitutes for the incomparable North Sea herring, which should have a red center bone and be of adequate size – about 8 in / 20 cm in length. A rather substantial dish, this fish and potato starter is ideal for winter, and confirms the Dutch version of a traditional American saying: "A herring a day keeps the doctor away."

1. Mix together the white wine, oil, and mustard in a blender. Immerse a few onion rings into this vinaigrette and leave to marinate.

2. Gut and fillet the herrings, remove the bones and use a circular cutter to cut rounds 1 in / 2.5 cm in diameter.

with Round Potatoes

3. Peel the potatoes, boil (but take care not to overcook) and cut into the same circles as the herrings.

4. To serve, arrange the potato circles in a ring around the plate, each with a herring circle on top. Garnish with the marinated onion rings and dress with the vinaigrette.

Cream Puffs with

Preparation time: 25 minutes, plus some time in advance
Cooking time: 25 minutes
Difficulty: ★★

Serves four

1/8 lb goose liver
scant 3/8 lb / 175 g of butter
1/2 / 125 ml cup milk
1/2 / 125 ml cup water
5/8 cup flour
5 eggs
1 cup / 240 g sugar
1/4 cup / 60 g cornstarch
salt to taste

While there is certainly no lack of recipes based on goose liver, this one may well become a favorite for many readers as it combines cream puffs with the noble goose liver in a completely novel way. Our chef, Constant Fonk, also had the interesting idea of seasoning the liver with salt as well as with sugar.

Duck's liver can be used as well here – the choice should be made according to your tastes; either way, select only goose or duck's liver that is of markedly high quality (for example, the French *foie-gras mi-cuit*, or semi-cooked). Of course, in a perfect world one would be able to prepare the liver mousse from scratch using fresh liver (*foie gras frais*), but, bearing in mind

the time that such an involved procedure would take, that is a luxury few of us can afford.

The dough for the cream puffs can be made in advance and then frozen. However, it entails two crucial steps: when reducing the sugar, use a casserole that evenly distributes the heat, and when making the liver filling, take great care that it is thoroughly blended. The other steps are relatively easy.

Surprising as it may seem, this appetizer is best eaten with your fingers.

1. Bring the milk, water, salt, half a tablespoon of sugar and a bit over a 1/4 lb / 175 g of the butter to a boil. Sift the flour through a sieve into a mixing bowl. Remove the liquid from the heat; fold in the flour with a wooden spatula. Stir until set, then fold in the eggs one by one.

2. Fill a pastry bag with the dough and pipe small cream puffs onto a baking tray covered with greased paper. Bake for 20 minutes at 355 °F / 180 °C; remove and set aside.

Goose Liver Mousse

3. Bring the remaining sugar, and the corn starch and water to a boil over very high heat until reduced to a clear sugar liquid. Dip the cream puffs into the liquid to glaze them, and place them upside down on a greased baking tray.

4. To make the liver mousse filling, in the blender or food processor, thoroughly mix a ¹/₄ cup / 65 g of butter with a ¹/₄ cup / 65 g of goose liver. Taste, adjust seasoning and fill the cream puffs with the mousse. Serving is simple: just arrange three cream puffs on each plate.

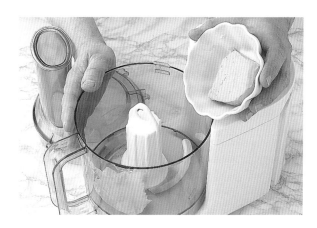

Langoustine Charlotte

Preparation time: *1 hour*
Cooking time: *30 minutes*
Difficulty: ★★★

Serves four
20 langoustines ($^1/_4$–$^1/_2$ lb / 120–240 g each)
2 1–1$^1/_2$ lb / 450–700 g female lobsters to
    yield: 1 cup / 250 ml lobster broth (also see
    sauce ingredients); lobster meat (also see
    sauce ingredients)
2 eggplants
1 red pepper
1 yellow pepper
1 small truffle
2 tomatoes
1 bunch of spring onions

$^3/_4$ cup / 200 ml lobster broth
lobster coral
2$^1/_2$ sheets of gelatin
a few saffron threads
half a bunch of thyme
half a bunch of chives
1 cup / 250 ml olive oil

For the sauce:
scant $^1/_4$ lb / 100 g lobster meat from the
    heads
$^1/_2$ cup / 125 ml lobster broth
1 tsp / 5 g mustard
$^1/_4$ cup / 50 ml aged red wine vinegar
$^3/_4$ cup / 200 ml peanut oil
salt, pepper to taste

Whether sweet or savory, essentially the preparation of a charlotte is always the same: a form is lined with vegetables, biscuits or breadcrumbs, filled with a stuffing, and then chilled or boiled so the charlotte can set. The classic dish appeared for the first time at the court of King George III of England in the eighteenth century; the monarch named it after his future wife, Charlotte Sophia. The tradition of making charlottes has continued to this day, branching out into many different versions.

Buy langoustines that are still alive to make sure they are genuinely fresh. They will be combined with cooked vegetables for a refreshing, Mediterranean appetizer that is an ideal way to start a meal of several courses.

Tomatoes, particularly when ripe and firm, are rich in nutrients. Once thought to be poisonous (see page 114 for more information), they became coveted in France for a time as aphrodisiacs. Here, their intense red lends vibrant color to this dish. The other vegetables also need to be as fresh as possible: the peppers, for instance, must be firm and smooth, without blemishes or cracks. If they still have their stems, check them carefully: if the peppers are fresh, the stems will always be very green.

1. Wash and clean the langoustines. Blanch the lobsters; separate the coral (roe) and the meat in the head; reserve the broth. Cut the eggplant into triangular chunks of $^3/_8$ in / 1 cm thickness. Fry briefly in olive oil and bake in a 260 °F / 70 °C oven. Peel and seed the tomatoes; briefly fry with thyme in olive oil. Cut the pepper into julienne strips and chop the onions, and briefly fry them together. Add 1 cup / 250 ml of the lobster broth and simmer; retain this broth.

2. Shell the langoustines; separate the tails. Mix some water with the retained pepper and onion juice and poach the langoustine tails in this liquid, then drain. To make the aspic, clarify the cooking liquid, season with saffron and add 2$^1/_2$ gelatin sheets per quart / liter. Refine the aspic with truffle, chopped chives, and lobster coral.

with Baked Eggplant

3. To shape the charlotte form, line the inside wall of a circular form (3 in / 8 cm in diameter and 1¹/₂ in / 35 cm high) with eggplant pieces, skin-side out. Fill the form with half a cooked tomato, a tablespoon of the thyme-infused oil, then the pepper and onions. Top with five or six langoustine tails.

4. Brush the charlotte with the aspic. To make the sauce, puree the poached meat from the lobster heads with mustard, vinegar, and the warm lobster broth in a blender. Adjust seasoning to taste, adding peanut oil, salt, and pepper. Remove the charlotte form, pour over the charlotte, and serve.

Crab Vegetables with

Preparation time: 1 hour
Cooking time: 20 minutes
Difficulty: ✷✷

Serves four

1 crab (approximately 6 lbs / 3 kg)
1 lb / 500 g leeks
1 lb / 500 g potatoes (such as Roseval or
  round white)
12 cherry tomatoes
juice of 2 limes
1/2 cup / 125 ml heavy cream

2 oz / 50 g lobster coral (cooked)
2 cups / 500 ml olive oil
scant 4 pints / 2 l vegetable broth
3 sprigs of flowering thyme (to yield
  1 tbsp / 15 g)
1 bunch of chives
1 bunch of dill
salt, pepper to taste

With its massive front claws and broad body, the Atlantic crab has one of the highest meat contents of all crab varieties. This peaceful crustacean, often seeming to be taking a siesta on the ocean floor, is easy prey for the fishermen of the English Channel and the Mediterranean, where it is caught in large numbers. It is available all year round, and has close relatives in the United States. Buy heavy, live crabs, and preferably female ones, since they contain coral. Crabs are cooked in broth so that their flesh remains tender. For easy extraction of the flesh, buy crabs that weigh at least two pounds (one kilogram); if you cannot find a crab weighing six pounds (three kilograms), buy two or three to equal that weight. Conveniently, the lobster coral called for in this receipe can be left over from lobsters used for another dish; it should be cooked.

The Roseval potato, a European variety, is harvested in the autumn and has pink or red skin and yellow, very dense flesh. It is preferably boiled whole, but is just as tasty in chunks. You can, of course, use a different variety, so long as it is not too starchy, as will be some varieties of Idaho (or russet potatoes) grown primarily for baking. Instead, look for round whites or reds, or Yukon Gold. For an extra dash of color, you might also try one of the red-fleshed potatoes, such as the huckleberry. Both the potatoes and leeks should be cooked *al dente*.

Prepare the accompanying dressing with olive oil only, as not only does it have superior digestive properties, but its delicate flavor imparts a Mediterranean subtlety to this appetizer. Chef Louis Grondard stresses using only cold-pressed olive oil, whose fine aroma is enhanced by the lime juice. Limes, incidentally, are very popular in Japanese and Mexican cuisine: both use lime juice as a marinade base for raw seafood.

This appetizer should, ideally, be consumed at once, although it can be stored for up to forty-eight hours.

1. Cut the leeks into rectangles and the potatoes into cubes. Cook separately in salted water and then rinse with cold water to arrest the cooking process. Both should still be quite crisp and firm after cooking. Mix the two vegetables. Fry the washed cherry tomatoes with thyme flowers over low heat in olive oil; chill.

2. Chop the chives. Bind the leeks and potatoes with a tablespoon of heavy cream in a bowl; season. Cook the crabs in broth and then extract the meat. Season the meat with olive oil, some of the chives, salt, and pepper.

Olive Oil and Limes

3. Place four circular forms (about 4 in / 10 cm in diameter) on aluminum foil and fill halfway with vegetables. Place the cooked crab meat on top, stir in a little heavy cream, sprinkle with lobster coral and chopped chives, and chill. Prepare a dressing with olive oil, lime juice, salt, and pepper.

4. Place the crab and vegetables in the middle of the plate. Arrange cherry tomatoes, the crab meat, and the claws in an alternating circle surrounding the crab and vegetable mixture. Sprinkle with the dressing and the rest of the chopped chives. Garnish with sprigs of dill, and serve chilled.

Preparation time: *1 hour*
Cooking time: *20 minutes*
Cooling time: *1 hour (optional)*
Difficulty: ★★

Serves four

4 spider crabs, 1¼ lbs / 600 g each
2 spider crabs, 2 lbs / 1 kg each
5 crabs, 1½–2 lbs / 700 g–1 kg each
1 squid, ½ lb / 250 g
½ lb / 250 g fresh seaweed, or ⅛ lb / 75 g
   dried seaweed

10 tomatoes
8 cloves of garlic
1 lemon
yolks of 2 eggs
½ cup / 125 ml olive oil
¼ cup / 50 ml wine vinegar
1¼ gallon / 5 l water
1 bouquet garni
1 oz / 30 g salmon roe
¾ oz / 20 g Sevruga caviar
1 bunch of basil
2 tbsp / 20 g coarse sea salt
1 tbsp / 10 g white pepper

Despite its hard shell, the spider crab has a very tender and delicate taste. It compensates for its gauche appearance by hiding behind algae and rocky outcroppings. The largest specimens, which have claw spans of up to ten feet (three meters), live on the coast of Japan; the next biggest, about half that size, can dive down a hundred and fifty feet (forty-five meters) and live predominantly on the south coast of England. For this appetizer, chef Phillipe Groult recommends well-developed spider crabs weighing between one and a quarter and two pounds (six hundred grams and one kilogram), preferably from the coast of Brittany, if you have access to them. Always buy live crabs, and cook them within twenty-four hours, keeping them refrigerated until then.

After being steamed or cooked in broth for fifteen minutes, the crabmeat and coral have to be carefully extracted from the

shell. The spider crab contains so much cartilage that the consistency and flavor of this dish needs to be refined; for this purpose, add squid, as well as the meat from king or blue crabs, particularly the claw meat. The spider crab coral can be used to make a traditional sauce that will blend quite well with any shellfish.

If indeed you are able to obtain female spider crabs (which you can recognize by a jagged ridge across the inside of its shell), this appetizer can be nicely ornamented with their own roe, set in the "lid" of the spider crab's shell. Spider crab roe is even more decorative than caviar or salmon roe. The crab is served on a bed of seaweed; if only male spider crabs are available, they can be served with fresh herbs.

1. Wash and scrub the spider crabs, cook in broth for 15 minutes; cook the other crabs for 20 minutes. Extract the meat from the small spider crabs without removing the legs, and then extract the meat from the remaining crabs (removing the claws and legs, but retaining whole claws from two crabs for garnish). Set the coral aside, pass it through a sieve, make an aïoli (two egg yolks whisked with crushed garlic and olive oil into a mayonnaise); blend the coral into it.

2. Chop three garlic cloves, peel and seed the tomatoes, gently fry together in olive oil. Add salt and pepper. Clean the squid and cut into thin strips (if possible freeze for an hour first to make it firmer); heat in the tomato liquid for five minutes.

Spider Crab

3. Mix together the squid, crab meat, and spider crab meat. Add all of the basil leaves and two-thirds of the aïoli. Using a cutter, cut a circle a bit under 3 in / 7.5 cm in diameter out of the shells of the four small spider crabs. Then remove this "lid."

4. Rinse the seaweed well; blanch in boiling water for two minutes, then rinse in cold water. To serve, stuff the spider crabs with the meat and aïoli mixture through the hole in their shell. Decorate with crab shells, salmon roe, and caviar. Serve on a bed of seaweed, and, if desired, fill the lids with crab eggs, brushing them with olive oil.

Tripe Salad with Goose

Preparation time: 30 minutes
Cooking time: 1 hour 30 minutes
Difficulty: ★★

Serves four

1 generous lb / 450 g tripe
⅝ lb / 300 g goose liver
⅝ lb / 300 g fava beans
1 onion
1 carrot
1 celery stick
1 clove of garlic
1 shallot
4 quail eggs
2 eggs

1 tbsp / 20 g hot mustard
1 tbsp / 20 g mild mustard
½ cup / 125 ml olive oil
2 cups / 500 ml white wine (Reisling)
1 tbsp / 45 ml balsamic vinegar
⅝ lb / 300 g breadcrumbs
3 tbsp flour
2 cups / 500 g mixed lettuces (Bibb and red
    leaf), or mesclun
1 bunch of chervil
1 bunch of thyme
¼ cup / 60 g bay leaves
 salt, pepper to taste

Tripe and goose liver are both very popular in Alsaçe, a region in northeastern France on the German border. The combination of tripe and a Riesling sauce has gained a reputation across the Alsatian border for good reason: it's fabulous. The dry but fruity Riesling, an Alsatian wine, is indispensable as a base for sauces, in particular with sautéed potatoes. It is somewhat remarkable that the Alsatian recipe for tripe has remained intact, uninfluenced by French cuisine: the Alsaçe region still retains its own strong character.

Tripe are the mixed trimmings from a cow's stomach that are carefully cleaned and blanched by the butcher. They should nonetheless be boiled in broth for an hour before preparation to impart some flavor into them. Normally they are prepared the day before and then left to chill in the refrigerator in their cooking broth. The small rectangles get coated with breadcrumbs and fried, with care taken to respect the indicated frying time, as excessive browning of the breadcrumbs will render them bitter.

The goose liver lends a certain softness to this dish. While not crucial, it provides a welcome contrast to the crispy tripe. The vinaigrette should be fairly sharp so as not to be dominated by the tripe's strong flavor.

If fava beans are available – your best chance for fresh, in-season favas is the summertime – choose ones whose pods are smooth, since the older the bean, the more the pod will bulge. Or substitute them with green beans or lentils. This dish is served at room temperature.

1. Blanch the tripe and boil for one hour. Cut into twelve 1 in / 2.5 cm squares and roll in flour, egg, and then breadcrumbs. Cut the remaining tripe into strips and simmer once more in the white wine and broth with egg white for 30 minutes; drain. Retain some cooking liquid.

2. In a blender or food processor, blend the shallot, wine, balsamic vinegar, salt, pepper, hot and mild mustards, a little cooking liquid from the tripe, and olive oil for a few seconds. Blanch the fava beans in salt water, rinse with ice water, and extract the beans from the pods. If the beans themselves have a tough skin on them, blanch or rub this off to reveal the tender bean.

Liver and Fava Beans

3. Cut the goose liver into four slices (they should be about ¹/₈ lb / 60 g each). Fry with the tripe squares in peanut oil for two to three minutes on each side. Fry the quail eggs sunny-side up. Heat the tripe strips and fava beans in the vinaigrette.

4. To serve, arrange the lettuce in a circle in the middle of the plate. Place the warm beans and tripe strips on top, then add three breaded tripe squares, then the fried goose liver. Top with a fried quail's egg. Garnish with chervil leaves.

Asparagus with

Preparation time: 35 minutes
Cooking time: 20 minutes
Difficulty: ★

Serves four

2 bunches of white asparagus, 2 generous lbs
   / 1kg each
¼ lb / 100 g fresh fava beans
2 shallots
¼ lb / 100 g smoked salmon
¼ lb / 100 g butter
⅞ cup white wine
½ cup / 125 ml vinegar
¼ bunch chives
salt, pepper, to taste

Chef Michel Haquin has always been inspired by the incredible range of goods available at the street markets. This elegant and exquisite appetizer is proof of his imaginative cooking.

Historically, asparagus has gone in and out of fashion: during the Middle Ages, it was not particularly appreciated, though it had been known since antiquity, and it only reappeared during the Italian Renaissance. Eventually, it found its way into French cuisine. Its popularity blossomed at the court of Valois, where it was thought to have aphrodisiac properties. Asparagus comes white, green or violet, always rich in vitamins and low in calories, making it both healthy and delicious. France produces a number of varieties, especially in the Anvers province. This recipe requires medium-sized stalks, which need to be thoroughly washed. They are served warm.

Fava beans are an ideal accompaniment. If the skin on the bean itself is too thick, it must be removed, as it is not very digestible and may impair the delicate flavor of the dish. The salmon should, if possible, be from Norway, as its refined taste will not overpower that of the asparagus. Finally, a small tip: premixing the butter in the blender or food processor will makes the sauce lighter and more emulsified. Serve the appetizer warm and consume soon, preferably right after it has been prepared.

1. Peel the asparagus and tie into bundles. Boil in salted water. Trim 2 in / 5 cm off the end and cut this bottom portion into ⅜ in / 1 cm chunks.

2. Shell the fava beans and blanch for a few seconds in boiling salted water. Rinse immediately with cold water and then peel. (If you are using dried fava beans, they will have to be soaked overnight first, and blanched slightly longer.)

Beans and Diced Leeks

3. Chop the shallots very finely; mix with white wine and vinegar. Bring to a boil, reduce, then add a little water. Remove from the heat and work into a sauce by gradually adding small chunks of butter. Whisk for a few minutes; season with salt and pepper.

4. Stir in the asparagus chunks. Add the beans and diced salmon. Mix well and place in a deep plate. Layer the asparagus tips on top and garnish with chopped chives.

Lobster

Preparation time: 30 minutes
Cooking time: 30 minutes
Cooling time: 24 hours
Difficulty: ★★

Serves four

2 lobsters, a generous 1 lb / 1 kg each
1 cucumber
8 tomatoes
$^1/_2$ red pepper
1 leek stalk
$^5/_8$ lb / 300 g onions
1 clove of garlic
3 slices of bread, crust removed
3 basil leaves

pinch of cumin
pinch of coriander
$^3/_4$ cup / 200 ml olive oil
$^1/_2$ cup / 100 ml red wine vinegar
1 cup / 250 ml cream
2 cups / 500 ml lobster soup (see basic
   recipes)
salt, pepper to taste

For the garnish:
1 red pepper
1 green pepper
1 cucumber
3 slices white bread
1 cup / 250 ml olive oil
half a bunch of basil leaves

Gazpacho was created in Seville, in southern Spain. Spanish farmers prepared this refreshing dish right in the fields, using a mortar to crush cucumbers, tomatoes, and onions into a pulpy liquid that they would pour into a clay pot, binding it with breadcrumbs and seasoning it with garlic and olive oil. The whole process, from clay pot to seasoning, imparted a fresh and particular flavor to the dish. Here, chef Michel Haquin uses the same original ingredients, but adds lobster to give it a marine nuance.

The cucumber has been known for more than three thousand years; today, it is particularly appreciated by diet-conscious consumers. Thanks to them, the cucumber – member of the pumpkin family – has become popular again, after having been rejected for a long time for tasting too bitter. These days we appreciate its beneficial properties, from its few calories to the large amount of water it contains, which of course is important for the gazpacho. But all the vegetables going into the gazpacho must be ripe and juicy.

If you happen to be out of fish stock you can also stretch the lobster soup with water, as the lobster flavor is very strong. This does not necessarily apply to all shellfish, but does to shrimp, crayfish, and langoustines as well; they would, incidentally, be a fine alternative to lobster in this recipe.

Gazpacho is an appetizer that is served chilled; some like to serve it as an intermediate course instead of a *digestif*.

1. Chop all the vegetables; peel and chop the garlic; chop the basil leaves. Stir in the basil leaves and the garlic. Cook the lobster quickly; extract the lobster meat from the shells. Add the claws and tails into the broth and prepare the lobster soup.

2. Add the red wine vinegar, olive oil, cumin, and coriander to the vegetable mixture. Season with salt and pepper. Remove the crust from the bread and retain for later; blend the bread with the other ingredients and leave the mixture to rest for 24 hours.

Gazpacho

3. After the 24-hour rest period, use a hand-held blender to mix well. Take about a quart of the gazpacho, and mix with the lobster soup. Adjust seasoning to taste, mix once more, add the cream and mix one last time; chill.

4. Peel the peppers and the cucumber, chop separately. Cut the retained breadcrust into small chunks and fry until brown in a little olive oil. Serve the gazpacho chilled in a deep plate, accompanied by separate small bowls of garnish. Set the lobster meat in the gazpacho; decorate with basil leaves.

Cool Tomato Broth with

Preparation time:	45 minutes, plus 24 hours for straining
Cooking time:	3 minutes
Difficulty:	☆

Serves four

2¹/₂ lbs / 1¹/₄ kg tomatoes
1 bunch of basil (to yield ¹/₈ lb / 50 g)
1 bunch of chervil (to yield a scant ¹/₄ lb / 100 g)
1 bunch of smooth parsley
3 sprigs thyme

1 clove of garlic
1 shallot
¹/₂ cup / 125 ml white wine
coarse sea salt to taste

For the vegetables:
2 carrots
4 tomatoes
2 zucchini
1 celeriac
¹/₂ lb / 250 g fresh fava beans
¹/₂ lb / 250 g small peas

This tomato broth can be served as an appetizer or as a digestive treat after the main course. It is simple to prepare and very refreshing. Make sure you buy very ripe, red, and tasty tomatoes, such as the Roma variety, which is sold on the stem – a sure indicator of ripeness. Romas have firm flesh and the sweet flavor that this dish requires. Nineteenth-century England considered the tomato, a member of the nightshade family, a toxic vegetable, and hygiene laws required any cook to boil them for three hours before consumption. Certainly, our knowledge of nature's products has improved since then, and the preparation of this dish is a little quicker than that, if one disregards the draining time.

The tomato broth requires some spicing up – enter the aromatic herbs, such as fresh basil, smooth parsley, and chervil. If you wish, add dill, fennel, and chives as well to this bouquet garni.

Crushed with your very own hands, the tomatoes only gradually release their juices, so they need to be strained through a muslin cloth for twenty-four hours. Use a muslin that is not too finely woven, so that a little of the flesh also passes through. The vegetables need to be cooked *al dente* so they retain their vitamins. If for some reason you can't obtain fresh fava beans, follow the instructions in previous recipes on dealing with dried ones.

1. Wash the tomatoes, remove the stems, and place the tomatoes in a bowl. Add the chopped herbs, shallot, and garlic as well as the wine and seasoning.

2. Squash the tomatoes by pressing them between your fingers until they are transformed into a pulp.

Chervil and Vegetables

3. Place the squashed mixture into a muslin cloth over a container and leave to strain for 24 hours.

4. For the vegetable garnish, peel and finely chop the vegetables. Skin the beans; remove the peas from the pods; cook the vegetables with the beans, and then the peas. Drain the tomato liquid; pour a portion into a soup bowl or cup, add the vegetable garnish and chervil leaves. Serve cold.

Cold and Warm

Preparation time: 30 minutes
Cooking time: 1–2 minutes
Difficulty: ★

Serves four

10 sea scallops
scant ¹/₂ lb / 200 g smoked salmon
juice of 1 lemon
1 cup / 250 g mesclun or mixed lettuce
¹/₂ cup / 125 ml olive oil
salt, pepper to taste

For the basil dressing:
1 bunch of basil
¹/₂ cup / 125 ml cold-pressed olive oil
salt, pepper to taste

For the vegetables:
1 onion (to yield ¹/₈ lb / 50 g chopped)
1 zucchini (to yield ¹/₈ lb / 50 g chopped)
1 eggplant (to yield ¹/₈ lb / 50 g chopped)
1 green pepper (to yield a scant ¹/₄ lb / 100 g
  chopped)
2 tomatoes (to yield ¹/₈ lb / 50 g chopped)

Based on the traditional British marriage of salmon and scallops, this easy-to-prepare appetizer pays tribute to the Scots' fishing methods and diverse smoking skills. The quality of smoked salmon depends on the pureness of the water it came from, its diet, and the wood used to smoke it. Our chef recommends smoking the salmon over wood from old brewery vats, which imparts a strong whisky aroma to the salmon without ruining its own flavor.

As for the scallops, chef Paul Heathcote recommends those found in the waters of northern Scotland, in Loch Linnhe for example, which are of medium size and usually smaller than their French counterparts. However, many markets sell scallops already shelled, so look for pinkish, rather than white flesh, which should have a fresh aroma. If you do buy them in the shell, once you have extracted them, the scallops must be stored in cloth to preserve their moisture. Afterwards, they are briefly heated in olive oil and lemon juice.

If they are only heated for a minute, the chopped vegetables will remain fresh and crisp. The basil dressing, which also forms the basis for the Mediterranean "pesto," imparts a southern flair to this northern dish.

1. Thinly slice the salmon; and form each slice into a rosette. Wash the mixed lettuce.

2. Cut the scallop flesh in half and heat on one side in olive oil and lemon juice. Place on absorbent paper towels and season with salt and lemon juice. Prepare the basil dressing: heat some oil, add the basil leaves, season and puree in the blender or food processor. Set aside to cool.

Scallop Salad

3. Peel the tomatoes and chop. Chop the vegetables, heat them briefly in a frying pan, and add the peeled tomatoes at the last minute.

4. To serve, set a heap of mixed lettuce in the center of the plate, top with a salmon rose, and arrange the warm vegetables in a ring of five small piles around the lettuce. Place a scallop on each. Pour dollops of the basil dressing in between the scallop heaps.

Salad of Sea Bream

Preparation time: 20 minutes
Cooking time: 30 minutes
Marinating/Pickling time: 2 hours total
Difficulty: ✶

Serves four

1 2 lb / 1 kg sea bream
2 lb / 1 kg coarse sea salt
scant ¹/₂ lb / 200 g green beans
1 bunch of radishes
scant ¹/₂ cup / 25 g lettuce
2 tbsp / 30 ml olive oil
4 potato skins (see below)

For the marinade:
scant quart / 1 l white wine vinegar
⁵/₈ cup / 150 g sugar

For the vegetable sauce:
1 small head lettuce
1 cucumber
1 green or red tomato
1 lemon
half a bunch of basil leaves
¹/₄ cup / 60 ml extra virgin olive oil
salt, pepper to taste

The sea bream, which lives on the rocky ocean floor, is mainly caught in the Atlantic and the Mediterranean. Its rather fat, firm and white flesh is very high in iodine.

Being particularly fond of marinated fish, our chef, Alfonso Iaccarino, wholeheartedly recommends this delicate salad. Instead of being cooked, the fish is first pickled in coarse sea salt and then marinated in white wine vinegar, giving it a distinctive flavor. How long the fish is marinated for depends on the thickness of the fillets: calculate about one hour per two pounds (one kilogram) of fish meat but err, if at all, on the side of underdoing it. The fillet should remain firm underneath the exterior layer. If no sea bream is available or if it is not to your taste, you can substitute it with a small perch.

The vegetable sauce is dominated by the cucumber, a vegetable known since antiquity (see page 112 for more information) but never really appreciated. Its bitterness can be neutralized by pickling the cucumber in honey or – as in this recipe – rolling it in salt and leaving it to infuse for ten minutes. You can then add it to the sauce along with a slightly acidic green tomato.

If you would like to vary the color of the sauce a bit, try adding beets, celery or carrots as well.

1. Clean and fillet the sea bream, and pickle in coarse sea salt for one hour; afterwards, rinse thoroughly in cold water. Prepare a marinade with vinegar and sugar and immerse the fillets in it; leave for one hour, regularly basting the fillets with the liquid.

2. Remove the fillets from the marinade and cut into thin slices. Chill for one hour.

with Vegetable Sauce

3. Wash the green beans and cook al dente. Julienne the beans and radishes into thin strips.

4. To make the potato cups, scrub the potatoes well; hollow out into thin shells; deep-fry in hot oil until crisp. To make the vegetable sauce, chop the lettuce, cucumber, basil and tomato in a blender. Add olive oil and salt. Heap some mixed lettuce in the middle of the plate, season, and place a few fish slices on top. Surround with the julienne of beans and radish. Serve with the sauce poured into an edible potato cup placed on top of the fish slices.

Smoked Breast of Duck

Preparation time: 30 minutes
Cooking time: 10 minutes
Pickling time: 24 hours (optional)
Cooling time: 24 hours
Difficulty: ★★

Serves four

2 breasts of duck
2 tbsp / 30 g dry black tea leaves
1 tbsp / 15 g hoisin sauce (ready-made)

For the vegetables:
8 fresh baby corn
10 cherry tomatoes
3/8 lb / 80 g snow peas

For the salt brine:
Salt for pickling (2 tsp / 10 g per 1 lb)

For the miso vinaigrette:
1 tbsp / 15 g white miso (see below)
1 tbsp / 15 ml vegetable oil
1 tbsp / 15 ml rice vinegar
2 tbsp / 30 ml broth

For the garnish:
half a bunch of smooth parsley
half a bunch of curly parsley
half a bunch of chervil

In days gone by, food was smoked in order to preserve it; now the process is primarily used to impart flavor. Here, chef André Jaeger demonstrates how this method can transform a breast of duck.

Smoking with tea is practiced in China to this day (with whole leaves, not broken ones). It lends a delicious flavor to the meat. The black tea sold in wooden crates is particularly suitable for this purpose, as its aroma is very strong. You don't need a smokehouse to do it: you can smoke the meat by placing it on a perforated rack in a covered frying pan, or make your own makeshift smokehouse from wood scraps. For better smoking, the duck breasts should be pickled in a salt brine for twenty-four hours to make the meat more tender. After smoking the breasts should be brushed with hoisin sauce, which consists of

fermented and perfumed soybeans with spices and is available in many Asian markets and health-food stores. The combination of hoisin sauce and duck meat might seem a little strange at first to a Western palette, but in fact it is a perfect match. After preparation, the meat should be left to rest so it becomes even more tender; it is then cut into slices with a pointed knife.

Miso, a paste made of fermented soybeans, comes in two basic varieties: red miso has a stronger flavor; white a milder one. For this recipe, the delicate, pale color of the white miso vinaigrette constrasts well with the hearty color of the duck, but, on the other hand, if your tastes run to the stronger flavor, use red miso instead.

1. Rub the duck breasts with salt; refrigerate for 24 hours. Then pour the dry tea leaves into a frying pan, place a flat sieve or perforated lid on top, place the salted breast on that, and cover.

2. Heat on the stove top until the tea leaves start smoking, and maintain the heat for 15 to 20 minutes. When smoke appears from the meat, reduce the heat so the duck will not cook prematurely.

with Vegetables and Miso

3. Cross-hatch the skin of the duck breasts every $^1/_4$ in / $^1/_2$ cm or so. In a skillet, heat the oil over high heat and fry the meat for five minutes each side, skin side down first. Leave to rest for ten minutes. Brush the meat with hoisin sauce and slice with a sharp knife.

4. To make the miso vinaigrette, mix all ingredients with the miso paste and stir. Wash the vegetables; quarter the cherry tomatoes and cut the corn into $^1/_2$ in / 1 cm slices. To serve, arrange the vegetables on the plates in mounds, pour over the vinaigrette, and place the duck breasts on top. Decorate with herbs.

Preparation time: 45 minutes
Cooking time: 15 minutes
Marinating time: 2 hours
Difficulty: ☆

Serves four

$^5/_8$ lb 300 g fresh tuna
half a cucumber
1 tbsp / 15 ml soy sauce
2 tsp / 15 g capers
$^1/_2$ cup / 100 ml Champagne vinegar
1 cup / 250 g mixed lettuce, such as mesclun
$^1/_2$ cup / 125 ml vegetable oil

For the tuna sauce:
1 small can of white tuna (packed in oil)
$^1/_2$ cup / 125 ml chicken broth
2 tbsp / 30 ml sesame oil
1 tbsp / 15 g wasabi paste
salt, pepper to taste

Our chef regards this dish as a combination of an Italian tradition – tuna sauce – and an Oriental custom – marinating raw fish. For this recipe, choose a very fresh red tuna with an agreeable and subtle scent, and, if you see the whole fish, with deep-red gills. The best pieces are from the upper back, which is the leanest part of the tuna's body.

You should instantly marinate this rather compact meat in soy sauce, according to Japanese tradition. Soy sauce, which comes in many varieties, essentially contains fermented, boiled soybeans and roasted barley or wheat. You may find its flavor a little on the strong side, particularly if you purchase soy sauce

in its strongest form, tamari. In this case, stretch the sauce with a little water. When looking for it in the market, it is best to choose a high-quality rather than a commercial supermarket brand; you may have good luck in Asian grocers or natural food stores.

With this recipe, we also introduce you to wasabi, or the Japanese equivalent of horseradish, which the Japanese grind into a powder and then often stretch with water into a paste. It is an indispensable component in sushi. The tuna sauce should rest for a while so the wasabi's taste can mellow.

1. Cut the tuna into 12 slices approximately $^3/_8$ in / 1 cm thick. Marinate the slices in soy sauce stretched with water (two-thirds soy sauce, one-third water) and set in the refrigerator for two hours.

2. Drain the tuna, oil it lightly, and grill very briefly, until it turns brown on the outside but before it starts to cook. Set aside.

in Spicy Sauce

3. Peel the cucumber, make small cucumber balls with a scoop and marinate in vinegar. Drain the capers. Wash the lettuce, spin-dry, and set aside. Crumble the white tuna.

4. Into a bowl or food processor add together the broth, sesame oil, wasabi, and the canned tuna as well as the oil it was packed in. Blend until the ingredients form an oily sauce. Add a pinch of salt. To serve, pour a little sauce on each plate, arrange the tuna slices, and garnish with cucumber balls, capers, and the mixed lettuce.

Salad with Prawns

Preparation time:	*30 minutes*
Cooking time:	*30 minutes*
Difficulty:	✫✫

Serves four

4 artichokes
40 prawns
scant $^1/_2$ lb / 200 g button mushrooms
salt, pepper to taste

For the prawn broth:
1 carrot
1 onion
1 celery stick
a few parsley leaves

For the sauce:
prawn shells
1 carrot
1 onion
1 bunch of tarragon
2 tbsp / 30 g concentrated tomato paste
$^1/_2$ cup / 100 ml cognac
$^1/_4$ cup / 50 ml sherry vinegar
1 cup / 250 ml broth
$^1/_2$ cup / 125 ml olive oil

Prawn breeders and chefs alike are confronted with the fact that some species of prawns are almost extinct. Freshwater prawns have all but disappeared from rivers due to water pollution.

That is why, when looking for prawns, a European cook would try to obtain either French prawns, an excellent variety with red legs, or Australian prawns with slightly thicker legs. For cooks in North America, another outstanding prawn would be the Hawaiian Blue, which is now being farmed to ensure its survival. In all cases, make sure they are fresh. Preparation begins with the removal of the intestines, which run as a small black thread under their tail; otherwise the broth will have a strong gall flavor. You should have a pot of boiling water ready, as the tails may start to release their contents if the prawns are not boiled immediately after the intestines are removed. The shells are retained for use in the sauce.

As for the artichokes, you could try to find an expensive import, such as the round, fleshy variety from Brittany, or, season permitting, violet artichokes from Provence, though California's varieties are also outstanding. And, if you prefer, you can make a salad of green beans instead.

1. Bring water to a rolling boil, Add a carrot, stick of celery, parsley, and onion. After removing the intestines, immediately boil the prawns.

2. Peel off the leaves of the artichokes and discard the fibrous parts of the heart (the choke), retain the heart, and cook the leaves for 20 minutes;. Shell the prawns, retaining them for the sauce. Into four individual forms, make a "chartreuse pie" using the prawn tails and claws with the chopped mushrooms; cook in a bain-marie for about ten minutes.

and Artichokes

3. To make the sauce, mix the prawn shells, carrot, onion, and concentrated tomato paste, gently pan-fry for a short time; flambé with cognac. Add a little broth and tarragon, reduce, and then pass through a fine-meshed sieve. Stir in the olive oil and sherry vinegar.

4. To serve, place an artichoke heart in the center of each plate and surround with cooked artichoke leaves. Place the chartreuse on top. Arrange the prawn tails decoratively; dress with the sauce.

Dough Cornucopia

Preparation time: 45 minutes
Cooking time: 30 minutes
Difficulty: ★ ★

Serves four

2 crabs, 1¹/₂ lb / 800 g each
4 flat rounds of dough, or puff pastry dough
   (see below)
2 grapefruit
1 orange

1 lemon
1 shallot
1¹/₂ tbsp / 20 g sesame seeds
⁷/₈ cup / 200 g whipping cream
1 cup / 250 ml vegetable oil
¹/₄ lb / 125 g butter
1 bunch of chives
half a bunch of chervil
half a bunch of tarragon
1 cup / 250 g mixed lettuce leaves
salt, pepper to taste

These cones stuffed with crab are irresistible. They look like little horns of plenty containing a special and delicious treasure, in this case crab meat. The flat dough discs we propose here are made from a Tunisian dough, by now popular and quite common all over Europe. The dough, made with flour, water, salt, and soy oil, is extremely versatile and can be worked into all sorts of shapes. It must be stored in a dry place, particularly if making it in advance. If you can not get this kind of dough, you can use ordinary puff pastry dough instead. Whichever dough you use, it has to be rolled into thin rounds to form the cones.

Around the globe, there is a veritable plethora of crabs: green, blue, red, and brown. These shellfish have an underdeveloped tail that disappears underneath the back shell, unlike the lobster or langoustine crayfish. Sometimes described by the French as "sleepers" because they hardly move, crabs are particularly tasty from April to July. Choose female crabs, as they have better developed shells and come with tasty crab roe, or coral. They should be very fresh – ideally, bought live.

To cook, the crabs are immersed in boiling water; the cooking time begins once the water comes to a boil again. It is important that the crab is left to cool in the cooking liquid so that the meat remains tender. Then take it out and cover with a moist cloth. Ideally, keep the crab in a warm place.

You could also use chopped tuna for this recipe (even freshly boiled and subsequently frozen tuna); instead of the grapefruit, you could substitute ripe avocados cut in quarters.

1. Plunge the crabs into fast boiling water and cook for 25 minutes. Afterwards, leave to infuse in the cooking liquid. Crack the shells and use a spoon to extract the meat. Prepare the dressing with oil, the juice of half a lemon and the shallot, which has already been cut into rounds.

2. Cut a circle 8–10 in / 20–25 cm in diameter out of cardboard and fasten into a cone; use as the form for four cones, wrapping them with aluminum foil.

with Crab Filling

3. Clarify the butter. Cut out the wafer-thin dough into enough of a disc to roll into four cones over the foil-covered forms. Sprinkle with sesame seeds and brush with clarified butter; bake at 355 °F / 180 °C for four to five minutes.

4. Mix the crab meat with the cream, chopped chives, orange zest, salt, and pepper. Fill the cones with this. To serve, place on on a plate with grapefruit slivers arranged on one side and the dressed salad leaves on the other. Garnish with tarragon and chervil.

Artichokes with

Preparation time: 10 minutes
Cooking time: 25 minutes
Difficulty: ★★

Serves four

16 small sardines (about 5 inches long)
scant ¹/₂ lb / 200 g coarse sea salt, crushed
4 tbsp / 50 g fresh-ground pepper
¹/₄ cup / 50 ml apple vinegar
1 sprig of tarragon
4 slices of rye bread
¹/₄ cup / 50 g sugar
salt, pepper to taste

For the garnish:
4 artichokes
scant ¹/₂ lb / 125 g lowfat quark (see below)
1 cup / 200 ml whole milk
1 bunch of chives
1 cup / 250 g mixed lettuce
2 red peppers
1 cup / 250 g sugar
salt, pepper to taste

For the vinaigrette:
1 cup / 250 ml olive oil
¹/₂ cup / 125 ml apple vinegar
salt, pepper to taste

Sardines are caught from April through September in the Atlantic and the Mediterranean. Up to ten inches (twenty-five centimeters) long, this fish frequently falls victim to its group instinct. Uniting to form gigantic schools that swim near the surface at night, they are easily attracted to any source of light and are thus caught in high numbers.

Sardines are sold whole. Check whether they are fresh: they must have stiff bodies, clean gills, and firm flesh. The smaller sardines are better than the fat ones as, logically, they have less fat and more taste. The fish tend to fall apart when being rinsed with running water, so we recommend you instead gently rub them with paper towels. They are then marinated in salt and apple vinegar – the latter used in small doses so it doesn't harm the meat. Salt was, incidentally, the original preservative for sardines, making them available for people living some distance from the coast.

That our chef, Patrick Jeffroy, recommends Breton artichokes is not a manifestation of any regional patriotism – he also acknowledges the premier quality of the violet artichoke from Provence. And, of course, if these are unavailable there are outstanding artichokes grown in California. In general, consume the artichokes quickly, as they will oxidate soon after cooking, deteriorating in both flavor and color.

Rye bread is the perfect accompaniment for marinated fish as well as for quark, which is a German unripened, soft cheese made from soured milk. Its compact yet light and fluffy consistency makes it similar to the French fromage frais. Though becoming more readily available outside of Germany, if you can't find it, substitute its French cousin; if all else fails, buy the freshest cream cheese available. The rye bread should be thinly sliced and then toasted to make it crisper.

1. Remove the leaves of the artichokes, discard the fibers from the heart, and cook the remainder in a milk-water mixture for 15 to 20 minutes. Finely dice the red peppers to yield about 1 tbsp / 15 g.

2. De-scale, gut and clean the sardines. Remove the head and central bone. Season with crushed coarse sea salt and freshly ground pepper. Sprinkle with a little sugar. Prepare the vinaigrette.

Marinated Sardines

3. Chop the chives. Bring the apple vinegar and the chopped tarragon to a boil and then pour over the sardines. Marinate for five minutes. Meanwhile, mix salt, pepper, and the chives with the quark, fromage frais, or cream cheese. Toast the rye bread slices.

4. To serve, slice the artichoke and fan across one side of the plate, punctutated by a dollop of cheese. Set a tall bouquet of salad leaves on the other side of the plate and cover it with a pyramid of four sardines. Sprinkle with the diced red peppers; dress the entire arrangement with the vinaigrette.

Preparation time: 45 minutes
Cooking time: 45 minutes
Cooling time: 30 minutes
Difficulty: ★★

Serves four

4 potatoes
2 leeks
³/₄ cup / 200 ml cream
³/₄ cup / 200 ml clear broth
generous cup / 300 ml chicken broth

To clarify the soup:
scant ¹/₈ lb / 40 g ground beef
1 tomato

2 leeks (to yield 2 tbsp / 20 g chopped)
2 carrots (to yield 2 tbsp / 20 g chopped)
¹/₂ celeriac (to yield 2 tbsp / 20 g chopped)
white of 1 egg
¹/₂ sheet of gelatin
3 ice cubes

For the vegetable garnish:
1 small zucchini
1 small carrot
1 turnip
half a bunch of chervil

For the meat garnish:
¹/₄ lb / 125 g chicken breast
scant ¹/₄ lb / 100 g cooked goose liver

The Alsace region has, thanks to its agriculture, rivers, and large game population, always considered food and drink one of its prime concerns and passions. And while Alsatian cuisine is certainly known for its famous choucroute, it is far from limited to it: chefs around the world regard its cuisine as one of the most creative, with countless recipes to be inspired by.

Our chef, Émile Jung, provides proof, as if proof was ever required, of this creativity with his Alsation soup platter, which has as a centerpiece a potato and leek puree. Leeks have been popular in antiquity, considered a symbol of strength and courage: Pharaoh Cheops rewarded leeks to his most courageous soldiers, and Emperor Nero consumed them to increase his vocal power. Harvested in spring, fall and winter, leeks in France are mainly cultivated in Normandy and Brittany. This recipe calls for only the sweet-tasting white of the leek.

Choose waxy potatoes for this dish to go with the leeks. The potato is deeply rooted in Alsatian tradition, having served its people well during times of war and famine: the Alsace region has been threatened time and again by its neighbors on both sides of the Rhine.

Preparation and seasoning requires some attention, though a few tips may make it easier: add ice cubes when clarifying the soup to prevent the egg white from stiffening, and make sure the aspic remains relatively runny (rather than letting it achieve its classic, firm consistency) so that it simply melts in the mouth and retains its delicate aroma.

1. To clarify the soup, chop all ingredients into coarse chunks and mix with the egg white. Stir in the ice cubes. Add clear broth and chicken broth bit by bit, constantly stirring. Retain a little of the liquid for the aspic.

2. Cook the soup for 20 minutes over medium heat, constantly stirring and then strain.

Soup Platter

3. Peel, wash, and dice the potatoes and cook with a scant ¹/₂ cup / 20 ml of the cleaned and chopped leeks. In a food processor or blender, prepare a puree from the leeks, potatoes, clear broth, and chicken broth, adding cream. Place in the middle of the plate with the aid of a 2 in / 5 cm in diameter circular form.

4. Gently cook the chicken breast in its own juices. Dice it, as well as the cooked goose liver, and arrange in a ring around the puree. Pour the slightly jellied broth (not yet an aspic) around the puree. Garnish with small carrot, turnip, and zucchini balls, and chervil leaves.

Tomato Consommé

Preparation time: *2 hours*
Cooking time: *8–10 minutes*
Difficulty: ★★

Serves four

For the tomato consommé:
2 cups / 500 ml double poultry consommé
$^3/_8$ cup / 100 ml olive oil
generous $^1/_4$ lb / 125 g tomatoes
generous $^1/_4$ lb / 125 g concentrated tomato
    paste
3 shallots

For the sushi:
2 nori sheets
$^1/_8$ lb / 50 g rice
$^1/_8$ lb / 50 g salmon
$^1/_8$ lb / 50 g crayfish
$^1/_8$ lb / 50 g monkfish
1 cup / 250 ml olive oil
1 orange (to yield 1 tsp / 10 g orange zest)
$^1/_8$ lb / 50 g ginger root
1 bunch of chervil
salt, pepper to taste

For the garnish:
2 oz / 50 g caviar (Ossetra or Sevruga)
2 oz / 50 g salmon roe

Easy on the palate and vibrant in appearance, Dieter Kaufmann's Japanese-derived appetizer is the ideal introduction to a rich meal. It combines a consommé, for which you should choose juicy and aromatic tomatoes such as globe or beefsteak (if available, our chef recommends ripe Italian tomatoes like San Marzano), with a classic of Japanese cuisine. One can now find sushi rice, also known as sweet rice, in many specialty markets, or use a fine-grain risotto or Camargue rice. The rice will be perfumed with ginger and orange zest during cooking. The type of sushi used in this recipe, *makizushi* ("rolled sushi") also known as *norimaki*, consists of thin strips of fish or vegetables rolled in sushi rice inside thin, crisp nori sheets; the rolls are cut into bite-sized slices. The contents can

be varied almost infinitely, so you can prepare several different rolls. If you prefer, or if the right rice is unavailable, try small lentils instead, and if you want even more variety you might try replacing the nori, or supplementing it, with blanched spinach or leek leaves, or celery strips.

The fish filling (raw salmon, monkfish, and crayfish) provides a harmonious color combination, but shrimp would work just as well. Whatever you choose, make sure it is extremely fresh, and a cut considered high enough quality to be used in sushi.

A final tip from Dieter Kaufmann: add a small frozen piece of meat to the consommé at the very last minute to clarify it.

1. Peel and seed the tomatoes. Sweat the chopped shallots in olive oil. Add the concentrated tomato paste and the tomatoes, simmer for five to six minutes, and mix with the poultry consommé. Pass through a fine sieve, add a small piece of frozen meat, and chill.

2. Cut the crayfish, monkfish, and salmon into small chunks. Grate the ginger and the orange zest; add to the rice water; cook the rice.

with Sushi

3. Unroll the nori sheets and carefully cut each into five strips. Put one layer of perfumed rice on the leaves and place either fish, vegetables or crayfish in the center. Roll into a tight, long cylinder. Do the same with the blanched spinach, leeks, or celery strips.

4. Cut the sushi into slices about ³/₄ in / 3 cm thick; place in a deep plate, and surround with tomato consommé. Mound caviar and salmon roe in the center. Garnish with chervil leaves.

Sturgeon Parfait

Preparation time: *1 hour, 30 minutes*
Cooking and chilling time: *3–4 hours*
Difficulty: ✲✲

Serves four

For the sturgeon parfait:
scant $^1/_2$ lb / 250 g smoked sturgeon
$^1/_2$ cup / 125 ml fish broth
$^1/_2$ cup / 125 ml Riesling sparkling wine or
    champagne
1 cup / 250 ml whipping cream
4 sheets of gelatin
$^1/_4$ cup / 50 g wheat starch
salt to taste

For the squid mousse:
scant $^1/_2$ lb / 250 g smoked squid
scant $^1/_4$ cup / 50 ml sepia ink (or food
    coloring, see below)
2 cups / 500 ml fish broth
$^1/_2$ cup / 125 ml Riesling sparkling wine or
    champagne
1 cup / 250 ml whipping cream
4 sheets of gelatin
2 tbsp / 20 g wheat starch
salt, pepper to taste

The sturgeon has been regarded as the "King of the Oceans" since the Middle Ages. It makes its habitat in the open seas, particularly the Caspian and Black Seas. During spawning season, the fish swim upstream from their saltwater homes to a freshwater spawning ground to produce caviar. There are two types of caviar: the roe of the Beluga sturgeon – a fish that can measure more than twenty feet (six meters) in length and has particularly delicious meat – and roe from the more common Sevruga, whose caviar is more fine-grained and less salty. These days, fresh sturgeon is not always easy to find, as opposed to smoked sturgeon, which is usually cured over beechwood smoke and cut into small pieces. This latter form is what Dieter Kaufmann's elegant recipe calls for. However, any smoked white-fleshed fish, such as monkfish, can be used for this recipe if no sturgeon is available.

Squid should be smoked over charcoal made from chestnut wood, a procedure that requires some patience, as does mixing the light mousse, which is dyed with a generous dose of sepia ink or food coloring at the last minute.

The trickiest part of the preparation is adding the right quantity of gelatin, which should lend the mixture firmness without impairing its fluffy and airy consistency. Therefore, use as little gelatin as possible and reduce the chilling time. Ideally, the parfait should be served at room temperature.

Keeping in mind the color contrast of the parfait and the mousse, tilting the terrine form at an angle when filling it with the second mixture will reward you with an unusual decorative effect.

1. Dissolve the starch in water. To prepare the sturgeon parfait, bring the fish broth and wine to a boil and bind with the starch to achieve a thick puree. Set aside to chill.

2. Remove the sturgeon's skin and dark exterior blemishes with a knife. Chop the rest (at least 1$^1/_8$ lb / 150 g) in the food processor; stir in the chilled puree. Chill once more for half an hour.

with Squid Mousse

3. While the sturgeon mixture is chilling, lightly whip the cream (not until completely stiff), soak the gelatin and then melt it in a bain-marie; keep warm. Carefully fold the cream into sturgeon mixture, adding salt if desired, and finally fold in the liquidized gelatin. Prepare the squid mousse taking identical steps, then add sepia ink or food coloring (in the case of food coloring, far less will be used than if you use ink).

4. Fill the terrine with the parfait, holding it at an angle to achieve a diagonal color division. Chill for two to three hours.

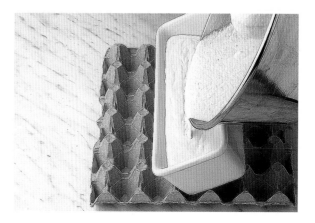

Duck's Liver Tart

Preparation time: 1 hour
Cooking time: 5 minutes
Cooling time: 12 hours
Difficulty: ★★★

Serves eight

1 duck's liver, 1¼ lb / 600 g
scant ½ cup / 100 g slivered almonds
1 cup / 250 ml cream
½ tbsp / 7 g starch
1¼ cups / 300 ml clear broth
³/₈ cup / 100 ml sweet muscat wine (see
   below)
scant ¼ cup / 50 ml cognac
4 sheets of gelatin
salt, fresh-ground white pepper to taste

For the confit of grapes:
1 lb / 500 g green seedless grapes
¹/₈ lb / 50 g sugar
2 cloves
half a lemon
2 sheets of gelatin
³/₈ cup / 100 ml white wine

For the génoise:
(see basic recipes)

Chef Dieter Kaufmann, also responsible for the last two recipes on the preceding pages, is the man behind the Traube restaurant – renowned throughout Germany for its passion for excellent wines. Kaufmann has a wine cellar with more than thirty thousand bottles, among them great French crus (Romanée-Conti, Yquem, Lafite and Pétrus) as well as top German wines, used in some of Kaufmann's recipes.

This appetizer was initially conceived as a proper pudding, with a layer of génoise (a versatile, spongy cake), and a sweet, almost caramelized wine aspic; it was modified for the birthday celebration of a close friend and then finally included on the restaurant's menu.

Duck liver contains less fat than goose liver, making it more appropriate for this dish. It is imperative that the filling is prepared at the right temperature, or the liver will become bitter. The cream is carefully folded into the mousse, which will be layered over the filling. Both layers need to be equal in height and balanced in flavor in order to achieve the desired effect.

Prepare the grapes ahead of time so you can then focus on the tart. If possible, Kaufmann recommends the excellent Chasselas grapes, which can keep in the refrigerator for more than a week; otherwise, look for a succulent, firm, green seedless variety that is ripe, but not overly so, unless you are preparing them the same day.

1. Chill half of the duck liver; strain the remaining portion and chill as well. Heat ³/₈ cup / 100 ml of clear broth with a scant ¼ cup / 50 ml of the muscat wine and the cognac, remove from the heat and carefully fold into the strained duck liver. Do not allow the liver to become too warm. Line the base of a circular cake form (about 4–6 in / 10–15 cm in diameter) with a thin layer of génoise and pour the duck liver filling into the form. Chiil for 20 minutes.

2. To prepare the mousse, heat another ³/₈ cup / 100 ml of clear broth and bind with the starch. Cut the remaining half of the duck liver into thin slices, add to the broth, and melt slightly. Puree in the blender and then strain. Add four pre-soaked gelatin sheets. Chill for 15–20 minutes.

with a Confit of Grapes

3. Whip the cream until half-stiff and carefully fold into the basic mousse mixture. Season with salt and pepper according to taste. Pour on top of the génoise in the cake form to make the second layer. Chill for 12 hours. To make the grape aspic, heat the rest of the clear broth with a pre-soaked sheet of gelatin, add a $^1/_4$ cup / 125 ml of muscat wine, and leave to cool. Glaze the tart with this aspic.

4. For the confit of grapes (which can be made ahead of time), mix the lemon juice, the remaining white wine, and cloves. Soak a gelatin sheet. Peel the grapes, remove any seeds and marinate in the wine-juice mixture. Make a caramel mixture from 2 tbsp of sugar and pour the grape marinade over it. Add a pre-soaked gelatin sheet and remove from the heat instantly. Remove the tart from the form and coat the outside with slivered almonds.

Marinated herring

Preparation time: *50 minutes*
Soaking time: *12 hours*
Marinating time: *1–2 days (more is*
                   optional)
Difficulty: ✮✮

Serves four

2 salted herrings, ⁷⁄₈ lb / 400 g each
8 potatoes
¼ piece of fresh horseradish root
1 carrot
1 white onion

1 red onion
3 bay leaves
2 tbsp / 20 g white peppercorns
2 tbsp / 20 g allspice corns
1 bunch of dill

For the marinade:
scant ½ cup / 125 g confectioners' sugar
⅔ cup / 150 ml brandy vinegar
1 cup / 250 ml water

The glassblower's guild lent its name to this recicpe from southern Sweden, conceived by chef Örjan Klein. Well-equipped with an array of glass containers, they presumably once had the idea of preserving herrings in them. In the nineteenth century, these preserved herrings were named *matjes* herrings, after the Swedish king Gustav V. The preparation method shown here is just as popular in Sweden as the traditional method of preparing herring in mustard or tarragon.

The best herrings are from Norway and Iceland, rich in healthy fats and salted before reaching the market. Thus they must be soaked in water for quite a while (and the water changed from time to time) in order to draw out the salt. They are then cut into small chunks to be preserved in a glass jar. You can enjoy every bit of these pickled including all the other ingredients in the glass, even the bones, which would have been discarded in other recipes.

The horseradish root lends a spicy note to this dish: cut it into thin strips to release all the juices. If the fish has been sufficiently soaked to remove all the salt, the sweet flavor of the red onion and the sharp taste of the horseradish should, in principle, strike a perfect balance. The red onion is used because sugar is so expensive in Sweden. The marinade should not fill the jar but should have room to move. And take note: do not marinate the mixture for more than a couple of days unless the container is completely airtight – in which case you can store the marinated fish for up to two months.

1. Gut the herrings and remove the fins. Soak in water for at least 10–12 hours, changing the water several times. Leave to air-dry and cut into 1 in / 2.5 cm slices; do not remove the bones and undamaged skin.

2. Cut the vegetables and horseradish root into fine strips. Cook the water, sugar and vinegar for 10 minutes, leave to cool and add the herring pieces.

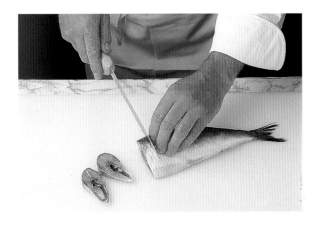

à la Glaser

3. Place the herrings and the other ingredients (vegetables, pepper, allspice corns, bay leaves, and horseradish) in a glass jar in alternate layers.

4. Pour the marinade into the glass container. Chill and leave to infuse for at least four to five hours. In the meantime, boil a few potatoes to be served with the pickled fish. To serve, arrange the marinated herring and vegetables on a plate, accompanied by potatoes and a dill garnish.

Baltic Herring

Preparation time: 50 minutes
Cooking time: 30 minutes
Marinating time: 12 hours
Difficulty: ☆

Serves four

7/8 lb / 400 g herring fillets
5/8 lb / 300 g small potatoes
1 bunch of dill
salt, fresh-ground pepper to taste

For the marinade:
3/4 cup / 200 ml white wine vinegar
2 1/2 / 600 ml cups water

For the dill sauce:
1 bunch of dill
1 tbsp / 15 g mustard
1 tbsp / 15 ml white vinegar
scant 1/2 cup / 100 g mayonnaise
   (see basic recipes)
2 cups / 500 ml milk (see below)
2 cloves of garlic

Serve with (if desired):
crispbread
Västerbotten cheese, or, if unavailable,
   Danish Tilsit

The Swedes celebrate the *Midsommar* – midsummer night – in great style, as it heralds the beginning of the warm season. The traditional midsummer night's dish is herring with potatoes and seasonal vegetables, followed by strawberry pudding.

Herring is inexpensive and easy to prepare; there is a huge, enduring population in the Baltic Sea. A member of the family *clupea*, it lives in the depths of the sea during summer, and then ascends as the temperatures fall with autumn and winter's coming. Our chef Örjan Klein's restaurant, Kostnärs baren, or simply "K. B.", as it is called, has had herrings on his menu for fifteen years. Instead of serving it in its natural, rather dull gray juices, he has concocted a green dill sauce that will please your

guests' eyes as well as their palates. For this recipe, the herring should be gutted and boned.

A final word about the extraordinary northern dill, whose sprigs develop even on frozen ground and reach a respectable size: its taste is more intense than that of the usual dill, so use a little more if you have bought the common variety. Also, make sure that you do not mix the milk, which should be almost ready to curdle, for too long, as you want to keep it from curdling and retain its very slight sour taste. Finally, the dill is added at the very last moment.

1. Remove the herrings' heads and skin. Cook the potatoes unpeeled and with a little dill in salted water.

2. Marinate the herrings for 12 hours in the mixture of white vinegar and water.

à la "K. B."

3. For the dill sauce, mix mayonnaise, the milk, mustard, garlic, and very finely chopped dill in the food processor; adjust seasoning to taste. Let the herrings air-dry and blend with the sauce.

4. To serve, place the herring fillets on the plates, generously covering them with sauce; place a few herring fillets on top for contrast if you prefer. Serve with potatoes. Garnish with sprigs of dill. Accompany, if desired, with crispbread and cheese.

Whitefish Roe

Preparation time: 25 minutes
Cooking time: 5 minutes
Difficulty: ★

Serves four

scant 1/2 lb / 200 g whitefish roe
7/8 lb / 400 g potatoes
1/4 cup / 60 ml crème fraîche
1 red onion (to yield 1/4 cup / 60 g chopped)
1/2 lb / 125 g butter
1 lemon
1 bunch of chives
salt, pepper to taste

Usually, fish roe is considered a luxury, used to decorate little canapés, embellish festive dishes, or add elegance to a meal. But, in Sweden, it is a popular and common ingredient, which is why it appears in this recipe. The dish, conceived by Örjan Klein, was inspired by the Russian blini the sturgeon roe having been replaced by whitefish roe, and the blini by the potato cake.

Whitefish has become increasingly rare. Not only does it have a unique, delicious taste, but its scales are distilled into an essence with which glass pearls are coated to give them the lustre of real pearls. In Sweden, the fish is called *lörja*, and is chiefly caught in the Baltic Sea.

The best whitefish roe comes from the fishing port of Kalix in northern Sweden, close to the Finnish border. When the roe is prepared, every egg is separated from the skin and cured with salt. The resulting salty flavor has a strong iodine element, and its color – yellow or red – is extremely bright (avoid gray roe). Although its flavor is more delicate than salmon or trout roe, the latter can be used alternatively. We also recommend you try whitefish roe with a dill sauce, prepared as described in the preceding recipe.

1. Wash and peel the potatoes. Slice thinly; cut the slices into very fine strips.

2. Press the potato strips well so that all the water oozes out (try sandwiching the strips between two boards, using a light book to weigh down the top one). Chop the red onion and chives.

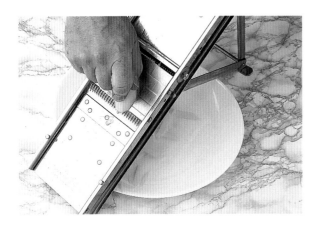

with Potato Cake

3. Form the potato strips into little cakes and sauté them in a frying pan that is, ideally, the same size as the cakes, if not much bigger, in order to keep the cakes' shape.

4. To serve, place a potato cake in the middle of each plate and dollop the whitefish roe, onion, and chives into separate mounds. Garnish with a sliver of lemon. Accompany the dish with a separate pot of bowl of crème fraîche.

Vegetable Terrine with

Preparation time: 1 hour
Cooking time: 2 hours,
                      30 minutes

Cooling time: 3 hours
Difficulty: ★★

Serves eight

4 fennel bulbs
5 zucchini
5 eggplants
4 lb / 2 kg tomatoes
2 red peppers
1 clove of garlic
7 sheets of gelatin
1 scant quart / 1 l olive oil
1 cup / 250 g pastis

1 bunch of thyme
salt, pepper to taste

For the mustard puree:
1 artichoke
1 carrot
1 onion
1 clove of garlic
2 large button mushrooms
1¹/₂ tbsp / 15 g mustard
scant ¹/₂ cup / 125 ml white wine
¹/₂ cup / 125 ml olive oil
1 cup / 250 ml milk
a pinch of coarse sea salt

Serve with: bread
chèvre (goat's milk cream cheese)

To garnish:
dill
chives

Terrines come in countless varieties, and have many admirers. A terrine might be filled with meat, fish, or simply vegetables, its aspic sweet or sour, its accompaniment a puree or a salad.

In the sixteenth century, people began listing all vegetables with edible leaves, stems, or bulbs, that did not have to be prepared with sugar. The list soon included three hundred vegetables, all with their own history and methods of preparation.

Choose fennel, zucchini, and eggplants that are very firm and unblemished. They will be steamed in a blend of their own juices and olive oil, imparting a Mediterranean aroma. Keep the vegetables *al dente* to contrast with the soft tomatoes.

Buy ripe and firm tomatoes and, above all, buy plenty of them: you will need around four pounds (two kilograms) raw to yield one-and-a-quarter pounds (six hundred grams) pickled. It is a good idea to prepare these the day before. They are well-seasoned before being placed on a baking tray and baked in the oven. If you like garlic, add it to the tomatoes, but be sure to blanch the garlic cloves in milk twice before cooking them into a paste, otherwise their flavor will be too overwhelming.

This appetizer should be served with a slice of country bread and fresh chèvre, or goat's milk cream cheese, sprinkled with dill and chives.

1. Discard the rough outer fennel layers and peel apart the inner layers. Peel and seed the peppers and chop. Gently fry the fennel in olive oil and add a little salt. Add a little pastis and cook for 20 minutes. Place the peppers in hot olive oil and gently fry for 20 minutes.

2. Cut the zucchini and eggplants in wide strips but discard the eggplant's seeded core. Gently fry in olive oil, add salt and pepper, and continue to gently fry for 15 minutes. Marinate the tomatoes in olive oil, garlic, thyme, salt, and pepper. Leave to infuse for two and a half hours in a low-oven – about 180 °F / 80 °C.

a Sweet Mustard Puree

3. To prepare the mustard puree, chop the artichoke hearts, carrot, onion, mushrooms, and garlic (which has been blanched in milk twice) into medium-sized chunks. Heat some olive oil, add the vegetables, and heat for ten minutes; with the heat still going, add the white wine, mustard, and a pinch of coarse sea salt. Cover with aluminum foil and cook gently for another 15 minutes. Puree in a blender or food processor.

4. Pre-soak the gelatin. Line the terrine form with foil or plastic wrap than can withstand high temperatures and fill, in layers, the eggplants, zucchini, fennel, peppers, fennel, zucchini, and then eggplants again, placing a layer of marinated tomatoes and a sheet of gelatin between each layer. Close the terrine form and cook in a bain-marie for 20 minutes at 350 °F / 180 °C. Serve in slices, accompanied by a spoonful of the mustard puree and a dollop of the chèvre.

Mackerel Fillets

Preparation time: 1 hour
Cooking time: 30 minutes
Cooling time: 2 hours
Marinating time: 6 hours
Difficulty: ★★★

Serves four

4 small mackerels
$^1/_4$ cup / 70 g coarse sea salt
2 oz / 40 g caviar
$^3/_8$ cup / 100 ml fish broth
$1^1/_2$ sheets of gelatin
1 egg white
4 eggs
1 bunch of flat-leaved parsley
salt, fresh-ground pepper to taste

For the marinade:
2 shallots
2 lemons
1 tsp / 5 g allspice corns

2 tsp / 10 g pastis
$^1/_2$ cup / 125 ml olive oil

For the onion mousse:
$^7/_8$ lb / 400 g small young onions
$^1/_4$ cup / 60 ml cream
$^1/_4$ lb / 60 g butter
salt, pepper to taste

For the fish vinaigrette:
$^2/_3$ cup / 150 ml fish broth
scant $^1/_4$ cup / 50 ml lemon juice
scant $^1/_4$ cup / 50 ml white wine vinegar
$1^1/_4$ cups / 300 ml olive oil

The readily available mackerel is a fine yet inexpensive fish with firm flesh. Our chef recommends a small mackerel, very similar to the sardine – firm and shiny, with pretty black patterning on its silvery skin.

Preparing the mackerel requires careful handling: it must first be washed thoroughly before being filleted, pickled in salt and finally marinated in olive oil and pastis. This process takes time, so it is advisable to start the day before. After marinating, the fish is thinly sliced; make sure the flesh has been completely cleared of allspice corns or onion pieces. Apart from marinating in salt, the salmon is prepared the same way.

Small, young onions are ideal for the accompanying mousse: after you have shed enough tears over cutting them, they are fried very gently and then left to reduce over a very low heat until soft enough to pass through a sieve. The resulting mousse should be fairly firm after the cream has been folded in. Incidentally, our chef, Robert Kranenborg, claims that all you need to do to avoid "crying" when cutting onions is to immerse them very briefly in boiling water to quell their sharp juice; another tactic is simply to wear goggles.

Chill this sublime maritime starter until just before serving it, and then let your guests enjoy it at their own pace.

1. Gut and fillet the mackerel and remove the bones. Cover with coarse sea salt, wrap in aluminum foil and put in the refrigerator for three hours. When that time is up, wash and dry the fish and place in a dish. For the marinade, chop the shallots and juice two lemons. Add the shallots, allspice corns, lemon juice, olive oil, and pastis to the mackerel and marinate for six hours in the refrigerator. Then skin and cut the fillets into small chunks, chilling once more for about an hour.

2. Pre-soak the gelatin. Make a fish broth, add the gelatin, and clear with egg white. Chill until stiff. Put four circular forms on a tray covered with plastic wrap, fill the forms with a thin layer of the very stiff aspic, then add a layer of caviar topped by a layer of chopped mackerels.

with Caviar Jelly

3. For the onion mousse, chop the onions and sauté. Add a little water and simmer for 30 minutes, then strain. Salt, pepper, and set aside to cool. Slightly whisk the cream, add a little pepper, and mix the cream into the onions; add coarse sea salt.

4. Hard-boil the eggs and chop finely. Fill the forms with their final layer of onion mousse, then tilt to tap the contents out. Garnish with the chopped egg and parsley. Finally, dribble on a few drops of the fish vinaigrette.

Oxtail Balls

Preparation time: 1 hour
Cooking time: 4 hours
Difficulty: ★★★

Serves four

half an oxtail
2 slices of goose liver pâté
4 tomatoes
1 celeriac
1 carrot
1 small leek
1 onion stuck with 3 cloves

1 tbsp / 15 g concentrated tomato paste
1 tbsp / 15 g poppy seeds
2 sprigs of thyme
1 bay leaf
half a bunch of flat-leafed parsley
1¼ cups / 300 ml red wine
scant quart / 1 l beef broth
½ cup / 125 ml sherry vinegar
⅜ cup / 100 ml walnut oil
fat for frying
salt, pepper to taste

Oxtail is not regarded too highly, although it is inexpensive, very tasty, and has a sublime consistency. Its upper portion bears the most delicious meat. Our chef, Étienne Krebs, recommends the tail from a young ox; when he makes this recipe, he looks for an ox of the Simmental breed from the Swiss region of Waadt. The oxtail has to cook for a long time, around four hours, over a very low heat, in order to draw out all the flavor and make it easier to separate the meat from the bone. Since only the meat will be consumed, it requires a bit of patience to discard all the fat and nerve tissue.

To make the celeriac ravioli you will need even, thin slices of celeriac: a slicing machine works well for this task; slice the celeriac as if you were slicing a ham. The celeriac itself should not be fibrous but firm and fresh. In Switzerland, the best

varieties are Alba or Mentor, if they have been cultivated traditionally; otherwise, get one in season (September through May) that is relatively free of knobs or blemishes. The celeriac flavor is the ideal accompaniment for the goose liver pâté, as quite a few recipes can attest to.

The choice of pâté depends on the consistency and the subtle differences of the slightly sweet flavors involved: a marinade of Madeira and sugar is a perfect contrast to the poppy seed crust that will coat the pâté.

Instead of the oxtail, you can make this dish with calf's tail; instead of ravioli, you might trying serving it with a julienne of deep-fried onions.

1. Quarter the tomatoes. Salt and pepper the oxtail on all sides. Place in a pan lined with tomatoes and spices, add wine, salt, and pepper, stir, and cook for four hours over very low heat. Peel the celeriac, slice extremely thin, and boil in broth for one to two minutes. Using a circular cutter, cut out 24 circles of about 3 in / 5 cm in diameter from the celeriac slices.

2. Let the oxtail cool a little, strain the meat juice, and reduce to an aspic. Separate the meat from the bone, discard the fat and nerve tissue, and dice into small chunks. Chop the vegetables finely. Mix the meat with parsley and add the vegetables, tomato paste, vinegar and 4 tbsp / 60 ml of reduced meat broth. Mix well and season to taste.

with Celeriac Ravioli

3. Place this filling on 12 of the celeriac slices and cover with the other 12 slices to make them look like ravioli. Then prepare the sauce: put a large portion of the remaining celeriac, vinegar, walnut oil, and a little meat broth in a blender or food processor and puree thoroughly. Fry about a ¼ cup / 50 g of the celeriac julienne and set aside.

4. Halve the liver pâté slices, form four balls, and roll with the palm of your hand in a mixture of celeriac julienne and poppy seeds. To serve, place three celeriac ravioli in the middle of each plate, place one ball of the liver pâté on top, and garnish with sauce.

Wishbone Meat

Preparation time: 20 minutes
Cooking time: 15 minutes
Difficulty: ★★

Serves four

⁵/₈ lb / 300 g wishbone meat (see below)
1 tb / 15 ml cream
¹/₄ lb / 50 g butter
2 shallots (to yield 1 tbsp / 15 g chopped)
1 bunch of parsley (to yield 1 tbsp / 15 g chopped)
1 tbsp / 15 g flour
salt, pepper to taste

For the artichoke fritters:
2 artichokes
2 cups / 500 ml olive oil
salt to taste

For the sauce:
1 artichoke base
¹/₄ cup / 50 ml walnut oil
1 tsp / 10 ml sherry vinegar
¹/₄ cup / 50 ml cooking liquid from the artichokes
salt, pepper to taste

One does not usually regard the wishbone in a chicken as a source of meat, but the meat on the wishbone is actually tender and tasty muscle meat that can be fried, grilled, or baked. It must be ordered in advance at your local butcher, particularly since one needs around eighty wishbone sections (they grow out the chicken's hip bones, symmetrically embracing the body) to get two pounds of meat.

For the fritters, choose large artichokes – our chef, Étienne Krebs, always opts for those from Brittany since they are the most common of French artichokes and have tasty and fleshy hearts. The California varieties will work just as well. The arti-

choke hearts can be run through a vegetable slicer to make thin slices, which are then deep-fried very briefly so they remain crisp. The walnut vinaigrette lends a refined note to this vegetable-poultry dish, but, in case you consider the walnut oil too strong, you can partly or entirely replace it with peanut oil.

This appetizer is highly original yet easy to prepare. It can be served with a seasonal salad, and is equally successful when made with sautéed calf sweetbreads.

1. For the sauce: separate an artichoke heart and simmer it quickly. Put all the ingredients for the sauce in a blender; blend into an emulsion that is not too runny. If necessary, strain the sauce through a fine-meshed sieve. Set aside.

2. Salt and pepper the meat; coat all sides with flour and add the cream.

with Artichoke Fritters

3. For the artichoke fritters: remove the leaves and dry sections from two artichokes; cut the raw artichoke hearts into thin slices and deep-fry in oil at 355 °F / 180 °C, leaving them to air-dry. Add salt and set aside.

4. Sauté the meat in butter until brown, then add the chopped shallot and parsley. To serve, simply pour a little pool of sauce on the center of a plate, and arrange the meat and fritters in a pyramid. Garnish, if preferred, with upright chive spears.

Preparation time: 40 minutes
Cooking time: 20 minutes
Cooling time: 12 hours
Difficulty: ★★

Serves four

2 lobsters, 1¼ lb / 600 g each
broth (for the lobster)
2 onions
1 bunch of leeks (⅞ lb / 375 g)
scant ½ lb / 200 g red peppers
⅛ lb / 50 g green beans

generous ¼ lb / 125 g spinach
1 bunch of carrots
1 cup / 250 ml olive oil
salt, pepper to taste

For the tomato sauce:
½ lb / 250 g tomatoes
2 tbsp / 25 g tomato paste
two dashes of Tabasco
2 tbsp / 30 ml vinegar
½ cup / 125 ml olive oil
a pinch of salt

Although the preparation of this appetizer is a little time-consuming, it does have some tempting advantages: you can modify the recipe according to season, using whatever vegetable is available and suitable, and the terrine will keep in the refrigerator for a few days.

The outside leaves of the leeks are particularly pretty, and their fiber is very beneficial for digestion. Paradoxically, leek is consumed more during the winter than the summer, though this vegetable does not like to be exposed to frost at all. The leek belongs to the family of lilies, along with its cousins, onion and garlic. Remove the green sprout so the leek tastes less bitter. And, when preparing the terrine, make sure the individual layers of vegetables are even and season every layer. For

full effect, the lobster tail is placed in the center. (See earlier lobster recipes for more information on lobsters.)

Finally, the terrine must be pressed down with a weight and set to cool for twelve hours, after which point it will have set enough to be cut into three-quarter-inch (two centimeter) slices that are served on a delicate tomato sauce. The tomatoes are, depending on the season, more or less juicy, so you should puree them in any case to obtain a smooth and even mixture.

1. Tie the leeks together in a bundle and boil in salted water for 8–10 minutes; rinse in cold water. Cook the onions, carrots, green beans, and spinach in the same cooking liquid; afterwards, very briefly dip into ice water. Line the terrine with plastic wrap, then halve the leeks and line the terrine with the leaves.

2. Plunge the lobster into broth that has reached a rolling boil. Peel the red pepper, cut into thin strips, and fry briefly in olive oil. Halve the carrots; line the corners of the terrine with the carrot pieces.

Lobster with Tomato Sauce

3. Continue to fill the terrine with the various layers of green beans, chopped onions, spinach, and peppers, then add the lobster tail before layering another series of vegetables.

4. Close the terrine with the overlapping leek leaves and plastic wrap. Place the terrine dish into another dish and press with a 10 lb / 5 kg weight; chill in the refrigerator for 12 hours. To prepare the sauce, chop the tomatoes in the blender, add the other ingredients, and puree into a fine thick sauce. Serve a slice of terrine on a bed of sauce; garnish with herbs.

Salted Haddock with

Preparation time: 3 hours 45 minutes
Cooking time: 4 minutes
Marinating time: 12 hours
Difficulty: ✲✲

Serves four to six

1 3 lb / 1¹/₂ kg haddock

For the marinade:
2 cups / 500 ml water
a pinch of sugar
5 tbsp / 75 g salt
4 black peppercorns
2 sprigs of dill

For the apple terrine:
white cabbage or lettuce leaves
3 cooking apples
4 tsp olive oil

2 tsp curry powder
1 sheet of gelatin

For the herb pocket:
5 black peppercorns
4 juniper berries or cloves
1 sprig of thyme

For the soured cream:
¹/₂ cup / 100 ml whipping cream
4 tbsp / 30 g salmon roe
juice of half a lemon
salt, white pepper to taste

For the garnish:
¹/₂ lb / 250 g horseradish root
1 bunch of chives

"Twelve hours is enough": that is Chef Erwin Lauterbach's recommendation for how long the haddock needs to marinate. The haddock is a cousin of the cod – and in fact is often confused with it. But as a distinguishing factor, haddocks have a long black stripe running along their side, and a black spot on their dorsal fin.

The haddock lives in large schools in the North Sea as well as in two straits targeted by Danish fishermen: the Skagerrak and the Kattegat. It is part of the daily diet of the Danish, who traditionally marinate haddock in salt brine. The British are also very fond of this fish, and usually smoke it before eating it.

As Chef Lauterbach would tell you, marinating haddock for too long can cause the flesh to become hard and turn white.

But a good haddock looks almost transparent. So take care when preparing this fish in stages – marinating it in salt brine is not as easy at it sounds.

For the apple terrine, you will need apples that remain firm during cooking. Chef Lauterbach regrets the Danish habit of importing apples, as he had found plenty of good apples growing in Denmark; certainly in North America there are countless varieties to choose from. Pick the apples you prefer so long as they are firm, and add a little curry to strengthen their flavor, which loses some of its intensity in this chilled dish.

1. Wash, descale and fillet the fish, but do not skin it. Remove the bones. Mix the ingedients for the marinade in a dish and marinate the fish for three hours. Blanch the cabbage or lettuce leaves in salted water with a teaspoon each of olive oil and curry powder. Leave to cool and let dry, then remove the large veins of the leaves.

2. Make a little pouch out of a paper coffee filter, fill with the herbs, and tie up. Cut the apples into six parts, peel, core, and bring to a boil with three teaspoons of oil, one teaspoon of curry powder, and the herb pouch in two cups of water; reduce the heat and simmer for a few minutes. Soak the gelatin envelope in cold water and mix with the cooked apples.

an Apple Terrine

3. Line the terrine with a thin layer of cabbage or lettuce leaves and set the rest aside. For the soured cream, whip the cream, add the lemon juice, season, and carefully fold in the salmon roe.

4. Fill the terrine with one layer of apples (it should leave about half remaining), cover with the rest of the lettuce or cabbage leaves, and finish with a layer of the rest of the apples. Cover, weigh down the lid, and chill. Leave the haddock fillets to dry and cut into small chunks. Slice the terrine before serving, season with grated horseradish root and chives, and serve with the soured cream.

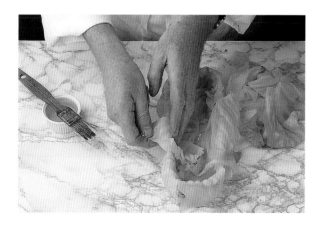

Shrimps and Cooked

Preparation time: 40 minutes
Cooking time: 20 minutes
Difficulty: ★★

Serves four

generous ³/₄ lb / 400 g shrimps (raw or
   cooked)
2 cups / 500 g salt (¹/₂ cup / 125 g per
   ¹/₂ gallon / 1 l of liquid)
1–2 tomatoes
¹/₂ red pepper
1 cup / 250 g lettuce leaves
1 shallot
2 tbsp / 15 ml mayonnaise (see basic recipes)
1 baguette
a dash of Tabasco
salt, pepper to taste

1 sprig of dill

For the spicy oil:
¹/₂ cup / 125 ml sesame oil
5 green peppercorns

half a bunch each: parsley, tarragon, basil, dill
half a clove of garlic

For the vegetables:
half a head of cauliflower
half a bunch of carrots
half a bunch of parsnips
1 parsley root (see below)
1 small zucchini
2 saffron threads
1 clove of garlic
1 sprig of dill flowers

For the saffron cream:
¹/₂ cup / 125 ml whipping cream
1 saffron thread
1 bunch of flowering dill

Our Chef, Erwin Lauterbach, has created a colorful recipe from an array of vegetables that complement each other perfectly, dominated by the dill flowers, which are much tastier than the leaves normally used in cooking. Available from mid-August to the end of October, they are perfect with lamb, seafood, and, of course, fish.

The shrimp, which can be bought uncooked or cooked, should – if they were bought uncooked – be boiled for about two minutes in salty water. Their size is not as important a consideration as their flavor – after all, there are more than three thousand varieties of crustaceans, from the small gray shrimp to the enormous sea crab. According to season or preference, you can substitute crab, crayfish or lobster for shrimps as well.

The mélange of vegetables is the dominant force of this dish. Chef Lauterbach combines a wide range, including parsnips, carrots, cauliflower, fennel, celery, and parsley root – a vegetable not always found in the United States, which is also known as Hamburg parsley. Parsley root is tan and somewhat carrot-shaped, with a spray of bright green, feathery leaves attached. If you can find it, its sweet, distinctive taste will certainly enhance this dish.

The intriguing saffron cream, unusual for Denmark, lends further contrast. To refine the dish even more, add a subtle sprinkling of cinnamon to the mayonnaise as well.

1. Clean the vegetables and simmer in salted water along with a sprig of dill flowers, a garlic clove, and saffron. After cooking, set the vegetables on a kitchen towel and chill. Cook the shrimps in their shells with a sprig of dill, and then shell them. Peel and seed the tomato and chop, along with the red pepper, into small cubes.

2. To prepare the spicy oil, put sesame oil, peppercorns, garlic, and herbs into a blender; mix well. Slit the baguette lengthwise and slice into four quarters; apply the spicy oil generously on each slice and grill in a frying pan until crisp.

Dill-vegetables

3. Finely chop the shallot. Mix the mayonnaise with a dash of Tabasco and the chopped shallot; chop all the vegetables and thoroughly mix with the mayonnaise. To make the saffron cream, add saffron and dill flowers to the cream and reduce by half. Strain and season to taste.

4. To serve, place a tall (2–3 in / 5–7 cm) and slender circular form on each plate, and layer as follows: first half the vegetables, then half the shrimps, then the remaining vegetables. Press firmly. Add a layer of the tomato-pepper mixture, then remove the form. Arrange the remaining shrimps, the grilled bread and the saffron cream on the plate. Garnish with lettuce leaves.

Goatfish Fillets on

Preparation time: 30 minutes
Cooking time: 5 minutes
Difficulty: ★

Serves four

1 dozen goatfish, scant ¼ lb / 100 g each
6 purple artichokes
2 shallots
1 lemon
¾ cup / 200 ml olive oil
half a bunch of chives
half a bunch of chervil
half a bunch of flat-leafed parsley
salt, pepper to taste

Goatfish (see page 30 for more information), also known as red mullet, is netted in the Mediterranean as well as in the Atlantic, using either simple fishing or drag nets.

Like a chameleon, the fish changes its color according to the type of ocean floor it is near: it colors light when on the sandy ocean floor; deep red when living in a rocky environment. Its excellent culinary properties, however, remain the same, particularly when used very fresh. Its delicate flesh should only be fried for a short time, in small portions, in hot, (but not exceedingly so) olive oil. Always fry it skin side down first.

Chef Dominique Le Stanc uses purple artichokes for this dish, a succulent version of the vegetable often consumed raw with a salt crust or pepper sauce. Furthermore, these artichokes stay crisp even when marinated in olive oil and herbs, and are surprisingly good when finely chopped. In order to maintain a delicate balance among the flavors, take care not to overdose the recipe with shallots or herbs – this applies particularly to the chives, which, while well-suited for decoration (they belong to the lily family), have a strong taste that can easily overwhelm other ingredients.

1. Gut the fish and remove the bones. Cut off the tail and fins with a pair of scissors. Finally, fillet.

2. After discarding the leaves, cut the artichoke hearts (including the outer layer of meat) into strips; marinate in olive oil and lemon juice (half a lemon should provide enough juice) for a few minutes.

a Bed of Artichokes

3. Arrange the artichokes in the middle of the plate in layers of decreasing size, distributing the chopped shallots, herb leaves and olive oil between them.

4. Very briefly fry the seasoned fillets in olive oil, skin side down first. Place the fillets on the artichoke strips and garnish with herbs.

Puff Pastry Tart with

Preparation time: 40 minutes
Cooking time: 15 minutes
Marinating time: 24 hours
Difficulty: ☆

Serves four

1¼ lb / 600 g tuna
3–4 lb / 400 g puff pastry dough (see basic recipes)
1¾ lbs / 800 g tomatoes
6 cloves of garlic
4¼ cups / 1 l olive oil
1 bunch of basil
half a bunch of thyme
2 bay leaves
salt, peppercorns

In the eighteenth century, an enormous earthquake shook Lisbon, Portugal, taking many lives and decimating the area's marine life. The tuna, which had been a resident since antiquity, disappeared from the Portuguese waters. Today, the (almost) undefeatable swimmer is still found in abundance in the Bay of Biscay and the Mediterranean, where it is considered a delicacy.

Choose fresh red tuna, available from April through November. The firmer the fish, the fresher; for this recipe, in which the tuna is served half-raw, the fish should be extremely fresh. When planning to make this dish, bear in mind the twenty-four hours the fish needs to marinate, since it will take that long for the meat to absorb the flavor of the herbs. And, as our chef,

Dominique Le Stanc, points out, tuna meat tends to dry out rather quickly, so it should never be overcooked. Here the cooking procedure is borrowed from Japan: the tuna is picked up with a fork (or cooking chopsticks) and quickly passed through an open flame, imparting an agreeably smoky flavor

The puff pastry slices forming the base of the tart should not be baked for too long, as overcooking can lend a bitterness to the pastry's taste. Our chef recommends you cut out the dough after it has been baked, rather than before, to achieve slices that match in size.

This simple appetizer, served at room temperature, is ideal for summer.

1. A day in advance, marinate the tuna in olive oil, bay leaf, thyme (about two sprigs), garlic, and peppercorns. If you prefer, prepare the puff pastry dough in advance as well, as it can chill up to 24 hours before using.

2. Roll out the dough. Cut out four 8 in / 18 cm circles, score with a fork, and chill for 20 minutes. Bake in the oven for 10–12 minutes (take it out before it begins to brown) at 400 °F / 210 °C.

Tuna, Tomatoes and Basil

3. Peel and seed the tomatoes, chop, and cook in olive oil, salt and pepper. While the tomatoes are cooking, swiftly pass the marinated tuna fillets through an open flame to sear them and impart a smoky flavor.

4. Add the herbs and a little oil from the marinade to the well-reduced tomatoes. Brush the puff pastry base generously with the tepid tomato mixture, and then cover with a layer of thin tuna slices arranged in a flat rosette. Brush with a little oil from the marinade to give the tuna a shiny film; garnish with basil leaves, and serve warm.

Trout and smoked eel

Preparation time: 20 minutes
Cooking time: 10 minutes
Cooling time: 2 hours
Difficulty: ✶✶

Serves four

2 ³/₄ lb / 350 g trout (see below)
¹/₄ lb / 120 g smoked eel
2 oz / 60 g whiting roe
4 eggs
1 egg white
1 zucchini
¹/₄ red pepper
¹/₄ green pepper
2 tbsp / 20 g butter
1¹/₂ tbsp / 30 g mustard

2 tbsp / 20 g mayonnaise (see basic recipes)
3 dashes tabasco
1 tsp / 5 ml custard (see basic recipes)
³/₄ cup / 200 ml cream

1¹/₂ sheets of gelatin
2 chive sprigs
pinch cayenne pepper

To cook the trout fillets:
1 shallot
2 tbsp / 20 g butter
³/₄ cup / 200 ml dry white wine
3 cups / 400 ml fish broth
1 bunch of lemon balm leaves
salt, pepper to taste

For the garnish:
1 bunch of lemon balm
dill
1 tomato

Fish can be prepared in countless ways, many of which are the province of our renown chefs. Michel Libotte offers this recipe based on trout and eel as yet another opportunity to encounter a seafood classic, fish in aspic, in a completely novel way.

Chef Libotte uses a particularly rare trout that is indigenous to the freshwater lakes of the Alps and Pyrennees. Known as the gold trout, the fish is related to the salmon, and is so rare that it has, at times, been considered extinct. If the fish is available in the United States, it will be a rare occasion indeed. So, instead, opt for adult brown trout or rainbow trout, or, in keeping with the gold trout's close relatives, for salmon or skate.

In terms of the other seafood involved, choose a whole smoked eel with shiny black skin, and when purchasing the whiting roe – which sits, in terms of quality, right between caviar and salmon roe – do not hesitate to buy frozen roe as it tastes just as good as the fresh version.

This appetizer is dominated by the fragrant taste of lemon balm, whose scent was designed to tempt bees into pollenating its white flowers. A common grass plant, it can be cooked before the white flowers are removed. And, incidentally, it forms the base for the French lemon liquer, L'Eau des Barbades.

1. Fillet the trout, chop the shallot and sweat in butter, and poach the fish, lemon balm leaves, and shallot in white wine and broth. (Retain the twelve most attractive lemon balm leaves for garnish.) Hard-boil the eggs and shell them.

2. Prepare the mayonnaise. Chop the peppers and poach for two minutes. Skin the eel, remove the bones, and chop into small chunks. Chop the chives. Put the hard-boiled eggs, soft butter, mustard, mayonnaise, Tabasco, custard, chives, chopped peppers, and eel into a blender and puree . Season to taste with cream and pepper.

in Lemon Balm Aspic

3. To prepare the aspic, blanch zucchini and slice into thin strips. Add the previously soaked gelatin to the trout's cooking liquid and clarify with an egg white. Line a tray or roasting pan with plastic wrap and place four circular forms on top of it. Line the inside of each forms with zucchini strips. Pour one ladleful of the aspic into the form and place the lemon balm on top, but make sure they are underneath the surface of the aspic. Chill to let the aspic set.

4. Cut the fillets into small triangles and place them, skin side down, on the aspic in the form. Top the form with the filling and smooth over with a spoon. Leave to chill. Whip the cream gently and season with curry powder, then add the whiting roe. To serve, place a puddle of cream in the center of the plate, and invert the aspic out of the form and on top of the cream. Garnish with tomato and dill.

Suckling Pig in Aspic

Preparation time: 20 minutes
Cooking time: 2 hours
Cooling time: 24 hours
Difficulty: ★★

Serves four

shoulder and neck of suckling pig
5 carrots
1 leek
$^1/_2$ celeriac
2 onions
1 gelatin envelope
1 bunch of thyme
1 bay leaf
1 bunch of flat-leafed parsley

1 tbsp cloves
$2^1/_2$ cups white wine
1 cup mixed lettuce
 salt, pepper to taste

For the vinaigrette:
1 leek
1 shallot
1 tomato
1 tbsp capers
2 tbsp white wine vinegar
$^1/_4$ cup peanut oil
$^1/_2$ tsp mustard
1 bunch of tarragon
salt, pepper to taste

This appetizer from chef Léa Linster is an example of the cuisine of Luxemburg, and reflects the country's Franco-German history. Based on suckling pig accompanied by an array of other ingredients, the aspic presents all of its contents, from meat to vegetables to herbs, as if you are looking at them in a shop window.

Give yourself ample time to prepare this dish, as it will take a while before all the piglet's meat comes off the bone. Since it comes off not in large, attractive pieces but in small chunks, it will take a little patience to find the choice pieces to use in this recipe. The dish's success depends on the aspic reaching a firm consistency. While a quick and easy preparation, the cooking

method nevertheless prohibits one from cooking the presoaked gelatin envelopes along with the other ingredients, as they would impair the flavor. It is, however, fine to cook the pig together with a knuckle of veal, which releases its own natural jelly into the broth-this would, as Chef Linster assures us, also produce a good, firm aspic.

The aspic's flavor should be subtle enough that it does not dominate the flavor of the meat; the same applies to the leek vinaigrette. Served on its own, suckling pig in aspic is a delicious appetizer, and served with sautéed potatoes it is a hearty main course suitable for all seasons.

1. If your butcher has not already done so, carve the suckling pig, separating the shoulder from the neck. Bring the meat to a boil in the wine before covering with water and continuing to cook until the meat is clearly softening and coming away from the bone. After cooking, take out the carrots and let the meat dry in the air as it cools. Carefully separate the meat from the bones and cut into chunks. Strain the cooking liquid and add the gelatin envelopes.

2. Cut the carrots into strips and chop the parsley. Fill a terrine form with layers of meat, carrot strips, chopped parsley, another layer of meat, and then another layer of each ingredient in the same order until all are used up. Cover with the cooking liquid and chill for twenty-four hours.

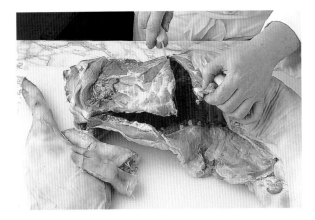

with Leek Vinaigrette

3. For the vinaigrette, beat mustard, vinegar, salt, tomato, and pepper with a whisk. Add peanut oil. Chop the vegetables and tarragon and add, along with the capers, to the vinaigrette.

4. To serve, slice the aspic and place one slice on each plate, with a pool of vinaigrette poured around it; serve with a small portion of mixed lettuce.

Lamb's Lettuce with

Preparation time:	*40 minutes*
Cooking time: 1	*2 minutes*
Difficulty:	✶

Serves four

4 chicken livers
$^1/_4$ celeriac
2 slices white bread
1 shallot
$^5/_8$ lb lamb's lettuce
$^1/_4$ lb butter
1 tbsp Marsala
1 bunch of flat-leafed parsley
salt, pepper to taste

For the vinaigrette:
1 shallot
1 tbsp mustard
1 bunch of tarragon
1 bunch of chives
$^1/_4$ cup peanut oil
2 tbsp vinegar
salt, pepper to taste

The lamb's lettuce used in this elegant appetizer from chef Léa Linster is a winter lettuce whose small round leaves inspire many culinary compositions. In France, where it also grows wild in fields, the most popular crop comes from Nantes, but German lamb's lettuce, sometimes referred to by Germans as "Rapunzel," is also good too. In North America, it is sometimes known as field salad, and, perhaps since it seems to thrive growing wild in cornfields, as corn salad. With its slightly nutty, tangy taste, the green is delicious with beets and small pieces of fried bacon or, as in this recipe, with chicken livers. For a slight variation use veal liver, the subtle aroma of which will meld well with the shallots and lamb's lettuce.

The strong green of fresh lamb's lettuce leaves forms a lovely contrast to the pale, cooked celeriac-a bulb which can be eaten raw as well as cooked, with a subtly sweet flavor brought out by the vinaigrette.

When frying the shallots and chicken livers, adding a touch of Marsala mixed with a dash of gravy imparts a delicate sweetness to the dish; Marsala, from Italy, is more subtle than the more popular Madeira. This intriguing hot-and-cold appetizer is easy to prepare, yet will provide a memorable start to any meal.

1. Wash the lamb's lettuce well and select the best leaves. Peel the celeriac, cut into large chunks, and boil in salted water. Afterwards, cut into small triangles.

2. Dice the white bread small for croutons and sauté. Prepare a vinaigrette of vinegar, salt, pepper, oil and mustard. Chop the shallots, tarragon, chives; add to the vinaigrette. Dress the lamb's lettuce and celeriac separately.

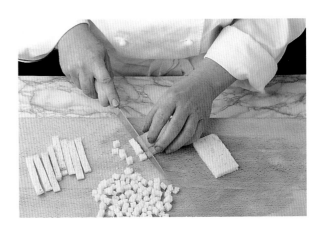

Celeriac and Chicken Livers

3. Fry the chicken livers with a chopped shallot in butter and add a dash of Marsala during frying. Keep warm.

4. To serve, arrange a bed of lamb's lettuce in the middle of the plate, placing the celeriac triangles, chicken liver pieces and croutons on top. Garnish with chopped parsley.

Rabbit and Celeriac

Preparation time: 1 hour
Cooking time: 45 minutes
Cooling time: 12 hours
Difficulty: ★★

Serves eight

1 lb / 500 g rabbit meat
⅝ lb / 300 g duck liver
1 lb / 500 g celeriac
2½ sheets of gelatin
1 cup / 250 ml mead (honey wine)
2½ / 750 ml cups chicken stock
1 lemon

For the aspic's aromatic garnish:
2½ cups / 750 ml chicken stock
1 carrot
1 onion
1 leek stalk
1 bouquet garni

For the side salad:
2 cups / 200 g mixed lettuce
½ cup / 100 g sprouts, such as sunflower or
   mung bean
½ cup / 100 ml vinaigrette

Honey has always been universally known for its healing properties; the bees that collected it were revered in antiquity. According to Greek mythology, mead – essentially the fermented essence of honey – was the preferred beverage of the gods on Mount Olympus, and they even allowed mere mortals to share this natural delight. Often available in shops that sell herbs and honey, mead here lends the aspic flavor and subtlety without dominating its own character.

For this recipe, created by Chef Régis Marcon, the quality of the rabbit is key: if possible, buy a free-range breeding rabbit from a farm. The bones and trimmings can be used for making the jelly, and the ribs should be cooked and retained for decoration. If you prefer, you can substitute chicken for rabbit, but make sure it is free-range chicken, as its quality will match that of the rabbit it replaces.

As for the terrine, we recommend you prepare it the day before so it can chill and set overnight. The final result will be a triangular slice, so, if you do not have a triangular form, make one by adding slanted, foil-wrapped cardboard along the sides of the terrine pan. Making a faultless terrine will require your full attention. One hint: carefully cut the celeriac and duck liver into proper rectangles so that the terrine will be perfectly lined up.

1. Cut the rabbit meat into chunks and set the ribs aside. Into a saucepan filled with cold water, put the meat along with the aromatic garnish for the aspic. Bring to a boil, then reduce the heat and leave to simmer for 45 minutes. Heat the chicken stock and add the sheets of gelatin. Once the stock has cooled, add the mead.

2. Peel the celeriac and cut into even ⅛ in / 3 cm slices. Cook the slices in salted water laced with lemon juice for three to four minutes, making sure they remain crisp; afterwards, place in a single layer of paper towels to dry.

Terrine with Honey Wine

3. Line a triangular terrine that has been covered with foil with the celeriac rectangles, then with the liver rectangles. Pour over the aspic and chill for one hour, then fill the terrine with rabbit meat and cover with aspic. Cover and chill for 12 hours.

4. To serve, sauté the seasoned rabbit ribs for three to four minutes. Invert the terrine and slice into 1¹/₄ in / 3 cm thick slices with a knife frequently dipped in hot water. Stand on a plate alongside a trio of ribs. Dress the salad with vinaigrette and serve on the side.

Artichoke Salad and

Preparation time: *30 minutes*
Cooking time: *20 minutes*
Difficulty: ★★

Serves four

8 artichokes
scant ¹/₂ lb / 200 g green beans
1 tomato
2 oz / 50 g truffles (see below)
1 bunch of flat-leafed parsley
1 tbsp / 15 g flour

2 tbs / 20 ml crème fraîche
salt, pepper to taste

For the vinaigrette:
juice of 1 lemon
2 tbsp / 20 ml peanut oil
1 tbsp / 10 ml walnut oil

Presented here, the artichoke in three roles: as a simple heart, as a puree, and in the form of fritters. Introduced via Sicily to France (see page 22 for other historical information), artichokes were first conceived of in France as a curative plant, good for melancholia, old age, and general infirmities; they were first cultivated in that fertile region in France known as the Dauphiné, long-famous for its produce and livestock.

The artichoke is actually a flower bud, and as such can be judged at market: one that is tightly closed has not passed its prime; one with leaves that are browning and loose should be passed over. In French markets the artichoke of choice comes from Brittany, a round and fleshy globe. Our chef, Guy Martin, recommends it highly although he himself is from the Savoie region. But North America has its own versions, such as the Californian-grown, deep-green globe artichoke in season from March through May.

In terms of truffles, two varieties will work here, one more expensive than the other. The elegantly flavored black Périgord truffles, or *tuber melanosporum*, are in season from January through March. They must be carefully chosen, however, since they are sometimes plagued by worm holes, which will destroy their quality altogether. The dark brown summer truffles, also known as Saint-Jean truffles, are less expensive. The very aromatic vinaigrette called for here should be as light as possible; adding too much lemon juice will disturb the delicate balance of spices and seasonings.

1. Remove the artichoke leaves and clean away the fibrous areas. Cook the remaining hearts in a mixture of water, lemon, flour, and salt for ten minutes, four at a time. To make the first four hearts into decorative pieces (the other four will be used for the puree), either use a circular cutter and knife to fashion them into smaller rounds, or just cut them into small, decorative chunks.

2. Prepare the dressing with lemon juice, peanut oil, and walnut oil; sprinkle some of it on the first four cut-up hearts. Puree the other four artichoke hearts in a blender; strain, and season. Vigorously whisk the crème fraîche and fold into the artichoke puree.

Mousse in Aromatic Oil

3. Wash and trim the green beans. Cook al dente, briefly rinsing in cold water to stop the cooking process. Peel, seed, and chop the tomato. Finely chop the truffles. Add the truffles to the remaining dressing and then sprinkle over the beans and chopped tomato.

4. To serve, place a trio of artichoke heart pieces in a triangle in the center of a plate; inside them, place a neat stack of the beans. Use a scoop to place a neat mound of artichoke puree on top. Garnish with parsley and chopped tomato. If you wish, you can accompany this dish with artichoke fritters.

Potato-truffle

Preparation time: *35 minutes*
Cooking time: *6–8 minutes*
Difficulty: ★★

Serves twelve

4 lbs / 2 kg potatoes
5 oz / 150 g truffles
generous 3 cups / 800 ml truffle juice
   (see below)
$^1\!/_2$ cup / 100 ml reduced veal stock
$^1\!/_4$ lb / 125 g mushrooms (optional)
salt, pepper to taste

The combination of the common potato with the noble truffle, presented here by our Chef, Guy Martin, provides for an intriguing and surprising culinary experience. Were one cooking this in a European kitchen, the ideal potato for this recipe would be the B. F. 15 or Bintje, but in a North American kitchen, there are many other varieties that will work, such as the newly popular Yukon Gold. Essentially, you should opt for a waxy potato that remains firms after cooking; as it is a crucial component in building the terrine, it will ensure that the terrine remains firm and that all the layers remain in place. The potatoes should be cut into slices of the same thickness as the truffle slices.

The truffle (see the previous recipe for more information), a member of the large mushroom family sometimes referred to as the "black pearl of the kitchen," can be found in numerous varieties at French speciality markets in Carpentras, d'Aups, or Cahors. Nearly all of its forms are imported, including the top-

notch black truffle. Searching for truffles has recently become a little easier with the introduction of specially trained truffle hounds, who are easier to keep than truffle pigs (though they must be trained not to devour the truffles the instant they find them!). Chef Martin recommends the black Périgord truffles above all others; when ripe in winter, they can weigh up to one or two ounces (twenty-five or fifty grams).

A light weighing-down and a sufficient amount of time spent chilling will give the terrine a chance to become firm. Slice the terrine with an electric knife in order to maintain the visual feature of the thinly sliced truffles and potatoes, as the fast-moving knife will not disturb the terrine's contents.

To make a less expensive version of this dish, replace the truffles with salmon or anchovy fillets, and season them alternately with pesto and basil.

1. Peel and wash the potatoes. Using a slicer, slice them lengthwise into extremely thin slices. Season with salt and pepper and then steam them in either a steamer or a pressure cooker.

2. Cut the truffles into thin slices using the same slicer.

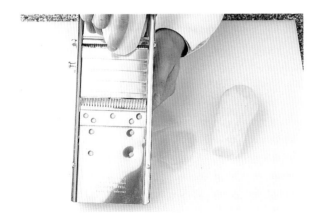

Terrine

3. Line the terrine form with moistened plastic wrap and layer with two levels of potatoes to every one level of truffles, continuing to fill the terrine form with alternating layers until all the ingredients are used up.

4. Reduce the veal stock and truffle juice to an aspic and pour over the terrine. Press lightly and set in the refrigerator to chill for several hours. To serve, slice with an electric kitchen knife and arrange on a plate. If desired, garnish with crisp-fried mushrooms.

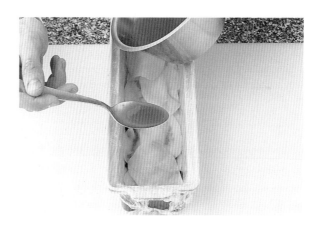

Bread with

Preparation time: 2 hours
Cooking time: 1 hour, 30 minutes
Difficulty: ★★★

Serves six

For the dough:
scant 1 1/2 lbs / 650 g wheat flour
1 package yeast
6 eggs
generous 1/4 lb / 125 g butter
1/4 cup / 50 ml olive oil
a pinch of salt

For the stuffing:
scant 1/4 lb / 100 g chorizo
generous 1/4 / 150 g lb cured ham
1/2 lb / 250 g slab bacon
half a chicken
1 onion
2 cloves of garlic
1/4 cup / 50 ml white wine
1/4 cup / 50 ml olive oil
1 bay leaf
2 sprigs of parsley
salt, pepper to taste

Portugal's golden age fell into the period of the "Great Discoveries" in the fifteenth and sixteenth centuries. Many traditions were developed during this era and have survived to this day, most of them being applied to the preparation and presentation of food.

When pigs are slaughtered in northern and northwestern of Portugal, this typical bread, called *fola*, is traditionally served. Originally, it was purely a bread, but as time went by, this bread became more like a cake, made from the simplest of ingredients. It is stuffed with chorizo, a hard Portuguese pork sausage, as well as different pieces of fresh pork meat. According to tradition, the dough of the bread is prepared in two stages, since, as with any yeast-rising bread, it must have sufficient resting periods in order to increase to the required

volume. So, after the initial kneading of the dough, let it rest for forty-five minutes, during which time it will double in size. And once it has been filled with meat it will require an additional forty-five minutes' rest before baking.

Chef Maria Ligia Medeiros has added chicken meat to the recipe as it will prevent the dish from drying out; you may also substitute the pork with poultry or rabbit meat, though in either case the sauce will have to be prepared with more fat. The bread is removed from the oven when it is brown, and then cut into thick slices with a long-bladed knife. It can be stored for a number of days, and eaten either hot or cold.

1. Dissolve the yeast in lukewarm water. Heap the flour on a smooth, clean surface, form a well, and into this sprinkle a pinch of salt and the dissolved yeast. Float the eggs in warm water for ten minutes, then crack and beat them vigorously before pouring into the well, slightly heat the butter and olive oil and pour this into the well with 1/2 cup / 120 ml of tepid water. Knead, cover the dough with a cloth, and leave to rise for 45 minutes.

2. Cut the chicken into chunks. Cut the onion into chunks and chop the garlic. Season the meat. Put with the olive oil, white wine, and the bacon in a casserole, mix to blend, and slowly simmer for 30 minutes, or as long as it takes for the chicken to soften.

Meat Stuffing

3. After cooking, skin the chicken and remove the bones. Puree the sauce with the herbs in the blender, then place the chicken meat back in. Cut the bacon and chorizo into $1/4$ in / $1/2$ cm thick slices, chop the cured ham, and soak all the meat in the sauce with the chicken.

4. Roll the dough into a circle of about 1 ft / 30 cm in diameter and place the meat on the dough. Fold together from the edges and place in an oval, buttered dish. Cover with a cloth and set aside to rise again for 45 minutes. Bake until brown (approximately ten minutes) at 395 °F / 200 °C, then reduce heat to 320 °F / 150 °C and continue baking for one hour. Cut into thick slices and serve hot or cold.

Pâté with

Preparation time: 20 minutes
Cooking time: 30 minutes
Cooling time: 12 hours
Difficulty: ★★

Serves twelve

2 lbs / 1 kg fish roe (hake, turbot, or sea bass)
1 carrot
$^{1}/_{2}$ lb / 250 g onions
2 oranges
4 tbsp / 50 g capers

generous $^{1}/_{4}$ lb / 150 g butter
zest and juice of two oranges
$^{3}/_{4}$ cup / 200 ml orange juice
generous cup crème fraîche
$^{5}/_{8}$ lb / 300 g mayonnaise (see basic recipes)
salt, pepper to taste

Considering the length of Portugal's coast line, it is no surprise that fish has attained prime status in Portuguese cuisine. This fish pâté, interpreted by chef Maria Ligia Medeiros, was probably originally created in the nineteenth century, when fish heads were still used because of their gelatin content. Today this pâté is prepared with fish roe, which is sometimes referred to as the "caviar of the poor."

Chef Medeiros first encountered this dish while dining at a friend's house; it was served with the *apéritif*, along with crème fraîche and toast. And being particularly fond of turbot roe – because, like the flesh, it has a subtle flavor – she has also included other fish from the Atlantic that produce delicious roe, such as sea bass and sea pike (sometimes called *charbonnier*, or "charcoal burner" in French, on account of its very dark skin). Mullet, however, would not be suitable for this dish, as its roe does not have the right consistency.

Finally, three further ingredients underline the pâté's flavor: capers, oranges and the mayonnaise laced with orange juice. The mayonnaise should be used sparingly.

1. Peel the oranges, remove the pith, and set aside. Rinse the fish roe and cook in salted water for ten minutes.

2. After removing the skin and veins of the fish roe, crumble it. Sweat the chopped onions in butter until golden brown. Coarsely grate the carrot and, if not done in advance, grate thin strips of orange zest; add with the crème fraîche to the onions and butter. Simmer for ten minutes, stirring constantly.

Fish Roe

3. Add the crumbled roe and orange juice to the pan and continue to cook for another ten minutes, stirring constantly so that nothing burns. In a blender or food processor, puree the entire mixture, then cook once more until the puree is reduced to a mash-like consistency that can easily be shaped.

4. Fill a terrine form with the mixture and chill overnight. Invert the next day. Squeeze the juice out of two oranges, and use to lace the mayonnaise. To serve, brush the terrine with the citrus mayonnaise, sprinkle the terrine with capers, slice with a thin, sharp knife, and garnish with orange slivers.

Scorpion Fish with Tapenade and

Preparation time: 1 hour
Cooking time: 8 minutes
Marinating time: 48 hours
Difficulty: ★★

Serves four

2 scorpion fish, 2 lb / 1 kg each
1 avocado
4 rice-flour wrappers (see below)
4 cherry tomatoes
2 tbsp / 20 ml vermouth
salt, pepper to taste

For the marinade:
3/4 cup / 200 ml olive oil
2 cloves of garlic
2 coriander corns
3 sprigs of thyme
2 sprigs of basil
1 sprig of rosemary
1 sprig of sage

For the tapenade:
generous 1/8 lb / 80 g olives
1/2 oz / 10 g capers
3/8 cup / 80 ml olive oil
1 tsp / 5 ml balsamic vinegar
salt, pepper to taste

Chef Dieter Müller of Germany is constantly looking to stretch his culinary horizons; one way he accomplishes this is to incorporate the traditional products from different regions into new recipes. Raised in a family of gourmets, Müller is quite familiar with the countries of the Mediterranean, and he often extends his repertoire with regional specialities from the region.

Scorpion fish, or rockfish, is an integral part of the bouillabaisse, that icon of French seafood tradition, and of the Provençal fish soup. The former was originally cooked right on the beach by fishermen, who used the fish unsuitable for the market, such as the large-headed, ungainly-looking scorpion fish. For this recipe you will need a relatively large scorpion fish with firm flesh. If none is available, look for another sub-species of rockfish, since there are many. It will be marinated in olive oil before being cooked.

Dieter Müller discovered rice-flour wrappers in Asia, where they are often used to wrap a whole range of dumplings and spring rolls; baked, they will provide the forms for the avocado mousse. Although avocado has a high fat content, it blends well with all kinds of flavors and is therefore very popular; it is also extremely easy to prepare. Choose a ripe but not yet brown fruit from California, Israel, or the Antilles.

The tapenade is, of course, typical of Provence, and will create a delicate aroma, conveying the Mediterranean, to the delight of your guests.

1. Wash, clean, and fillet the scorpion fish; remove the bones and skin. Wash the fillets and leave to dry on a kitchen towel. Marinate in olive oil for 24 hours, after which the fish should be seasoned, wrapped in basil and sage leaves, and finally wrapped and then rolled up in layers of plastic wrap and then aluminum foil.

2. Leave the fillets to infuse for ten minutes in water at 155 °F / 65 °C. Remove from the saucepan and set aside to cool. For the tapenade, remove the olive pits, chop the olives very finely, and mix with the other ingredients. Place in an air-tight container and set aside for the next day.

Avocado Mousse in Rice Leaves

3. Cut the rice-flour wrappers into small squares-about 4 x 4 in / 8 x 8 cm, form into little containers by shaping them around a cork, and bake in the oven for five minutes. Mix the avocado with the vermouth, salt, and lemon juice until it becomes a light mousse. Fill the rice-flour wrappers with the avocado mousse using a pastry bag with a star-shaped nozzle.

4. Cut the scorpion fish fillets into medallions that are $^3/_8$ in / 1 cm thick. Place a small bouquet of salad leaves and two medallions on a plate and garnish with tapenade. Place a rice leaf filled with the avocado mousse on one side, and cherry tomato on the other. Sprinkle with olive oil.

Tartare with Green Sauce and

Preparation time: 45 minutes
Cooking time: 12 minutes
Chilling time: 3–4 hours
Difficulty: *

Serves four

generous ³/₄ lb / 400 g beef fillet
a pinch of white pepper
1 tsp / 5 ml balsamic vinegar
3 tbsp / 50 ml cold-pressed olive oil

For the green sauce:
1 bunch of basil
2 bunches of parsley

half a clove of garlic
²/₃ cup / 150 ml cold-pressed olive oil
1 tbsp / 15 g pine nuts
1 tsp / 5 g capers
1 tsp / 5 ml balsamic vinegar
salt, pepper to taste

For the garnish:
2 tomatoes
1 cucumber

For the decoration:
puff pastry (see basic recipes)
4 black olives

Chef Dieter Müller, at his restaurant of the same name, claims to have introduced his fellow countrymen and women in Germany to Mediterranean flavors that they had never tasted before. Here, he presents a green sauce made of basil leaves, parsley, tomatoes and olive oil, similar to the Mediterranean pesto. The green coloring comes primaily from the parsley; to get the desired bright green you must use twice as much parsley as basil.

Marinating the raw meat for three or four hours imparts an array of aromas to it and also "cooks" it, as it were. Of course, the meat is still raw when served, and still very juicy. But it has been prepared in several stages. First, it is ground (if the butcher has not done it for you), then mixed with garlic and

basil; then the capers are added; then finally, the sauce. The meat has to be extremely fresh: if you can't get fresh beef, then don't prepare this recipe. Germans prefer the meat from Friesian animals, comparable to the other European varieties such as the French Charolais or the Swiss Simmenthal. Friesians are known in the US as holsteins; look for free-range beef that is relatively free of hormones. If you prefer veal, it works quite well prepared this way.

Finally, two crucial tips from Chef Müller: only use extra virgin olive oil, as it will impart a special spicy note to the meat, and, if possible, use aged balsamic vinegar that is at least five years old for full effect.

1. Make enough puff pastry to have a 3 in / 7.5 cm piece on each plate. Wash the fillet of beef. If not ground already, cut the meat into chunks and pass through the meat grinder on a fine blade.

2. Put all the ingredients for the sauce into the blender and mix until you have a smooth puree. Blanch, then peel and seed the tomatoes, set aside to dry. Cut out four pieces with a serrated cutter, place on a baking tray covered with aluminum foil, and bake for 12 minutes at 440 °F / 220 °C.

Tomato and Cucumber Slices

3. Place the ground meat in an oval earthenware dish. Add the pepper, vinegar, oil, and a little salt and, using a fork, mix well in a circular motion, then smooth over with a spoon.

4. Cover with the green sauce and marinate and chill for three to four hours in the refrigerator. Cut out portions of the tartare with a circular cutter that measures 3 in / 7.5 cm in diameter. Place the portions on a plate and surround with a ring of alternating tomato and cucumber slices. Sprinkle with olive oil and serve with a piece of puff pastry garnished with chopped black olives.

Smoked Duck Carpaccio

Preparation time: 30 minutes
Cooking time: 15 minutes
Cooling time: 2¹/₂ days
Difficulty: ★★

Serves four

2 thick duck breasts
¹/₂ lb / 250 g cooked duck liver (optional)
8 artichokes
4 fresh porcini mushrooms
¹/₂ cup / 120 ml walnut oil
1 cup / 250 g pine nuts

1 bunch of parsley
1 bunch of chervil
4 bay leaves
2 tbsp / 30 g white peppercorns
2 tbsp / 30 g coarse sea salt
sawdust for smoking

For the vinaigrette:
¹/₂ cup / 100 ml cold-pressed olive oil
¹/₄ cup / 50 ml white wine vinegar
¹/₄ cup / 50 ml gravy
¹/₄ cup / 50 ml truffle juice
salt, pepper to taste

Jean-Louis Neichel was on his shady patio one day, meditating on the classic *carpaccio*, when he came up with this idea for a new variation on the traditional theme. As a chef (in Barcelona) who is particularly fond of smoked meat, he opted for smoked duck; his reinterpretation of this Italian dish is both novel and, surprisingly, not at all that difficult to prepare.

For one thing, it is quite possible to smoke meat without a professional smokehouse; all you need is a combination of a casserole, a baking tray, and a grill. After lining the bottom of the casserole with sawdust, a baking tray is placed upside-down in the casserole, with a grill set on top of the tray. The casserole is then lidded tightly. Five minutes of slow heat are all it takes to create the necessary amount of smoke. The duck breast is then placed in the casserole, on the grill. The casse-

role is lidded tight again, and set aside in a cool place. It is vital that the duck be smoked for only five minutes – otherwise the meat will start to cook, betraying the nature of a true *carpaccio*. Once the meat is smoked, the fat is removed and the meat is seasoned with white peppercorns and crushed bay leaves. To make it easier to slice the duck wafer-thin, it is placed in the freezer to firm up for just a few minutes (as too much cold will destroy the meat).

Both artichokes and fresh porcini mushrooms are typical summer vegetables though fresh porcini, also called cèpes, are a rare sight in most markets and quickly snapped up for their wonderful, woodsy flavor. Prepared with walnut and olive oil and sprinkled with toasted pine nuts, they may be accompanied by duck liver if so desired.

1. Skin the duck breasts, sprinkle with salt, and coat with a covering of white peppercorns. Crush the bay leaves and sprinkle over the meat as well. Loosely wrap in aluminum foil and place in the refrigerator to infuse and chill for 48 hours.

2. After the duck breasts come out of the refrigerator, rinse them thoroughly under cold running water. To smoke them, distribute a layer of sawdust over the bottom of the smoking dish (a lidded casserole works well), and brown the sawdust on a slow heat for five minutes. Place the duck meat on the grill and remove the lidded casserole from the heat. Let the meat smoke for five minutes. Wrap in aluminum foil and chill for another 12 hours.

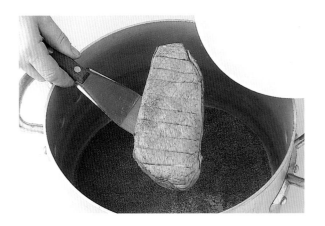

with Artichoke Salad

3. If adding duck's liver to the dish, prepare it according to your preference. Strip the artichokes of leaves and choke; wash the fresh porcini and cut both artichoke hearts and mushrooms into thin slices. Prepare the vinaigrette. Roast the pine nuts by placing them on a tray in the toaster, or in a dry frying pan on low heat either on the stove top or in the oven; whichever method you prefer, take care not to let these tender nuts burn.

4. To serve, cut the duck breasts into wafer-thin slices, arrange on the plates; toss the porcini and artichokes in walnut and olive oils, and sprinkle with roasted pine nuts. Place the mushrooms and artichokes (and duck liver if you are serving this as well) on the plates, sprinkle with vinaigrette and a little coarse sea salt, and garnish with parsley and chervil leaves.

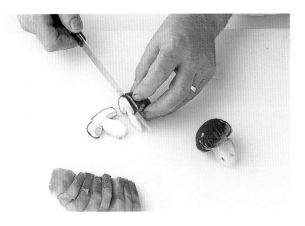

Mediterranean Salad

Preparation time: *30 minutes*
Cooking time: *8 minutes*
Difficulty: ★

Serves four

12–16 jumbo shrimps
12 cockles
20 clams, winkles, or other seasonal mollusks
$^1/_2$ lb / 250 g mixed lettuce
$^1/_4$ lb / 120 g green beans
$^1/_2$ lb / 250 g button mushrooms

2 tomatoes
1 stick of celery
1 orange (see below)
1 tsp / 5 g sesame seeds (see below)

For the vinaigrette:
$^1/_4$ cup / 60 ml sweet wine vinegar
$^1/_2$ cup / 125 ml cold-pressed olive oil
1 tbsp / 15 g mustard
salt, pepper to taste

This seafood salad, typical of the seafood-based Catalan cuisine, is a marvellous summer appetizer. Featuring jumbo shrimps, which are very popular in Spain and often served as an appetizer, it also reflects the Catalan facility for salads. Coming in endless varieties, the cuisine's summery salads provide chefs with countless opportunities to stretch their creativity.

The Spanish are particularly fond of the algae-nuanced taste of extremely fresh jumbo shrimps. In fact, the shrimps are often served with their heads intact; evidence of how fresh they are, since the head is like a freshness-gauge. If the head is colored black, then do not attempt to eat the shrimp. Frozen, the shrimps come only as tails. In order to preserve their excellent flavor, the delicious crustacean should ideally be steamed or boiled in a broth of sea water.

The molluscs underscore the iodine flavor of the jumbo shrimps, and the marine aspect of the dish. You can certainly use other shellfish for this dish, such as crayfish or langoustines. Cockles, though not as popular in the United States as Europe, as generally tasty, as are other molluscs such as winkles. With all shellfish, placing them while still alive in sea water for a couple of days can help them get rid of the sand in their shells, since they will be able to move around as they normally would, only without picking up more sand.

1. Wash the lettuce. Cook the green beans al dente. Peel and chop the celery and the tomatoes. Clean the mushrooms and cut into thin strips.

2. Prepare the vinaigrette and mix with the vegetables in a salad bowl. Cut the orange peel to yield thin strips of orange zest; marinate.

# of Jumbo Shrimp

3. Clean the jumbo shrimps, discarding the intestinal vein, but do not remove the head. Steam them until their shells are bright red. Clean the cockles, clams, and other shellfish well, and soak in water.

4. Roast the sesame seeds for a few minutes, either in a dry frying pan on the stove top or in the oven, or in a toaster. In a frying pan over a high flame, heat the cockles, clams, and other shellfish with a little unpeeled garlic for two minutes. To serve, place the mixed lettuce on the plates, add the vegetables, and dress with vinaigrette. Sprinkle with the roasted sesame seeds and marinated orange zest strips. Arrange the seafood on the plate.

Crayfish

Preparation time: 30 minutes
Cooking time: 1 hour
Drying time: 1 hour (optional)
Difficulty: ★★

Serves four

40 crayfish
a pinch of cayenne pepper
$^1/_2$ cup / 120 g coarse sea salt

For the salad mayonnaise:
1 egg yolk
1 lemon

1 tbsp / 15 ml ketchup
$^1/_4$ cup / 60 ml peanut oil
1 tbsp / 15 g mustard
salt, pepper to taste

For the garnish:
4 hearts of lettuce
2 tomatoes
1 clove of garlic
1 bunch of chives
$^1/_4$ cup / 60 ml olive oil
thyme flowers from 1 bunch of thyme

Crayfish have a greenish color, providing them with effective camouflage in their river habitat; but they turn a conspicuous bright red when cooked. In France, the process of cooking them is described as a "cardinalizer," as the crayfish's red color resembles the color of the cardinal's vestments. These days, crayfish are hardly caught in France anymore; most of those consumed in France are now imported.

For this recipe we recommend you buy live, medium-sized crayfish. Make sure you discard the intestinal vein on the underside of their tail, as it releases gall that will render the flesh very bitter, making it unfit for consumption. The smaller the crayfish, the shorter the cooking time; cooking them for too long will make their flesh become rubbery.

Mayonnaise, a sauce of universal popularity, was created in 1756 by Count Richelieu's cook while on the Balearic Islands.

The conquest of Port Mahon was just about to take place, hence the name – mahonnaise – which turned into mayonnaise later on. Prepare the mayonnaise at the last moment, as it can not be stored, and its consistency is likely to change over a short period of time. However, preparing a smooth mayonnaise is an easy process provided that all the ingredients have the same cool temperature.

The dried tomatoes dressed in olive oil provide an Italian flair. Ideally, these should be dried in the Mediterranean sun, but that is, of course, not always possible. In Europe, the Roma variety would be the tomato of choice for this dish; in the United States, Holland or any other tomato that has been ripened on the vine will work well. One could also, for a slightly richer taste, get real sun-dried tomatoes and then soften them in hot water and olive oil before using. If you prefer to dry the tomatoes yourself, the process will take about an hour.

1. Remove the intestinal vein of the crayfish and cook them in salted water seasoned with cayenne pepper. Take them out of the cooking liquid and let them sit for ten minutes. Let them drain, then shell, setting aside four crayfish shells to use for decoration. Set the crayfish tails aside in a dish covered with aluminum foil.

2. Prepare a light mayonnaise with the egg yolk, mustard, lemon, peanut oil, salt, and pepper. Season with ketchup and set aside. Blanch the tomatoes, hollow them out, and place on a baking tray lined with aluminum foil.

Salad

3. Fold the crayfish tails into the mayonnaise and leave to infuse for five minutes. Place an opened lettuce heart on each plate and arrange the shrimps on the lettuce. Slice the cloves of garlic.

4. Finally, briefly fry the tomatoes with thyme flowers and sliced garlic in olive oil, then dry the tomatoes in the oven for one hour at 175 °F / 80 °C. Place a decorative crayfish shell on each plate, arrange the tomatoes around the lettuce heart, and sprinkle with chives.

Salad with Roasted

Preparation time: 30 minutes
Cooking time: 30 minutes
Difficulty: ☆

Serves four

4 whole quails
¼ lb / 120 g Puy lentils
⅛ lb / 50 g young spinach leaves
1 bouquet garni
1 bunch of chives

For the lentil dressing:
2 tomatoes
1 shallot
1 tsp / 5 g Dijon mustard
1 tsp / 5 ml sherry vinegar
1 tbsp / 15 ml peanut oil
1 tbsp / 15 g chopped chives
salt, fresh-ground pepper to taste
coarse sea salt

Here, we present a salad created by Chef Pierre Orsi that is based on roasted quail. This low-fat bird has come to play a different role in cuisine than in the past, when it was hunted from April through October and considered almost an everyday ingredient in cooking. Today, there are far fewer wild populations, but the number of quail being farm-raised has increased.

Quail meat is often fried on a skewer, but there are many other preparation methods. The firm, light-colored flesh is ideal for smoking, and the different kinds of wood used for smoking impart an array of strong and unusual flavors to the meat. One certainly does need a proper smokehouse: see "Smoked duck carpaccio with artichoke salad" on page 182 for more guid-ance. Or, if you prefer, you can substitute the smoking process with a little extra frying time, which will impart the birds with a similarly deepened flavor.

For this recipe we use the most famous green lentils of all, the Puy lentil from Le Puy in central France, which grows in volcanic soil and is a source of much French culinary pride. Puys should never be overcooked, just blanched and cooked very slowly so they retain their crisp consistency. Season sparingly with a mild mustard. The young spinach leaves called for in this recipe are washed and dried thoroughly; their fresh character combines well with the quail.

1. Chop the shallot and chives. Blanch the lentils and gently cook with the bouquet garni for 30 minutes; set aside to drain. Season with oil, sherry vinegar, chopped shallot, salt, and freshly ground pepper. Blanch, peel, and then chop the tomatoes. At the last moment, add a teaspoonful of Dijon mustard to the lentils and chopped chives along with the chopped tomatoes.

2. Flambé the quail, halve, and remove the bones. Fry gently for 30 minutes in a casserole, skin side down. Towards the end of the cooking time, season the quail on all sides; fry on a higher flame on both sides until the skin turns a golden brown.

Quail and Puy Lentils

3. Wash the spinach well and select the best, most intact leaves. Slice the quail fillets and mix with the meat from the legs.

4. To serve, warm four plates. Arrange a semi-circle of spinach leaves in a petal pattern on each plate, and mound the lentils over the spinach stems. Surround with quail pieces and slices. Sprinkle with freshly ground pepper and a few grains of coarse sea salt, and garnish with remaining chopped chives.

Oysters with

Preparation time: 30 minutes
Cooking time: 40 minutes
Difficulty: ★★

Serves four

20 oysters
4 oz / 120 g Sevruga caviar
scant $^1/_2$ lb / 250 g whiting
$^5/_8$ lb / 300 g seaweed (see below)
2 celeriac bulbs
whites of 4 eggs
$3^1/_2$ sheets of gelatin

For the fish broth:
$^3/_4$ lb / 400 g fish bones (from a plaice)
$^2/_3$ cup / 150 ml white wine
$^1/_8$ lb / 60 g butter
8 shallots
2 carrots
1 bunch of parsley

The fertile Gulf of Morbihan in northwestern France produces countless oysters for French consumption. For this recipe, our chef, Georges Paineau, advocates using the freshest oysters available – ideally, they should go directly directly from the net on to your plates. One hint when buying oysters: if they don't snap shut when you tap their shell, don't buy them. In general, oysters are at their best in spring and fall, as in the summer they can be a little milky, so choose other molluscs unless you are sure you have a good source for clear, fresh oysters in the summertime.

There are two stages in the preparation of this recipe that could prove a little difficult: clarifying the fish broth, and making the jelly. In terms of the broth: on no account should the egg white be allowed to become stiff and sink to the base of the saucepan when you are clarifying the liquid. To prevent this, stir the broth rigorously in the beginning. And in terms of the aspic:

add it to the caviar before it has completely set, when it still has a syrupy, runny consistency.

Sevruga caviar is particularly suitable for this recipe because it is coarse-grained and has a memorable, outstanding taste. It is, however, rather expensive. Instead, Chef Paineau recommends you substitute a julienne of carrots or spinach, sweated in butter.

The seaweed pictured here for the decoration is rather common in France, hailing, as is a third of all French seaweed, from the Breton island of Molène. Other varieties produced there include the popular nori, which is also one of the varieties readily available in the United States. Much of the seaweed available in markets comes dried; follow the instruction on the package to remoisten it before use.

1. Chop the aromatic garnish for the fish broth. Sauté the plaice bones, add the aromatic garnish and the white wine and cover with water; cook for 20 minutes before straining. Soak the sheets of gelatin in cold water and begin clarifying the broth with the egg whites.

2. Chop the whiting meat, mix with the gelatin, and pour the boiling fish broth over this mixture. Stir and bring back to a boil. Cook for ten minutes over high heat and then strain. Leave the broth to become tepid.

Caviar Aspic

3. Peel the celeriac, chop finely, and heat briefly. Wash the seaweed three times in clear water and then blanch. Open and shuck the oysters, making sure you catch the juice from the oyster shell in a container; pass this juice through a muslin cloth and add 2 tbsp / 10 ml of it to the fish broth.

4. Chill the aspic and leave to set until it takes on a syrupy consistency. Arrange the seaweed on the plates and decorate with a dollop of caviar and chopped celeriac. Place the oysters on the plate and pour the aspic, not yet completely set, over the oysters and chopped celeriac.

Cream of Chicken Soup with

Preparation time: 30 minutes
Cooking time: 1 hour, 30 minutes
Difficulty: ★★

Serves four

For the cream of chicken soup:
1 chicken, about 3 lb / 1½ kg
1 gallon / 2 l water
3 carrots
1 bunch of celeriac greens
1 onion
4 cloves

1 clove of garlic
1 bouquet garni
2 tbsp / 30 g flour
2 tbsp / 30 g butter
1 cup / 250 ml whipping cream
salt, pepper to taste

For the whisked egg whites:
8 egg whites
1 bunch of watercress
salt to taste

In France, whisked egg-whites are normally served with custard as a pudding. In days gone by they were prepared with biscuits or dry brioche dipped in liqueur and accompanied by fresh berries. Our chef, Georges Paineau, has created instead a soup with whisked egg whites that are salted. This is, perhaps, an unusual concept, but nonetheless it works very successfully in combination with cream of chicken soup.

Start by preparing a nice large and meaty chicken that forms the main component of the broth's taste, underscored by the other ingredients added in careful doses. The roux for the soup should not contain too much flour, as the soup will then become too thick. If by accident you add too much, however, just compensate by adding a bit more cream or chicken stock.

The egg whites must be whisked briskly to make them stiff enough; salt is added to make the firm froth more durable. The watercress – a green that is rich in both iodine and vitamin C – adds a lovely pastel green color and a tangy note to the egg whites. Almost all of the watercress available in Europe is produced in France and the United Kingdom, particularly in Scotland. In the United States, it is available year round. Choose small-leafed watercress, which is much more flavorful. Wild watercress would be ideal since it has an intensely sharp taste, but it is difficult to find. In any event, the cress must be folded into the whisked egg whites very carefully to prevent them from losing their firmness and collapsing. A last tip: poach the whisked egg whites in water at a maximum of 175 °F / 80 °C, to prevent the egg white from spoiling.

1. Peel the onion and garlic. Gut and prepare the chicken; put into a saucepan filled with cold water, add carrots, the celeriac greens, onion, cloves, garlic, and bouquet garni and bring to a boil. Cook for one hour, then remove the chicken from the cooking liquid and cut the meat into fine strips; set aside.

2. Make a roux with 2 tbsp / 30 g each of butter and flour, and pour the chicken stock into it. Cook for 20 minutes. Stir in the cream and continue to cook for ten more minutes. Strain and set aside to cool.

Watercress and Whisked Egg White

3. Strip the watercress stalks of the leaves, wash the leaves, and drain well. Beat the egg whites until very stiff, adding a little salt during whisking. Carefully fold in the watercress leaves.

4. Scoop out portions of the whisked egg white and poach for one and half minutes on each side in water no hotter than 175 °F / 80 °C. Drain. To serve, arrange the strips of chicken meat on four plates, adjust the seasoning of the soup, and pour over the meat. Add two or three scoops of whisked egg white to each plate.

Langoustine Rosette

Preparation time: 45 minutes
Cooking time: 30 minutes
Difficulty: ★★

Serves four

24 langoustines
4 lb / 2 kg mussels
1 onion
¼ tsp / 10 g saffron threads
2 cups / 500 ml Muscadet
2 cups / 500 ml whipping cream
salt, pepper to taste

For the vegetable garnish:
1 celery stick
half a bulb of fennel
half a red pepper
1 shallot
1 tbsp / 15 g small capers
1 bunch of chervil

Langoustines, which are often confused with prawns, shrimps, and crayfish, are rarely available alive outside coastal regions. Unlike crayfish, they do not look like a miniature lobster; unlike shrimps and prawns, they have slender, enlongated, front claws. Choose medium-sized langoustines to complement the mussels in this dish; the langoustines are cooked very briefly in a broth seasoned with thyme, bay leaf, and a few parsley stalks. A dash of white vinegar (distilled from turnips) can make the langoustine flesh a bit firmer, but in any case they should not be cooked for too long.

Mussels, bred for European consumption predominantly in the English Channel, the North Sea and the Atlantic, are available from July through January. Our chef, Paul Pauvert, prefers the mussels from around Mont St. Michel or from the Bay of Aiguillon, where the Irishman Patrick Walton invented artificial mussel banks back in the thirteenth century. In the United States, where there isn't the same passion for this mollusc as there is in Europe, mussel shoals are in abundance along many coasts; markets often carry them in large quantities as well. Always sold alive, mussels have shiny, tightly shut shells and should be thoroughly washed before preparation.

Saffron is one of the most expensive spices in the world – if not the most expensive – as it comes in minute quantities and must be entirely picked and handled by hand. To yield two pounds (one kilogram) of saffron threads, 150,000 stamen must be collected from as many flowers (crocuses, actually). But the reward is a color and aroma like no other, heralded for centuries since King Solomon used it in his gardens.

1. Chop the onions and wash the mussels. Cook the langoustines in broth for three to four minutes. Drain, set aside to cool and then shell. Heat the mussels with the onion in wine until they open up, then shuck.

2. Add cream and saffron to the cooking liquid, reduce and leave to cool.

with Saffron Mussels

3. Place a large circular form on each plate and pour a little sauce inside. Chop the celery, fennel, shallot, and red pepper.

4. Mix the chopped vegetables with a few capers and sprinkle over the sauce. Arrange the langoustines and mussels in a rosette over the sauce. Garnish with a centerpiece of chervil leaves. Serve chilled.

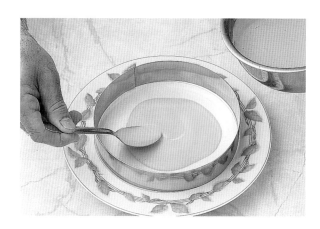

Salad of Duck Fillet

Preparation time: 1 hour
Cooking time: 10 minutes
Difficulty: ✩

Serves four

2 breasts of duck
1 orange
half a bunch of watercress
2 tbsp / 30 g butter
1 tsp / 5 g coriander seeds
salt, pepper to taste

For the pear salad with pine nuts:
2 ripe green pears
scant $^1/_2$ cup / 100 g pine nuts
1 tbsp / 15 ml sherry vinegar
3 tbsp / 45 ml peanut oil

For the julienne:
1 carrot
1 celery stick

The Chinese are credited with raising ducks, and the bird was already a popular meat in antiquity: the Romans particularly enjoyed duck brain and breast. In feudal times duck was traditionally served for Christmas. In the late nineteenth century, four ducks on a ship from Peking to Long Island gave the latter region its own indigenous species. Today there are many subspecies, all of which can be traced back to either the mallard or the muscovy, and the popularity of duck is widespread.

The breast is the choicest part: the breast of ducks raised for making foie gras is particularly full and meaty. The French used to cook the duck breast for hours and then preserve it; contemporary recipes may even call for the duck breast to be smoked. For this dish, the breast is fried skin side down first, so the meat can draw all the fat, and then only briefly fried on the other side. The meat is then set aside to sit before it is sliced, a step that keeps the meat tender.

As they are just the slightest bit acidic, green pears are an ideal accompaniment for substantial and hearty dishes such as this one. Make sure to sprinkle the chopped pears immediately with lemon juice to prevent their turning brown. This lovely fruit salad with pine nuts is dressed with sherry vinegar, whose subtle aroma – not unlike that of Madeira – underlines the pear's flavor. Depending on the season, you may garnish this dish with watercress, coriander, blueberries, or pomegranate seeds.

1. Peel and finely chop the pears; mix with the pine nuts. Prepare a vinaigrette with sherry vinegar and peanut oil; dress the pears with three-fourths of the vinaigrette.

2. Fry the duck breasts in butter – skin side down first and then the other side briefly – but only until rare; leave to rest for a short while and then slice against the direction of the grain.

with Pears and Sherry

3. Prepare a julienne of carrots and celery and then blanch the vegetables. Prepare a little zest of orange the same way.

4. Moisten the meat with the remaining vinaigrette. To serve, place the pear salad in the center of the plate and sprinkle with some of the julienne of carrots and celery. Lay the duck slices around the mound of pears. Garnish with the blanched julienne of the zest of orange, and place a few watercress leaves with coriander seeds in-between the meat slices.

Crayfish and Snowpeas

Preparation time: 1 hour
Cooking time: 1 hour 15 minutes
Difficulty: ★★

Serves four

16 crayfish
3¹/₂ oz / 100 g Périgord truffles
2 lb / 1 kg snowpeas

For the crayfish stock:
crayfish claws and shells
half a bunch each of fennel, leeks
¹/₄ bulb of celeriac (to yield scant
     ¹/₂ cup / 100 g chopped)
2 shallots
¹/₂ clove of garlic
1 tbsp / 15 g tomato paste

1 sprig each of tarragon, thyme
1 tsp / 5 g sugar
³/₄ cup / 200 ml white wine
¹/₈ lb / 50 g butter
salt, pepper to taste

For the broth:
¹/₂ cup / 100 ml vinegar
generous cup / 300 ml dry white wine
7 pints / 3 l of water
1 bunch of dill
half a bay leaf
10 crushed peppercorns
1 leek, 1 onion
¹/₄ celeriac bulb
1 tsp / 5 g sugar

For the vinaigrette:
¹/₂ cup / 100 ml each truffle juice, light veal
     stock
1 tbsp / 15 ml each fruit vinegar, balsamic
     vinegar, olive oil
1 tbsp / 15 ml grapeseed oil

Crayfish have been very popular since the Middle Ages. During the nineteenth century they became so fashionable that they were consumed in vast quantities; after the Belle Epoque, however, they became rare and expensive. The wild crayfish has all but disappeared from most areas now, the most famous being a crayfish with red legs that was caught in summer and fall. Ideally, choose live crayfish. For this recipe you need crayfish that weigh at least two ounces (sixty five grams) and no more than a scant quarter-pound (one hundred and fifteen grams). As usual you must remove the intestines before preparation. Cook the crayfish at the last minute so they do not have a chance to dry out.

Snowpeas, known as "mange-touts" in France because one can eat the whole snowpea, are ripe in May and June. Originally the snowpea was imported to France from Italy in the seventeenth century. There are countless varieties of the vegetable – for example, there is one with light-colored pods and one with violet flowers, and there is also a kind that does not contain threads and is thus referred to as the "gourmet pea." Choose thick, bright-green pods without blemishes, and, for this recipe, remove the threads that run along their top line.

Made even more elegant by Chef Horst Petermann's including Périgord (black) truffles, this is an ideal summer appetizer, ideally suited to complement meat dishes such as veal.

1. For the crayfish stock: sweat the chopped vegetables in a little butter for two to three minutes, then add the crayfish claws and crushed shells, all the spices and the tomato paste. Cook this mixture for another two or three minutes before adding the white wine, then covering with water. Simmer for 30–40 minutes, and add salt and pepper to taste. Strain and then reduce to 4 tbsp / 60 ml of crayfish stock.

2. Wash the snowpeas, remove the threads, and cook very briefly in salted water. Set aside on a kitchen towel to air-dry and cool. Bring the broth to a boil with all ingredients, and leave to infuse for one hour. Cook the crayfish for two minutes in the broth, then discard the heads and shells.

with a Truffle Vinaigrette

3. With a long-bladed knife, chop the truffles as finely as possible. To prepare the vinaigrette, pour the veal stock into a casserole, add half of the chopped truffles, reduce by half, and set aside to cool. Add the other half of the chopped truffles and remaining ingredients, and mix well. Bring to a boil once more and simmer for one hour. Add the crayfish, cook for two or three minutes, and leave to cool.

4. To serve, arrange the snowpeas in a star shape on each plate, sprinkling with a little vinaigrette. Place the crayfish in the center of the star and sprinkle with the remaining truffle vinaigrette. Pour the crayfish stock in a ring around the outside of the snowpea star.

Terrine of

Preparation time: 2 hours
Cooking time: 4 hours, 20 minutes
Marinating time: 1 7 hours
Setting time: 48 hours
Difficulty: ★★★

Serves twelve

3–4 lb / 1¹/₂–2 kg ox tail meat
¹/₈ lb / 50 g bacon, thinly sliced
1 bunch each of carrots, celery, leeks
2 shallots
1 clove of garlic
5 juniper berries
1 sprig of thyme
¹/₂ bay leaf
1 tsp / 5 g tomato paste

For the foie gras:
2¹/₂ lb / 1.2 kg uncooked foie gras
1 tbsp / 15 g salt
1 tbsp / 15 g chopped herbs (of your preference)

1 quart / 1 l milk
1 quart / 1 l water
¹/₄ cup / 50 ml port
¹/₄ cup / 50 ml cognac

For the garnish:
4 small artichokes
1 bunch of broccoli
1 bunch of young carrots
¹/₂ lb / 200 g small turnips
generous 2 tbsp / 30 g fresh walnuts
¹/₂ lemon

For the vinaigrette: (see basic recipes)

Foie gras, the fattened liver of a goose or duck, has enjoyed special culinary status since antiquity. A duck foie gras is smaller than a goose's: firm, smooth duck liver should weigh between one-and-a-quarter and two pounds (five hundred and fifty grams and one kilogram). Its color will vary, ranging from yellow to pink to ivory, depending on the kind of corn it was fed. Duck livers also tend to have a bitter taste, but this is easily neutralized by marinating in a mixture of milk and water. The duck liver is then marinated once again, this time in a mixture of port and cognac, to impart even more spice and flavor to the meat.

The ox tail should, if at all possible, be from a young animal whose flesh is still tender; it may be male or female. After an extended cooking period over slow heat the meat will easily separate from the bone. To form the terrine, it is weighed down evenly so that later, it is easier to invert and to slice. Use an electric carving knife to slice the terrine without disturbing its shape.

Since they will be used as a decorative arrangement on the plate, the vegetables should be carefully prepared: cut small florets from the broccoli head, and precise, pretty shapes from the carrots, turnips, and artichoke hearts. These last three will be gently heated in olive oil and then sprinkled with lemon juice; the remaining vegetables will be blanched. Finally, sprinkle this appetizer with a little vinaigrette, and serve with a few slices of toasted bread.

For clarity, we present this dish's preparation in logical steps, but you should begin preparing the foie gras first, as it will need a long marinating time. And as with all terrines, this one needs a long (two days) time to set as well.

1. Salt and pepper the ox tail and briefly fry in olive oil, turning so that all sides are cooked. Remove the meat and heat the vegetables in the same saucepan; drain the vegetables and transfer back into the saucepan along with the meat. Add the herbs, spices, and tomato paste; leave to infuse over medium heat for a few minutes. Flambé with cognac.

2. Add wine if you need to ease the reduced gravy off the base of the saucepan. Place everything in another, larger saucepan for slow cooking, fill with enough water to cover, lid, and cook in the oven at 350 °F / 170 °C for four hours, or until the meat is completely tender. Leave to cool, separate the meat from the bone, and trim off the fat. Press the meat. Skim the gravy and set aside.

Foie Gras

3. Marinate the foie gras in a mixture of water and milk for five hours; remove the tendons, season with a mixture of chopped herbs and salt, add port and a dash of cognac, and marinate for 12 hours. For the garnish, blanch the broccoli florets, carrots, and turnips; sauté the artichoke bases in olive oil. Sprinkle with lemon juice and cook over medium-low heat for ten minutes.

4. Line the terrine form with the thin bacon slices so that they overlap the edge of the form. Fill the terrine with alternating layers of the marinated foie gras and pressed ox tail meat. Press every layer firmly and finish off with a layer of foie gras. Fold the overlapping bacon slices over the top of the terrine to close it. Cook in a bain-marie at 180 °F / 95 °C for 16 minutes. Cover, leave to cool and let sit for 48 hours.

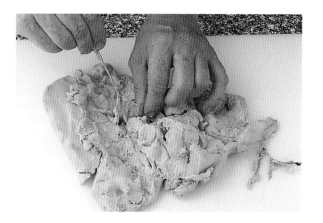

Caviar – Presented

Caviar is one of the most delicious and elegant cold appetizers of all. Chef Armen Petrossian proposes four different ways to present this delicacy. And caviar will combine exquisitely with:

salmon
smoked fish
vodka
foie gras
truffles

Only Petrossian, who, in 1920, made caviar famous in France and beyond, could possibly present this rare and sublime product in such a beautiful manner. For the presentation of caviar, it is not enough to have an aesthetic eye for detail; it is equally imperative to serve caviar at exactly the right temperature and without any additional ingredients that might impair its delicious flavor. Ideally, it should be served in the original container.

Petrossian has devised several ingenious and functional methods of presenting caviar in its original container, without having to add crushed ice directly to the caviar. You can, for example, present caviar in a serving dish that contains an insulation material instead of crushed ice. The dish is covered with a lid, so the insulation is invisible. The lid has a mold in its center into which the caviar container is dropped. Usually, there is ample space for three of these dishes on most dinner tables (see main picture). Furthermore, there are individual serving dishes, enabling the guests to help themselves: a handmade glass bowl or a silver-plated metal dish, both designed to hold a two ounce / fifty gram caviar container. The silver-plated dish also exists in a five ounce / one hundred and fifty gram version, which can be placed in the middle of the table (see photo 3).

Further serving dishes in the Petrossian design range include ring or star forms for making ice rings or stars that are designed to hold the caviar containers. These are forms that are filled with water and then put into the freezer. The ice is then simply inverted and can thus guarantee that the caviar will be kept at the right temperature throughout the evening (see photos 1 and 2). Finally, the range also includes a caviar serving spoon and a caviar spoon (see photo 4), which, along with the serving dishes, turn the enjoyment of caviar into a unique experience.

1. This ice ring holds all the caviar containers in the Petrossian range and keeps them chilled: the 4 oz / 125 g, 8 oz / 250 g, and 16 oz / 500 g containers. All that is required is filling the form with water, and subsequently inverting the ice ten minutes after it has been taken out of the freezer. Incidentally, the ice ring is also ideal for chilling taramasalata or fresh fruit.

2. This interesting ice star with a slightly raised center was inspired by the tentacles of the starfish. In order to prevent temperature shock, the form should not be inverted under running hot water but be allowed to warm up for ten minutes at room temperature.

by Petrossian

3. Classic in appearance, this serving dish carries the name of Petrossian; it is designed to hold a 2 oz / 50 g caviar container, which fits neatly into the silver ring in the center. The elegant shape allows no special chilling devices, so the caviar must be served instantly.

4. Caviar should always be eaten with the correct cutlery to ensure maximum enjoyment of this sumptuous delicacy. This gold-plated cutlery does not impair the flavor of the caviar, and the rounded contours facilitate serving the caviar without squashing it.

Trout Gazpacho

Preparation time: 45 minutes
Cooking time: 15 minutes
Difficulty: ★

Serves four

8 crayfish
1/2 lb / 240 g fillet of salmon (lake) trout
generous 1/2 lb / 260 g tomatoes
1 cucumber
1/2 red pepper
1 onion
1 clove of garlic
2 tbs / 30 g bread crumbs

2 tbsp / 30 ml olive oil
1 tbsp / 15 ml vinegar
1 drop of Tabasco
salt, pepper to taste

To garnish:
1/2 green pepper
1/2 red pepper
1/2 yellow pepper
3 tomatoes
4 sprigs salicornia (see below)
4 sprigs flat-leafed parsley
half a bunch of chives

Although he is Swiss, our chef, Roland Pierroz, was inspired by Andalusian tradition when he devised this recipe. The dish's originality lies in the combination of crayfish and lake trout (*salmo trutta lacustris*), a large trout whose diet of shellfish turns its flesh pink and thus becomes known as a salmon trout.

But there is, actually, a link to Roland Pierroz's homeland: the lake or salmon trout is very common to Switzerland's Alpine lakes, where, thriving in the high altitude's cold waters, it grows quite large. If cooked over low heat for only a short time the pink and tender flesh tastes delicious, and retains its color.

Unfortunately, crayfish are rarely caught in the wild, having all but disappeared from rivers; the crayfish sold today are usually farm-raised.

For the gazpacho, Roland Pierroz recommends using shapely, round peppers of different colors with smooth and shiny skins. Salicornia, a type of edible, coastal plant called a samphire, is also sometimes called glasswort or sea bean; its spiky green leaves bear the hint of the sea in their salty taste, particularly when salicornia is at its peak season in the summer. The gazpacho should be served chilled but should not be frozen, otherwise the careful blending of ingredients will be lost when the mixture disintegrates back into its individual components.

1. Peel the tomatoes, retaining three for decoration. Halve the remaining tomatoes, hollow them out, and chop up the pulp. Wash the red pepper, remove the seeds and the pith. Peel the onion and cucumber, seed the cucumber; chop both.

2. In a blender or food processor puree all the vegetables. Add the bread crumbs and olive oil and blend once more. Stir in the vinegar, salt, pepper, garlic and a dash of Tabasco. Strain and chill.

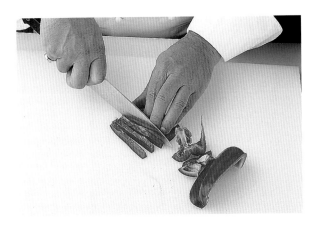

with Crayfish

3. In a stainless steel saucepan, bring salted water to a boil. Cook the crayfish in the water for one minute, remove them from the saucepan, shell them, and then place the meat in a little cooking liquid; set aside. Steam the trout fillets for three minutes: they should remain slightly pink inside. Wash the green and yellow peppers, remove the stalks, seeds and pith.

4. Chop the peppers and the three retained tomatoes into separate piles. Wash the salicornia, drain, and keep cool. To serve, pour the gazpacho into a deep plate and add one piece of trout fillet and two crayfish tails. Decorate with crayfish shells and a sprig of parsley and sprinkle with the chopped peppers, tomatoes, and chives.

Preparation time: 1 hour
Cooking time: 10 minutes
Difficulty: ★★

Serves four

16 small squid (measuring 3–4 in/8–10 cm)
8 langoustines
2 tomatoes
1 red pepper
1 eggplant
8 baby zucchini
1 onion

$^1/_2$ cup / 125 ml olive oil
1 bunch of chives

For the vinaigrette:
1 lemon
$^3/_4$ cup / 200 ml olive oil
$^1/_2$ cup / 125 ml walnut oil
2 tsp / 10 ml soy sauce
1 bunch of chives
1 sprig of basil
salt, fresh-ground pepper to taste

Ratatouille, of which this appetizer is a variation, is a Provençal dish. Essentially, it comprises a vegetable ragout that is cooked very slowly in olive oil and seasoned with Provençal herbs. There are as many recipes for ratatouille in Provence as there are chefs, and the ingredients vary significantly from recipe to recipe.

There is one thing, however, common to all versions of ratatouille: the ingredients are always fried separately before they are mixed together to be slowly cooked into an even, smooth vegetable mixture. Soft-fleshed zucchini are the exception: they must be blanched in boiling water and then immediately rinsed with cold water. Our chefs, the Pourcel brothers, prepare their ratatouille following these traditional steps and then add their signature, which is a cluster of delicious langoustines.

In this appetizer, the squid is actually filled with the ratatouille; in Sète, southern France, the squid are usually filled with cured sausage. The former is an ideal preparation method, as filling the squid with ratatouille will ensure that the squid does not become too dry and, furthermore, it provides a nice accompaniment for the langoustines.

Related to the octopus and differing mainly in size, squid is available in many types. For this recipe, we use sepiola, caught in large numbers in the Mediterranean, though if none are available, choose any smallish variety that seems fresh (with unclouded eyes, and an ocean smell). The squid is fried for only a short period of time, and the filling, as well, is not cooked for too long, as that would rob it of its intense flavor.

1. Peel all the vegetables and chop finely, discarding the core of the zucchini. Fry all the vegetables but the zucchini in separate batches in a non-stick frying pan. Shell the langoustines, discard the intestines, then chop finely. Mix all the vegetables together for the ratatouille. Prepare the vinaigrette.

2. Gut the squid, wash thoroughly under running water, and set aside. Blanch the heads and then chop them finely before adding them to the ratatouille.

Squid

3. Use a pastry bag to fill the squid with the ratatouille; close using a wooden toothpick. Heat gently in olive oil for ten minutes or until brown; season and bake in a hot oven to brown if necessary. Slice the zucchini into long, thin slices (use a slicer or the slicing side of a food grater for the best results), cook in salted water and then immediately rinse with cold water.

4. Sauté the zucchini in butter, season, and set aside. Retain the liquid released by the squid during cooking and stir into the vinaigrette. To serve, place the zucchini in the middle of the plate and surround with three stuffed squid. Sprinkle with the vinaigrette and garnish with chives.

Asparagus Salad

Preparation time: 20 minutes
Cooking time: 10 minutes
Difficulty: ✭

Serves four

16 flat oysters (see below)
⅝ lb / 300 g smoked salmon
2 lbs / 1 kg green asparagus
3 tomatoes
1 lemon
¼ cup 50 ml crème fraîche
1 bunch of chives

For the vinaigrette:
½ cup / 125 ml olive oil
½ cup / 125 ml rapeseed oil
half a bunch of basil
1 lemon
salt, pepper to taste

The oyster season, traditionally in the fall and winter, inspires many unusual and classic culinary compositions. By now, the saltwater mollusc's dietary benefits are well known, which is why oysters can be wholeheartedly recommended. This applies to the flat as well as the rounder varieties, both of which are offered in market stalls in Europe in equal measure.

The flat type of oyster the Pourcel brothers call for here is native to France; in the United States, it is available in varieties such as Belon and Marennes. But, ever loyal to their origins, the Pourcel brothers propose the use of oysters from Bouziges, bred in the oyster banks of Thau, near Sète, in southern France, these may also be available in the United States, particularly from high-end seafood markets. The Bouziges can be distinguished from other varieties by their size and their slightly flaky shell; their flesh is also much more piquant and crisp than that of the Atlantic or English Channel oysters.

In this recipe oysters are combined with asparagus. Choose asparagus stalks that are not too long, yet with fully developed tips, so they do not crowd each other during cooking and possibly disintegrate. If the asparagus is cooked too long it will be difficult to handle without squashing it, and it will also lose its soft yet bright green color. This aspect of the preparation, as well as the vinaigrette, can be done in advance. And if you want to take the vinaigrette one step further, try lacing it with truffle oil or sea urchin roe to refine its aroma.

The smoked salmon – preferably Scottish – should be very thinly sliced so that it releases its delicate aroma to fullest effect and the other ingredients can absorb its flavor. Serve this appetizer chilled.

1. Trim the end off the asparagus and peel (if you have one, an asparagus peeler works best); wash and then tie into four bundles. Immerse the four bundles in boiling water and cook for five to six minutes. Rinse with cold water and set aside.

2. Open and shuck the oysters, cut into three parts each and set aside. Peel the tomatoes and chop the pulp finely.

with Oysters

3. Trim the asparagus tips to lengths of about four inches each. Cut the remaining sections of the stalk into round slices and mix with the tomatoes. Chop the chives and add about a $^1/_4$ cup / 60 g, and mix this and the cut tomatoes and asparagus with the crème fraîche, lemon juice, and oysters. Blend well and add salt and pepper to taste.

4. Stir the vinaigrette and stretch with a touch of boiling water. Divide the asparagus-oyster mixture into four portions. To serve, use a circular form of about 4 in / 10 cm in diameter in the middle of each plate to make a flat mound of the mixture; top this with slices of smoked salmon. Distribute the asparagus tips and vinaigrette around the plate and garnish with chives.

Artichoke Leaves

Preparation time: 1 hour 15 minutes
Cooking time: 1 hour
Difficulty: ★

Serves four

6 large artichokes
32 crayfish
1 tbsp / 15 ml sherry vinegar
3 tbsp / 45 ml olive oil infused with basil
1 bunch of basil
1 bunch of parsley
salt, fresh-ground black pepper
   to taste

For the sauce:
$1/8$ lb / 50 g dried tomatoes
   (to yield 2 tsp, chopped)
1 tsp mustard
$1/4$ cup white wine vinegar
$1/2$ cup strained tomato juice
juice of 2 lemons
salt, fresh-ground black pepper
   to taste

For the tomato juice:
$2^1/_2$ lbs / 1.2 kg large tomatoes
1 fennel
4 cloves of garlic
half a bunch of tarragon
$1/2$ cup / 125 ml olive oil
salt to taste

For this recipe, use large artichokes – our chef, Stéphane Raimbault, eschews the small violet artichokes from southern France for Brittany's round and fleshy *maître* ("master") variety, which can weigh up to one pound (four hundred and fifty grams). As this may be a rarity in American markets, look for the largest artichokes you can find.

The artichoke is a type of wild thistle that was initially known as a plant with healing properties before it became a garden vegetable and a delicacy (peruse earlier artichoke recipes in this volume for more information). It must be consumed soon after cooking as it will quickly turn brown.

To remove the stalks, pull rather than cut them out, otherwise the stringy fibers, or choke, will not be completely removed.

Scrape the leaves thoroughly with a spoon to extract all the pulp, which is then squashed with a fork (as is the pulp from the artichoke heart) to retain its fibrous consistency.

Chef Raimbault, again working with the foodstuffs plentiful in Europe, recommends a Turkish crayfish that has a long, slim tail for this dish. But in the United States, the crayfish from the Mississippi are outstanding as well. These freshwater crustaceans, which look like miniature lobsters, must first be cleaned of their small, black intestines underneath the tail. They are then steamed for a short time. And, if crayfish are unavailable, any crustacean can be used to make this artichoke-based appetizer, such as shrimp, lobster, or langoustine.

1. Cook the artichokes in salted water and steam the crayfish for two minutes. Set aside five attractive artichoke leaves per person for decoration (they will be arranged into a star-shaped cup). Scrape the pulp off the rest of the leaves.

2. Chop the tomatoes and some of the basil. Mix all the ingredients for the sauce in a glass bowl and whisk. Add the chopped tomatoes and a little chopped basil as well as a pinch of freshly ground black pepper. Squash the artichoke hearts with a fork, and season the artichoke pulp with sherry vinegar.

with Crayfish

3. Slice the garlic and fennel for the tomato juice; halve the tomatoes as well. Fry the garlic and fennel in olive oil, add the tomatoes and cook in the oven for one hour. Afterwards, puree finely in a blender or food processor.

4. To serve, pour the tomato sauce onto four large plates; place the artichoke leaves in the middle in a star shape and fill the center with artichoke pulp decorated with basil. Surround with the crayfish and garnish with parsley.

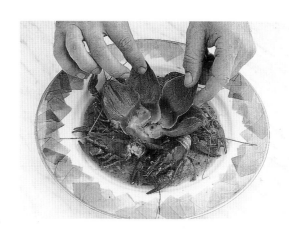

Faux Parfait With

Preparation time: *14 minutes*
Cooking time: *2 minutes*
Cooling time: *15 minutes*
Difficulty: ✶

Serves four

8 king (or large) prawns
2 avocados (fuerte variety)
16 small tomatoes (globe variety)
4 cherry tomatoes
2 small onions
1 lime
12 small basil leaves
salt, cayenne pepper to taste

For the vinaigrette:
3 tbsp / 50 ml lime juice
4 tbsp / 60 ml cold-pressed olive oil
5 tbsp / 75 ml sunflower oil
1/4 tsp / 2 g paprika
salt, cayenne pepper to taste

This unusual recipe is a novel take on the traditional parfait – normally a dessert – using the classic combination of avocado and prawns. The Aztecs regarded the avocado as a fruit of the gods; though laden with fat (which puts some people off), it is not so high in calories. Of the two varieties, the black, pitted-skinned Haas and the green, smooth-skinned Fuerte, the latter has a bit less fat, and is the one that Stéphane Raimbault has chosen for this dish.

Choose ripe avocados with a shiny and smooth skin. You can check the fruit's ripeness by gently pressing with your thumb: if it is hard, it needs more time, if it can be easily dented, it is almost too ripe. The olive-shaped scoops of avocado flesh that we will use in this recipe should immediately be sprinkled with lime juice before they have a chance to oxidize and turn brown.

The remaining pulp is squashed with a fork and also mixed with lime juice.

Choose the largest prawns (called jumbo shrimp in many markets) you can find: if they are too small, they will be hard to cut into medallions. The Mediterranean variety is firm-fleshed and rich in iodine, and has a strong flavor that combines well with the avocados. If at all possible, buy fresh, not frozen prawns, since they will be steamed only briefly in an aromatic broth. Despite their slightly brittle shell, they are easy to peel.

This appetizer can also be prepared with other shellfish, provided they are large enough. You could, for example, use langoustines or lobster instead. The vinaigrette is also flexible, and can also be modified in a variety of ways.

1. Steam the prawns, set aside to cool, shell and cut a portion into small medallions. Place a circular form of 3 in / 7 cm in diameter in the middle of each appetizer plate; line the inside walls of the form with the shrimp medallions. Set the remaining prawns aside.

2. Cut half of the tomatoes into ovals and the rest into thin slices. (The cherry tomatoes will be used for the decoration.)

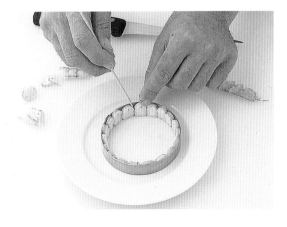

Avocados and King Prawns

3. Chop the onions. Peel the avocados, scoop out half into small, olive-shaped balls with an oval scoop and immediately moisten these with lime juice. Squash the remaining avocado pulp with a fork and mix with the chopped onions. Add salt and mix with lime juice and the remaining prawns.

4. Fill the circular forms lined with the prawn medallions with the avocado puree, and arrange the tomato slices on top in the form of a rosette, crowned with a cherry tomato. Garnish with basil leaves. Remove the form and place the olive-shaped avocado scoops and oval tomato pieces around the "faux" avocado parfait like sun rays. Sprinkle with vinaigrette.

Beef Salad with

Preparation time: 1 hour
Cooking time: 45 minutes
Difficulty: ✶

Serves four

1 lb / 500 g fillet of beef
half a bunch of celery
1 clove of garlic
2 tbsp / 30 ml cold-pressed olive oil
1 tbsp / 15 ml light olive oil
$^1/_2$ tsp / 3 g salt
1 tsp / 5 g crushed peppercorns

For the garnish:
$^1/_4$ lb / 100 g arugula
$^1/_4$ lb / 100 g parmesan

For the vinaigrette:
$^1/_4$ cup / 50 ml cold-pressed olive oil
$^1/_4$ cup / 50 ml white truffle oil
$^1/_4$ cup / 50 ml balsamic vinegar
$^1/_4$ cup / 50 ml beef gravy
salt, black pepper to taste

For this dish our chef, Paul Rankin, recommends Scottish beef: Angus beef from Aberdeen, to be more precise. Angus cattle spend their days grazing on healthy fields and the selection process is very strict indeed, so the meat's excellent quality is assured. Feel free to use other top-quality beef if Angus is not available: there are a number of breeds in the United States, particularly recently, that are raised free-range, and prime cuts (the highest quality of meat), once the province of only select butchers, are now available in many different markets.

This recipe is based on the tenderloin or short loin cut, a fillet of beef muscle that runs alongside the backbone. Fry the fillet for a minute on each side over very high heat to cook it rare, which, according to British tradition, means very brown and crisp on the outside, and quite tender and pink on the inside. This can be achieved by heating a frying pan (preferably grid-

dled) over an extremely high heat and, when it is really hot, frying the meat and seasoning it while frying.

Chef Rankin's recipe was inspired by the Italian *carpaccio*, and contains a range of transalpine products, such as white truffle oil from the Piedmont region, balsamic vinegar from Modena, and Parmesan from the Reggiano region. All these ingredients should be of the highest quality and be dispensed exactly in the quantities indicated.

Instead of fillet of beef, you can also use other cuts, such as rumpsteak or short loin; whichever cut of beef you decide to use, do not trim the fat off before frying as it will help the meat retain its flavor and juices during the cooking process. If you want to try further modifications, try using venison or, more simply, grilled chicken for a different culinary slant.

1. Wash the fillet and halve lengthwise, seasoning with crushed peppercorns and oil. Fry in a very hot frying pan for one minute each side until dark brown on the outside but still rare on the inside. Set aside to cool at room temperature until tepid.

2. Peel the celery and cut into medium-sized chunks; add to salted water. Bring to a boil with a whole, unpeeled clove of garlic and leave to simmer until the celery is cooked. Remove from the heat, add olive oil and black pepper, and leave to infuse for at least one hour.

Celery and Truffle Oil

3. Shortly before serving, cut the fillet into slices around a ¼ in / ½ cm thick. Carefully whisk the ingredients of the vinaigrette in a bowl. Wash the arugula and discard any yellowing or decaying leaves. Shave the Parmesan to yield about 2–3 tbsp / 30 g.

4. To serve, arrange the salad in layers on four plates: the beef fillet first, and then the celery, arugula, and Parmesan, until all ingredients have been used up. Generously pour the vinaigrette over the salad and serve immediately.

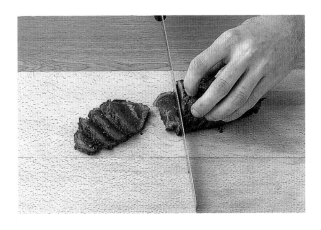

Lukewarm Salmon

Preparation time:	20 minutes
Cooking time:	2 minutes
Difficulty:	☆

Serves four

generous $3/4$ lb / 400 g fresh salmon fillet
1 zucchini
1 tomato
$3/4$ / 200 ml cup walnut vinaigrette
1 bunch of chervil
salt, fresh-ground pepper to taste

The quality of a salmon depends on the voyages it has made during its lifetime, and how many it has undergone, for the best wild salmon meat is from a salmon that is three years old or younger, according to aficionados. If it has traveled upstream its flesh will be particularly good; after spawning, when it has exhausted all its fat, it has to return to the open sea to recover.

Given the changes in our waterways, such as pollution and dams, wild salmon are not as abundant as they used to be, but for this recipe, wild salmon is particularly suitable, as it has a rich flavor acquired by migrating between freshwater and the sea. Use the fillet, the part just behind the head, which should be cut into even slices of sufficient thickness and then cooked

in the oven. Watch over the process carefully so as not to destroy the salmon's delicate flavor, which will fade from over-cooking. Some gourmets prefer tuna for this kind of preparation.

The vegetables that our chef, Jean-Jacques Rigollet, has chosen for this dish include summery tomatoes and zucchini. Select a ripe tomato and a medium-sized zucchini with firm flesh and few seeds. Growing in abundance in the Mediterranean river valleys, zucchini form the basis of many a popular dish such as ratatouille; the Italians, Greeks, and Spaniards also know many culinary applications for this simple and delicious vegetable.

1. Prepare the vinaigrette. Peel and seed the tomato and chop into small dice of uniform size. Slice the unpeeled zucchini thinly and evenly (use a slicer if you prefer) and gently sprinkle with the vinaigrette.

2. Arrange the zucchini slices in a large ring on each plate.

with Zucchini

3. Cut the salmon into four slices. Season with salt and freshly ground pepper, place on a baking tray, and bake for around two minutes in a very hot oven.

4. To serve, place one salmon slice on each of the plates, sprinkle the remaining vinaigrette over the zucchini rounds, and dot each zucchini round with a piece of diced tomato. Garnish the salmon with chervil leaves.

Saddle of Rabbit in

Preparation time: 1 hour
Cooking time: 20 minutes
Cooling time: 2 hours
Marinating time: 6 hours
Difficulty: ★★

Serves four

2 saddles of rabbit, a scant
   ³/₄ lb / 350 g each
¹/₂ lb / 250 g crushed rabbit bones
4 small artichokes
2 shallots

¹/₄ lb / 100 g mixed lettuce, such as mesclun
white of 2 eggs
2 sheets of gelatin
2 cups / 500 ml white wine (Chinon blanc)
³/₄ cup / 200 ml vinaigrette
1 bunch of rosemary
1 bunch of chervil leaves
salt, pepper to taste

During the Middle Ages, wild rabbit was hunted in France whenever game was rare; today it has taken on a slightly higher status. Breeders now offer a variety of domesticated species. It is best to choose young rabbits that have been raised on a farm, since the animal will carry a seal of quality. Preparation should not begin until at least forty-eight hours have passed since the animal was slaughtered, as meat well hung will be much more tender.

The saddle, a particularly good piece of rabbit meat, is located directly above the leg. This round section should be loosely tied with string before being marinated for about six hours. Towards the end of the cooking time the vegetables are added to the rabbit and cooked for another two minutes; the broth is then clarified with whisked egg whites and finally strained. The liquid is left to cool and set, which results in a lovely, clear aspic.

Of the other ingredients, all are essential. The artichoke hearts will provide an intriguing contrast to the meat and aspic. Before slicing their bases, they should be thoroughly chilled. The rosemary is an indispensable partner for rabbit and most other meat dishes. Mesclun, often comprised of young lettuces once found in wild meadows, strikes an interesting note in a dish of a meat once hunted in the same such meadows. And finally, the white wine (our chef is a Chinon blanc aficionado) lends a perfect balance to the rabbit and the aspic.

1. Chop the shallot and divide the rosemary into sprigs. Wash the rabbit saddle, tie with string, and place in a casserole or large saucepan, along with the crushed bones, 4 sprigs of rosemary, and the chopped shallot. Cover with white wine, sprinkle with salt, and simmer for 20 minutes. Remove from the heat.

2. Soak the gelatin in cold water, add to the rabbit cooking liquid (from which the rabbit and bones have been removed and set aside), and then strain the liquid through a muslin cloth. Strip and clean the artichokes; slice and cook the artichoke hearts, and leave to cool.

White Wine Aspic

3. Untie the rabbit meat, pour the aspic over the meat and chill. Season the artichoke hearts and the mixed lettuce separately with vinaigrette.

4. Cut the jellied meat into medallions. To serve, place a mound of sliced artichoke heart in the center of the plate on a broad bed of mesclun and surround with an arrangement of rabbit medallions. Garnish with chervil leaves and sprinkle with diced aspic.

Salad of Monkfish with

Preparation time: 30 minutes
Cooking time: 10 minutes
Difficulty: ✲

Serves four

1 monkfish (a generous 2 lb / 1 kg; see below)
1 lb / 500 g spinach
1 tomato
1 bunch of chives
1 tbsp / 10 g butter
3 tbsp / 50 ml vinaigrette
a dash of sherry vinegar
2 tbsp / 30 ml gravy (from a meat or
   chicken dish)
salt, pepper to taste

Chef Jean-Claude Rigollet has unearthed this appetizer from the rich culinary tradition of Touraine, the Loire valley that has produced excellent wines – such as the red Chinon and the white Montlouis – and food since Roman times. Graced by long visits from the court, Touraine cuisine became known for its luxurious dishes, many based on fish. This appetizer, centered around monkfish and bright-green baby spinach, is intended to prepare the palate for the courses to come, and thus provide a suitable introduction to a memorable meal.

As all the goodness and delicacy of a fish – particularly monkfish, with its dense, compact meat – as well as its flavor and consistency can be easily destroyed by too much handling, care is a top priority. If you prefer, get your fishmonger to fillet the monkfish, or, you may even substitute the monkfish with a goatfish (or red mullet), filleted by the fishmonger. Like the monkfish, the goatfish should be prepared by being fried very

briefly. The monkfish should be carefully washed and all the bones and skin removed before cooking, during which time you should make sure the fish is not losing its tenderness. In order not to dominate the presence of the fish, baby spinach leaves should be used, ideally harvested in spring or summer. Spinach, a once unpopular "fasting" green that was only eaten during the fasting season, is a tender and dark vegetable perfect with a well-seasoned fish. Among its many benefits, it is rich in both vitamins and minerals. Only use small spinach leaves, as the larger leaves do not have the same delicate flavor.

The vinaigrette is made with a neutral oil such as peanut oil, so the aroma of the strained gravy (for example, from a grilled chicken or pork) is not overpowered. For the sauce to have the correct consistency and a smooth emulsion, the oil should only be stirred into the vinaigrette shortly before serving.

1. Wash the monkfish thoroughly, fillet with a sharp knife (if it has not already been done), and cut into even slices.

2. Peel the tomatoes and chop the pulp into small dice. Prepare the vinaigrette. Wash the young spinach leaves well, season with the vinaigrette, and distribute on the four plates. Bake for around 20 seconds in a hot oven.

Gravy and Baby Spinach

3. Salt and pepper the monkfish and then sauté in butter, without browning, on both sides.

4. While the fish is still in the sauté pan, add the vinegar and gravy. To serve, arrange the fish on the plates in a ring on top of the baby spinach, and sprinkle with chopped tomato and sprigs of chives.

Grilled Duck Liver with

Preparation time: 30 minutes
Marinating time: 6 hours
Cooling time: 27 hours
Cooking time: 5 minutes
Difficulty: ★★

Serves four

For the grilled liver:
generous ³/₄ lb / 400 g duck liver
1 quart / 1 l whole milk
a pinch of salt
a small pinch of sugar
a pinch of pepper

For the salad:
¹/₄ cup / 50 g lentils
¹/₄ cup / 50 g pearl barley
¹/₂ lb / 250 g air-cured bacon (or 12 slices)
¹/₄ bunch of chives
1 shallot
1 tbsp / 15 g lard
1 to 2 tbsp / 15–30 ml sherry vinegar
2 tbsp / 30 ml peanut oil
salt, pepper to taste

To garnish:
1 bunch of chives
4 nasturtium flowers

Our chef, Michel Rochedy from the restaurant Chabichou, has always regretted the loss of quality that normally occurs when heating poultry liver, be it from a duck or a goose. One day, by accident, he discovered to his pure delight that browning the liver with a flame torch prevented the meat from going hard during cooking, yet allowed the liver to release the full extent of its subtle flavor. Since then he has been preparing liver this way, to outstanding results.

Rochedy has provided here a step-by-step guide for the preparation of the liver so that other cooks may understand how it works. First, the liver is marinated in milk mixed with ice cubes, for improved chilling. Then the liver is loosely wrapped in plastic wrap (on no account must the liver be squashed even slightly), and placed in the freezer. Once the liver has been

taken out of the freezer, it is set on a rack and grilled with the flame torch; hold the flame a bit under an inch (two and a half centimeters) away from the liver (Rochedy holds it approximately three-quarters of an inch (two centimeters) away, to be specific). The liver is left to rest for a few moments and then returned to the freezer. Or, if you prefer a simpler method, the liver could be pan-fried the usual way after marinating in milk.

Both the liver and the cured bacon should be very fresh; the latter will be quickly fried in a bit of lard. The spices complete the picture: the mixture of coarse sea salt and fresh-ground pepper gives a sturdy seasoning for the liver. The nasturtium flowers (which are edible) are grouped with chives for a fanciful decoration – or, if none are available, you can use violets, as pictured.

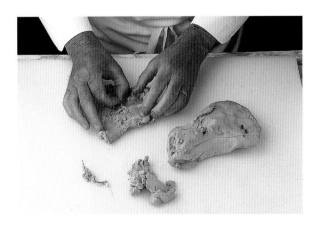

1. Marinate the liver for six hours in milk; drain. With a sharp knife, clean the liver of tendons and veins. Season with salt, pepper, and sugar.

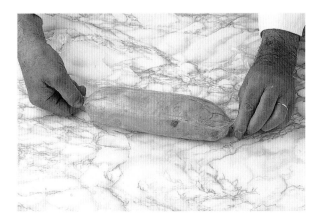

2. Wrap the liver in plastic wrap and roll into a long "sausage"; put in the freezer for three hours to firm up. Cook the lentils and pearl barley in plenty of water; drain after cooking and set aside.

Lentil and Pearl Barley Salad

3. Take the liver out of the freezer, remove the plastic wrapping, and grill with the flame torch as specified above, or pan-fry in the conventional manner. Re-wrap the liver, roll up, and chill for another 24 hours.

4. Chop the shallot and chives. Season the lentils and pearl barley with the shallot, chives, vinegar, peanut oil, salt, and pepper. Brown the bacon in the oven at 395 °F / 200 °C until crisp. To serve, place two slices of duck liver on each plate, accompanied by a few slices of bacon (they should have cupped slightly while in the oven) with a scoop of lentil and pearl barley salad inside them. Garnish with a "bouquet" of chive sprigs and nasturtium blossoms.

Salad of Lobster and

Preparation time: 30 minutes
Cooking time: 10 minutes
Difficulty: ★★

Serves four

1 dozen scallops
2 lobsters, generous ³/₄ lb / 400 g each
1 cup / 200 g mixed lettuce

For the lobster broth:
1 onion
1 carrot
1 stalk of leek stalk
1 stick of celery
1 sprig of thyme
1 bay leaf

1 lemon
salt, pepper to taste

For the leek vinaigrette with truffles:
1 small leek
2 shallots
¹/₂ oz / 10 g truffles
1–2 tbsp / 20 ml truffle juice
2¹/₂ tbsp / 40 ml sherry vinegar
¹/₃ cup / 80 ml peanut oil
salt, pepper to taste

To garnish:
half a bunch of parsley
half a bunch of chervil
half a bunch of chives

The combination of lobster and scallops is a classic, and it is served as part of the most elegant meals. As our chef, Michel Rochedy, will attest, only the freshest seafood of the highest quality, professionally prepared, will do.

Whether it comes from Canada or Brittany, lobster (after being plunged head-first into already boiling cooking liquid) must never be left in the cooking pot for too long, as it takes only eight minutes to destroy the wonderful flavor that helps to justify its high market value. Apart from lemon juice or perhaps a dash of white wine, you might consider adding a little seaweed to the cooking liquid to emphasize the iodine flavor of the lobster. For a slightly different-flavored variation, the lobster can be substituted with langoustines.

Although termed a cold appetizer, this salad should actually be served warm. Its flavor is further refined with chopped truffles and truffle juice. In order to facilitate serving, Chef Rochedy recommends you brush the lobster and scallops with oil and put them under the grill for just a minute or so. He also suggests that you gently heat the vinaigrette.

If you want to add another component to complete the composition, the salad could be served with a few thin slices of perch or sturgeon.

1. Prepare the lobster broth. Bring to a boil and cook the lobster for five minutes, then take the lobster out of the broth and shell. Shuck the scallops and clean them thoroughly.

2. Cut the scallops into slices and arrange these in a rosette shape on a non-stick tray or a circular form. Place half a lobster in the middle of each rosette. Select the best leaves from the mixed lettuce and wash them thoroughly; let them air-dry.

Scallops with Truffles

3. For the vinaigrette, finely chop the shallots, place in a hot frying pan, pour sherry vinegar over and reduce the liquid. Chop the truffles, reserving about a dozen slices for garnish. Add peanut oil, truffle juice, and half a tablespoon of chopped truffles. Chop the leek finely. Warm the vinaigrette and season to taste with salt and pepper. Add the leek.

4. Toss the lettuce with the vinaigrette in a roomy bowl. Preheat the over to 395 °F / 200 °C and heat the lobster-scallop rosettes for two minutes. To serve, heap a little salad in the middle of each plate, and careully set the rosette on top. Sprinkle with the truffle-laced vinaigrette. Decorate with chopped chives, chervil leaves, and truffle slices.

Lukewarm Tartare of Langoustines

Preparation time: 20 minutes
Cooking time: 2 hours
Difficulty: ★★

Serves four

1 dozen langoustines

For the broth:
langoustine shells
1 each of onion, carrot, leek, fennel bulb,
   celery stick
2 cloves of garlic
1/4 cup / 50 ml olive oil
half a bunch of basil

For the tartare:
juice of 2 lemons

1/2 cup / 100 ml olive oil
half a bunch of chives

For the soured cream sauce with salmon roe:
1 1/2 oz / 40 g salmon roe

1 egg yolk
juice of 2 lemons
1/2 cup / 100 ml cream
1 tsp / 5 g mustard
1/3 cup / 80 ml peanut oil
langoustine broth
salt, pepper to taste

For the potato wafers:
1 large potato
3 1/2 tbsp / 50 g butter

To garnish:
1 bunch of chives
1 bunch of chervil
1 cup / 200 g edible blossoms such as violets
   or nasturtiums (optional)

Chives, like garlic, belong to the lily family, originally from more exotic regions but today very common in Europe and North American. Our chef, Michel Rochedy, was raised in Saint-Agrève, in Ardèche, France, and has appreciated this herb since childhood. Today, he incorporates them into his recipes whenever he can, as in the appetizer presented here.

The chives should not, however, be allowed to dominate the delicious flavor of the langoustine tartare. To prepare the tartare, langoustine tails are first chopped and then very quickly cooked over very low heat: because the heating process is so brief, there is no danger of the langoustine meat toughening up. If you prefer, you can use tuna, crab, or spider crab instead:

prepare any of these the same way, ensuring their flesh will remain tender.

The potato wafers provide a delicious contrast to the seafood aspect of this dish, as well as a nice visual, textural feature. Mixing the sauce with the salmon roe can be tricky, so take care to do it gently so the eggs are not smashed. In Scandinavia and Russia, salmon roe is just as popular as caviar. Not all salmon species, however, produce roe of the same large size, or with a good, intense aroma. Of all the different types of salmon, this roe comes from one particular species that lives in the Pacific.

1. Shell the langoustines and separate the heads from the tails. Set aside the shells from four langoustine heads and four tail fins, which will be used later for garnish. Make a broth using the shells by frying the shells in olive oil, mixing with herbs and spices, covering with water and then simmering for two hours. Strain the broth afterwards.

2. To make the soured cream sauce, prepare a basic mayonnaise with egg yolk, mustard, peanut oil, salt and pepper, adding the juice of two lemons, the cream, and a bit of langoustine broth (1/4–1/2 cup / 60–20 ml). Shortly before serving, gently fold in the salmon roe.

with Soured Cream Sauce

3. Coarsely chop the langoustine tails. Peel the potato and transform into wafers (one improvised way to do this is to use a slicer to get extremely thin rounds, and then impress perforations on them with a meat tenderizer). Fry the wafers in butter in a non-stick frying pan until brown and crisp; drain on paper towels.

4. To make the tartare, chop the chives and squeeze the juice from two lemons. Mix the oil, lemon juice, chopped chives, and the langoustine tails. Heat over a very low flame in a saucepan for two minutes and then drain. To serve, place a portion of tartare in the center of each plate and top with an arrangement of potato wafers. Decorate the plate with a langoustine head and tail fin. Finally, pour over the soured cream sauce.

Plaice à

Preparation time: 30 minutes
Cooking time: 10 minutes
Difficulty: ☆

Serves four

1 plaice, 1 1/2 lb / 700 g
1/2 lb / 200 g green beans
8 young turnips
8 spring onions
2 artichokes
2 bunches of radishes

1 head lettuce, such as Bibb or Boston
1 lemon
1/4 cup / 60 ml olive oil
1 cup / 250 ml white wine
1 tbsp / 15 g butter
1 bunch of chervil
salt, pepper to taste

This appetizer *à la jardinière*, which simply means "with vegetables" contains many fresh and crunchy examples: carrots, turnips, green beans, and other young seasonal vegetables. Combined with a classic olive oil vinaigrette, they form an aromatic and tasty mixture with which to fill the lettuce.

Like many vegetables, lettuce was not initially eaten fresh, but, until the time of Louis XVI, cooked before consumption. Only later was it recognized for its nutritional benefits, such as a high vitamin A and minerals content. Now considered an important component of a healthy diet, fresh and crunchy lettuce should be washed thoroughly several times. The final time, it should be washed with water laced with vinegar to remove the fertilizer with which it is, unfortunately, often treated. Afterwards, dry it by dabbing carefully with a kitchen towel, so as not to break the leaves.

The artichokes combine well with the spring vegetables. Adding white wine prevents their pale flesh from oxidizing: a bit less acid than lemon juice, wine is a good alternative to the normal sprinkling of lemon juice used to keep the artichoke from browning.

Finally, a word about the plaice, a flat fish that belongs to the flounder family: choose a thick piece to fillet with firm flesh and skin that is still firmly attached to the flesh – a sure sign of freshness. Serve this appetizer either chilled or at room temperature.

1. Have the fishmonger fillet the plaice. Cut the fillets into even strips and set aside. Strip the artichokes of everything, from leaves to chokes, until only the hearts remain; quarter these and cook them in a mixture of olive oil, water, and white wine.

2. Blanch the green beans in boiling salted water and then rinse in cold water. Peel the spring onions and turnips; slice the turnips and radishes; set aside. Wash the lettuce well. Prepare a vinaigrette with olive oil and lemon juice.

la Jardinière

3. Thinly slice the spring onions and cook with the artichoke hearts. Briefly fry the strips of plaice, sprinkle with vinaigrette, and toss well.

4. Shape a bowl out of the lettuce leaves and place one on each plate. To prepare the filling, drain the cooked vegetables and add the strips of plaice, sliced turnips, and radish. Toss with the remaining vinaigrette. Fill the lettuce bowls with this mixture, and decorate with chervil leaves.

Smoked Salmon and

Preparation time: 30 minutes
Cooking time: 10 minutes
Difficulty: ☆

Serves four

16 large langoustines
1 lb / 450 g fresh salmon fillet
2 bunches of asparagus
1 pink grapefruit
1 bunch of chervil
1 bunch of chives

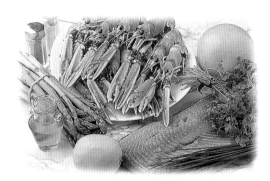

For the dressing:
juice of 1 lemon
¹/₂ cup / 125 ml olive oil
salt, pepper to taste

While smoking food was originally done for preservation purposes, today this method is used to impart a special flavor to food. The smoking process can span from a few minutes in a pan in the oven to several days in a smokehouse, depending on the desired effect. In this case, a few minutes will suffice (see earlier smoking recipes for more information), lending the salmon and langoustines an intensified, but not altered, aroma.

Only use absolutely fresh langoustines, which should be large, translucent and have shiny eyes. The shellfish, caught in the Mediterranean and the Atlantic, are available year round. Since smoking the langoustines does not actually cook them, the tails should be steamed for a minute or two.

The salmon adds a colorful visual element to this dish and is easy to prepare if not too thinly sliced into its sixteen slices.

These should be thick enough that they don't disintegrate during smoking. Our chef, Joël Roy, does not hide his preference for Scottish salmon, whether fresh from the river or from a salmon farm, he considers it by far the best. And like the langoustines, the fish should be absolutely fresh.

Chef Roy is particularly fond of asparagus as an accompaniment, be it the green, white, or violet variety. The spears, depending on their thickness, are cooked in salted water for between four and six minutes, then immediately rinsed in cold water to arrest the cooking process. A final tip for the olive oil and lemon dressing: only add the chopped chive at the last moment, otherwise it will be attacked by the acidic lemon juice and lose its aroma.

1. Shell the langoustines, separate the tails and heads, and then steam the tails for two minutes. Slice the salmon fillet into 16 slices.

2. Wrap the langoustines in the salmon slices and fasten with wooden toothpicks. Prepare the dressing with lemon juice, olive oil, salt, and pepper.

Langoustines in an Asparagus Fan

3. Smoke the langoustines and salmon rolls for five minutes and then season with a touch of pink grapefruit juice. Peel and trim the asparagus and cook for about five minutes in salted water.

4. To serve, fan out five spears of asparagus on each plate and place a langoustines and salmon roll between each asparagus spear. Stir the chives into the dressing and season the dish. Garnish with chervil leaves.

Steamed King Prawns with

Preparation time: 2 hours,
                             30 minutes
Cooking time: 40 minutes
Difficulty: ☆

Serves four

16 king (or large) prawns
1 pig's trotter
3 bunches of green asparagus
1 bunch of baby carrots
1 shallot

1 onion
1 bunch of parsley
$1/8$ lb / 50 g butter
1 quart / 1 l veal stock
2 cups / 500 ml port
1 cup / 250 ml olive oil
salt, pepper to taste

To garnish:
1 lb / 450 g small onions
1 bunch of arugula

Tangy and spicy arugula has been popular since the Romans; its flavor has been described as reminiscent both of dried fruit and wild radish leaves. Called rocket in Europe – *rocchetta* in Italian and *roquette* in French – it belongs to the mustard family, and came to the Mediterranean from southern and central Europe. Its pungent intensity combines well with the strong flavor of the giant prawns, who are able to "tame" the arugula's sharp flavor enough to balance it.

The prawns most Europeans know come from the Mediterranean: deep pink in color, they have flesh that tastes different from that of shrimps and are smaller than langoustines. Their fleshy tail is very firm and quite flavorful, and shelling them can be a bit tricky. The crusteacean can be prepared in many different ways: cooked briefly in boiling water, grilled, steamed, or in true Catalan fashion, fried with garlic and parsley.

Small green asparagus (you need thirty-two spears for this dish) is the perfect partner for king prawns. Wild asparagus, which is sometimes still found in the forests, would be ideal. The woody stalks should be trimmed off and the tips cooked very briefly so they remain crisp. Unfortunately, in Europe, small green asparagus is usually available for only about four weeks a year, beginning in mid-June, and mostly in southern regions. Hothouse asparagus, however, is available year round, and, due to regional farming, the growing season in the United States has been extended from February into the summertime. But, if for some reason you cannot get your hands on green asparagus, young leeks could be an interesting alternative.

1. Cook the pig's trotter with a carrot and an onion for two hours. Take out the trotter and add a sliced carrot and parsley to the water, bring to a boil and cook the prawns for three to four minutes in that liquid. Trim the meat off of the trotter bone and chop into small dice. Melt the small onions for about 30 minutes in olive oil over low heat.

2. Cook the remaining carrots al dente. Peel and trim the asparagus, cook in boiling water, and immediately rinse in cold water. Melt a little butter in a frying pan, add olive oil, and gently fry the asparagus and carrots.

Pig's Trotter and Asparagus

3. Shell the prawns and remove their intestinal veins. Chop the shallot. Fry the shallot with port in a frying pan and reduce, then add the veal stock and the diced meat.

4. Reduce once more, remove the meat from the heat and fold in the remaining butter. To serve, arrange the meat and stock decoratively on the plates. Dress the arugula, place in the center of the plates, and arrange the prawns around it. Garnish with baby carrots and melted onions.

Preparation time: 20 minutes
Cooking time: 40 minutes
Difficulty: ★★

Serves four

5 small artichokes
1 large bunch of Swiss chard
2 cloves of garlic
2 shallots
1 egg
1 egg yolk
⅝ cup / 150 g ricotta

scant ¼ lb / 90 g Parmesan
1 tbsp / 15 ml truffle juice
1 cup / 250 ml extra virgin olive oil
¼ lb / 100 g mixed lettuce
half a bunch of marjoram
salt, pepper to taste

For the dough:
½ cup / 125 g plus 1 tbsp flour
⅛ cup / 20 ml olive oil
scant ½ cup / 100 ml water
a pinch of salt

Our chef, the Italian Ezio Santin, usually serves this affectionately named tart for his family, albeit a much larger version than the appetizer tarts he presents here. The latter, which have to be smaller to suit gastronomic requirements, are nevertheless just as delicious as the large-sized model. The dish is a specialty from the Ligurian coast, a fertile region in northwestern Italy that is bordered by France and Tuscany. Rich in local produce, the area yields, for example, the thorny artichoke, which is reminiscent of the artichoke's ancestor, the thistle. Though certainly hard to find in American markets, if you find them, by all means buy them all. For the thorny artichoke, available in Italy from November through March, is much-loved for its frail delicacy. Just like its French counterpart, it is cleaned with lemon water before preparation.

Swiss chard, from the beet family, is a low-calorie vegetable that contains a lot of iron and vitamins A and C; it is abun-

dantly cultivated in Liguria. Chard's subtle iodine flavor will meld well with both the Parmesan in the tart, and the olive oil in which the artichokes are fried.

Of the two quintessential Italian cheeses presented in this recipe, the ricotta is used merely to bind the filling of the tart. A fresh, white cream cheese made with sheep's milk, ricotta remains relatively compact when cut, and, when combined with marjoram, one has a classic hallmark of Ligurian cuisine. As for the Parmesan, Chef Santin recommends the *Grana padano* variety from northern Italy with its complex flavor; it is still made by hand and matures in the dairy for eighteen months. Occasionally, it is available in high-end American markets, but if not, look for any incomparable Parmigiano Reggiano.

1. Wash the Swiss chard well and separate the leaves. In a saucepan, heat a quartered clove of garlic in olive oil. When the oil is hot, add the Swiss chard and toss with a fork for three to four minutes, then remove from the saucepan. Retain the cooking liquid and coarsely chop the Swiss chard.

2. Clean the artichokes, pluck the leaves, quarter, remove the choke and halve the quarters. Peel and finely chop the shallots and sweat with a clove of garlic and 5 tbsp / 75 ml of olive oil in a frying pan. Add the artichokes and truffle juice. Season with salt and pepper, continue cooking for eight minutes, then remove the clove of garlic.

Artichoke Tart

3. Fold in the ricotta and continue cooking. Chop the marjoram. Remove from the heat and stir in the Swiss chard, Parmesan, chopped marjoram, the whole egg and the egg yolk. Combine this mixture with the Swiss chard's cooking liquid and mix well. Season with salt and pepper. Prepare the dough.

4. Take four round earthenware forms and line their bases with thin layers of dough, leaving plenty to overlap the edges. Fill and close with the overlapping dough, using any extra as a cap over the top of the tart. Bake in the oven for 35–40 minutes until brown and crisp. Remove from the oven and leave to cool. Serve, if desired, with a small salad tossed in vinaigrette, topped with shaved Parmesan.

Tomato-eggplant terrine

Preparation time: 10 minutes
Chilling time: 2 hours
Cooking time: 4 minutes
Difficulty: ✳

Serves four

3 small eggplants
1¼ lbs / 600 g tomatoes
1 cup / 100 ml extra virgin olive oil
¾ cup / 200 g vegetable aspic
1 bunch of flowering basil
salt, pepper to taste

This cold appetizer from chef Nadia Santini, with its fresh ingredients such as tomatoes, eggplant, and basil, will be particularly welcome in summer. Ripe and tasty tomatoes are crucial for its success. Choose tomatoes that are deep red. Once scorned superstitiously as a poisonous fruit, it was then adopted in earnest by the French, who call them "love apples," as do the Italians, who gave them the name *pomodoro*. To maintain the integrity of the tomato's delicate pulp, it should not be blanched. Instead, though it is, alas, a little harder to peel raw tomatoes with a knife, it is worth it, since this way consistency and intense flavor will not be impaired at all.

The eggplants should be long rather than round, as they will be used in long strips to line the terrine. Long eggplants also con-

tain fewer seeds and are easier to cut into even strips that will not split or break during baking. When lining the terrine with the eggplant, the strips should not only overlap beyond the edge of the terrine, but they should also overlap each other for increased stability.

Basil blossoms and the extra virgin oil lend this dish a refined touch. Extra virgin olive oil, still produced using traditional methods, neutralizes the tomatoes' natural acidity and slightly emulsifies the terrine. Olive oil is an indispensable ingredient in Italian cooking, and comes in many grades; the extra-virgin kind is called "green gold" by the Italians.

1. Peel the eggplants and slice lengthwise. Heat half of the olive oil in a non-stick frying pan and fry the eggplant strips in batches (since they won't all fit in the pan). Season and leave to dry on a kitchen cloth.

2. Line a terrine form with the eggplant strips; they must overlap each other as well as lay over the edge of the terrine. Peel the tomatoes with a sharp knife, discard the juice and seeds. Bring water to a boil in a casserole and dissolve the vegetable aspic in it.

with Basil Blossoms

3. Fill the terrine form with the tomatoes. Add the aspic and close the terrine with the overlapping eggplant. Separate the edges of the terrine slightly with a spoon so the jelly is distributed evenly throughout. Chill for two hours.

4. Remove the terrine from the refrigerator. Invert and cut into $^1/_2$ in / 1 cm slices. To serve, place a slice in the middle of each plate, surround with a light pool of olive oil and garnish with basil flowers.

Preparation time: 30 minutes
Marinating time: 3–4 hours
Cooking time: 20 minutes
Difficulty: ✲

Serves four

2 lbs / 1 kg monkfish tail
¹/₂ lb / 250 g pink shrimp
1 cup / 200 g mixed lettuce leaves (optional)
half a bunch of chervil
salt, pepper to taste

For the vegetables
Assorted seasonal vegetables: peas, green
    beans, turnips, zucchini, tomatoes
¹/₄ cup / 50 ml vinaigrette or mayonnaise
    (see basic recipes)

For the marinade:
generous cup / 300 ml whole milk
¹/₂ tbsp / 10 g sweet paprika
¹/₂ tbsp / 10 g black peppercorns

Cooked, the meat of monkfish, with its incomparable consistency, is not dissimilar to langoustines in appearance or taste. But, as the fish is not particularly attractive, with thick, gray skin, plenty of scales and an easy-to-remove backbone, fishmongers often sell the tail section only. Served with a selection of seasonal vegetables and shrimps, the monkfish, prepared with care, will be transformed into an appetizing prelude to a festive summer meal. It's not at all uncommon in Portuguese cuisine: Portuguese fishermen used to make a sort of hot pot with it, called *cozido*.

The completely skinned monkfish fillet must be tied with string until it looks like a sausage; this precaution will make for easier slicing later. Dose the paprika carefully when adding it to the ingredients and when working it into the fish to give it that special coloring. On no account must hot paprika or cayenne pepper be used, as they are both too hot for this dish.

1. Wash and skin the monkfish thoroughly; if there are bones, only use the fillet. Tie into a tight "sausage" with string.

2. Prepare a marinade with milk, the paprika, pepper, and salt. Marinate the monkfish for three to four hours; afterwards, rub the fish on all sides with the paprika.

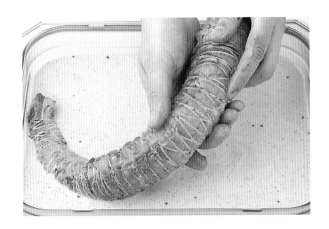

Monkfish Salad

3. Transfer the fish, including the marinade, to a casserole, bring the contents to a boil and leave to simmer for 20 minutes. Meanwhile, prepare and cook the shrimp in the usual way.

4. Remove the monkfish from the cooking liquid, set aside to dry on a kitchen towel and then cut into $1/4$ in / $1/2$ cm slices. Wash, trim, and lightly cook the seasonal vegetables. To serve, arrange a few monkfish slices and a few shrimps on each plate, accompanied by the cold salad of seasonal vegetables dressed with vinaigrette or mayonnaise.

Preparation time: 20 minutes
Cooking time: 25 minutes
Difficulty: ☆

Serves four

4 crabs, 1¹/₄ lb / 600 g each
2 eggs
2 gherkin pickles
2 tsp / 10 ml whiskey
1 tsp / 10 g custard
1 bunch of flat-leafed parsley
1 pimento
salt to taste

For the crab broth:
1 onion stuck with cloves
¹/₄ cup / 50 ml white wine
1 bunch of parsley
1 tsp / 5 g peppercorns
salt to taste

Fishing forms an integral part of Portuguese life, as Portugal's coastline is some 340 miles / 547 kilometers long with waters that yield prime quality fish and seafood in abundance. It is therefore not surprising that a large part of Portuguese cuisine is dedicated to seafood, and that the Portuguese know many methods for preparing the myriad crab varieties that populate Portugal's coast.

Like all crab species, the common crab is essentially a ten-legged shellfish with an underdeveloped tail. It is characterized by the lovely color of its meat when fried, by the oval shape of its shell, and by the enormous front claws, the meat of which is a particular delicacy. In reality the crab leads a very dull life, just sitting on the ocean floor and waiting for its prey, hardly bothering to move at all. When the prey is close enough, the crab throws itself upon the unsuspecting creature, having, usu-

ally, a distinct advantage on account of its weight and the large claws. The largest crabs, at home in French and British coastal waters, can be as heavy as twelve pounds / six kilograms. This recipe, from Chef Maria Santos Gomes, calls for much smaller fare.

Our chef is particularly partial to the rich, creamy area directly beneath the lower shell, and to the coral-rich ovaries in a female crab, which are used to form the basis of many sauces because of their subtle flavor. The crab meat is complemented by the tart pickle, which the British have been producing since the seventeenth century. You can make pickle yourself and store it for up to three months, or look for high-quality examples at your market. The mélange of flavors in this appetizer is rounded out with a dash of whisky.

1. Cook the crab for around 25 minutes in salted water along with the peppercorns, parsley, the onion stuck with cloves, and the white wine. Leave to cool in the cooking liquid. Afterwards, remove the legs and shell. Retain the front claws for decoration.

2. Extract the crab meat and the coral, chop, and mix with the creamy substance from the crab belly.

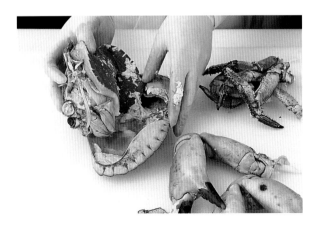

Stuffed Crab

3. Hard-boil the eggs. Add the pickles, whiskey, custard, pimento, and half a chopped hard-boiled egg. Adjust seasoning to taste.

4. Mix everything carefully. Fill the crab shells with this mixture and garnish with the remaining chopped hard-boiled egg and a center strip of parsley. Arrange on the plates with the front claws on either side.

Greek Platter

Preparation time: 1 hour 30 minutes
Cooking time: 20 minutes
Soaking time: 12 hours
Difficulty: ★★

Serves four

For the taramasalata:
1 oz / 20 g smoked cod roe
2 potatoes (to yield 3 tbsp / 40 g mashed)
1 onion (to yield 1 tbsp / 10 g chopped)
2 tbsp / 30 ml olive oil
1 lemon
1/2 cup / 125 ml white vinegar

For the tzatziki:
1 cucumber (to yield 1 tbsp / 12 g chopped)
2 tbsp / 20 g strained Greek yogurt

2 tsp / 10 ml olive oil
1 clove of garlic (to yield 1/2 tbsp / 5 g chopped)
2 tsp / 10 ml vinegar
salt and pepper

For the eggplant salad:
1/2 eggplant (to yield 2 tbsp / 20 g chopped), 1/2 onion (to yield 1 tbsp / 10 g chopped), 1/4 red pepper, 1/4 green pepper
juice of 1 lemon
2 cloves of garlic
1/2 cup / 125 g mayonnaise (see basic recipes)
salt, pepper to taste

For the gigantes:
1 oz / 30 g dry beans
1/2 onion (to yield 1 tbsp / 10 g chopped)
1 clove of garlic (to yield 1/2 tbsp / 5 g chopped)
1 tomato (to yield 2 tbsp / 30 g purée)
1 tbsp / 15 g tomato paste
1 bunch of parsley
salt, pepper to taste

Greece's prime status in the history of the Mediterranean region has also helped its cuisine gain a leading role in that part of the world. Created from several cultures, some going back to ancient history, Greek cuisine encapsulates a culinary panorama, with many contrasts. Such diversity is manifested in this platter of appetizers by chef Nikolaos Sarantos. With its many ingredients – some rich and some delicate – it could almost be regarded as a main course in itself.

Taramasalata is well known in Germany and France; there is a French Mediterranean version called *poutargue*. Here, it is served in dollops and, unlike the store-bought version, is white. The smoked cod roe that forms taramasalata's base is naturally white, and is dyed a deceptive pink for commercial use. Stored in a chilled environment for several months, the cod roe is then whisked with mayonnaise and olive oil and enhanced with garlic to make this ambrosia-like concoction.

Chilled tzatziki, or yogurt sauce with cucumber, provides the palate with a refreshing break. To make it, a strong-flavored yogurt is strained over a few days until only a concentrated mass is left. The cucumber is left in a bed of coarse sea salt for an hour or so, so that it releases all its water; thus the tzatziki will become a little firmer. The eggplant, which you should buy on the thick side, with a shiny skin, will be marinated the same way. In Greece, a classic side dish is eggplant filled with feta cheese, and grilled until soft.

The large white beans are available in most Greek food markets, and are used in soups, salads and vegetable mixtures, and served hot or cold. Completing the picture are the anchovies, sardines and olives used as a garnish – and, above all, do not forget to serve this appetizer with the obligatory Greek drink, ouzo.

1. To prepare the taramasalata: cook and mash the potatoes (you need about three tablespoons); chop the onion; juice the lemon. In a bowl, mix together the cod roe, potato, onion, and lemon juice, whisking – as you would a mayonnaise – with olive oil and vinegar.

2. To prepare the tzatziki, mix cucumber with vinegar and salt and leave to infuse for one hour. Drain, and mix well with the strained yogurt, olive oil, chopped garlic, and vinegar.

# of Appetizers

3. Roast the eggplant in the oven and then dice finely. Chop the onion, thinly slice the green and red peppers and mix all with mayonnaise, lemon juice, and chopped garlic.

4. To prepare the gigantes, soak the beans in water overnight. Chop the onion and garlic; puree the tomatoes. Heat, add the soaked beans, and cover with water. Add parsley, salt, and tomato paste. Cook in the oven for 20 minutes. To serve, arrange the different appetizers on a plate and garnish with anchovies, sardines and, to add even more variety, feta cheese and squid tentacles.

Shrimp Dolmas with a

Preparation time: 15 minutes
Cooking time: 15 minutes
Difficulty: ★★

Serves four

24 vine leaves
$^1/_2$ / 100 g cup short-grain rice
20 shrimp
8 crayfish (optional)
2 egg yolks
1 tbsp / 15 g butter
$^1/_4$ cup / 50 ml cream

2 cups / 500 ml fish broth
$^1/_4$ cup / 50 ml ouzo
$^1/_2$ cup / 100 ml white wine
$^1/_2$ cup / 100 ml vegetable oil
half a bunch of dill
juice of 1 lemon
salt, pepper to taste

For the filling:
2 carrots (to yield $^1/_4$ cup/ 50 g)
2 zucchini (to yield $^1/_4$ cup / 50 g)
2 leeks (to yield $^1/_4$ cup / 50 g)
1 onion (to yield $^1/_4$ cup / 50 g chopped)

Vine leaves are a traditional ingredient of Greek cuisine. But they are so easy to prepare that they have become popular all over Europe. A vine leaf filling based on rice can be varied almost infinitely if a few basic rules are observed. If fresh, the vine leaves should first be blanched in boiling salt water to make them flexible. If no fresh vine leaves are available, choose some that have been marinated in salt brine: these will have to be thoroughly soaked in water before they can be used. Cover the dolmas with a plate during cooking to prevent them splitting, an action caused by the expansion of the rice grains inside. Use light colored short-grain rice, as it will cook quickly.

The individual ingredients of the filling should be cooked separately, as all require different cooking times; for example, if you cooked the shrimps with the rice they would wind up overcooked, the meat tough. Therefore the filling should only be mixed at the end, immediately after the shrimps have cooked just long enough to become soft. There is a tried and true trick for rolling the dolmas: fold the edges of the vine leaf inwards, holding the filling down with your fingers while rolling up the leaf lengthwise, as if you were hand-rolling a cigarette.

The aniseed flavor of Greece's national drink, ouzo, underscores the shrimps' aroma and rounds off the balance of flavors in this appetizer. And, if you have a surplus of crayfish, use two of them on each plate as a garnish, as pictured here.

1. Blanch the vine leaves in salted water. Sweat the chopped vegetables for the filling in butter. Add the rice and (chopped) dill, mix gently, and add salt to taste. Pour over the fish broth, bring to a boil, and leave to simmer. Dice eight shrimps, briefly fry in butter, add the white wine, mix with the rice and finally stir in half of the ouzo.

2. To make the dolmas, drop a tablespoon of filling onto each vine leaf and roll up the leaf. Line the base of a casserole with vine leaves, place the dolmas in the casserole, and cover with vine leaves.

Butter, Lemon and Ouzo Sauce

3. Add a little broth, oil and the remaining ouzo. Cover with a plate (to prevent the vine leaves from splitting) and cook for about ten minutes.

4. To prepare the sauce, reduce the fish broth, add cream and lemon juice, and reduce further. Remove from the heat, add the egg yolks and fold in the butter. Strain, add chopped dill and a dash of ouzo, and adjust seasoning to taste. Pour the sauce on the plates, arrange the dolmas, and garnish with julienned zucchini, sprigs of dill, and, if you prefer, two cooked crayfish per plate.

Bavarian Cream with

Preparation time: 3 hours
Cooking time: 1 hour
Cooling time: 3 hours
Difficulty: ★★★

Serves four

12 crayfish (about ¹/₄ lb / 100–120 g each)
12 violet artichokes
1 each large artichoke, tomato, shallot, clove
    of garlic
2 button mushrooms
1 lemon
12 green olives, 30 black olives
¹/₂ cup each vermouth (such as Noilly Prat),
    ¹/₂ cup white wine
1 cup / 200 ml chicken stock
1¹/₂ cups olive oil (1 cup for deep-frying)
¹/₃ cup / 80 ml cream

2 sheets of gelatin
1 sprig each of thyme, rosemary
¹/₂ cup flour
1 bunch of parsley
salt, pepper to taste

For the shrimp broth:
¹/₂ lb / 250 g assorted vegetables for making
    stock
1 tsp / 5 g cumin
1 sprig of dill
salt, pepper to taste

For the artichoke mousse:
2 each button mushrooms, shallots
¹/₂ stalk of leek
2 sticks of celery
1 bunch of cilantro
1 sprig of parsley

For the vinaigrette:
¹/₂ cup / 125 ml red wine vinegar
¹/₄ cup / 50 ml Madeira
¹/₂ cup / 125 ml olive oil

Bavarian cream is really a pudding made with heavy cream, milk, and fruit. Here, our chef, Fritz Schilling, has transformed it into a savory sauce to combine with artichokes. Incidentally, the artichokes' slightly sweet aftertaste is due to a substance in the vegetable closely related to dextrose called inulin. Chef Schilling uses a large, fleshy Brittany artichoke for the sliced artichoke hearts (or just choose a very large globe artichoke), and the small violet ones from Provence (look for small, purple artichokes as an alternative) for the puree.

Schilling prefers to use olive oil from the first cold pressing, as it is ideal for cooking vegetables and lends the dish a Mediter-

ranean note. Adding crayfish to this dish would be impossible if one were limited to German or northern European crayfish, since they are almost extinct. Germans use imported crayfish instead, whose quality is still excellent.

Reducing the stock and getting the right dose of gelatin are crucial steps when preparing the Bavarian cream: at all cost, avoid making it stale and heavy. Chilling the cream well in advance will leave you with enough time for any necessary modifications, such as adding a little more chicken stock if it tastes too gelatinous.

1. Clean the artichokes, and set the large one and two small ones aside. Quarter the remaining artichokes, sweat with the vegetables intended for the artichoke puree in olive oil, and then stir in the chicken stock. Add the vermouth, white wine, and herbs, and reduce. Puree in the blender, strain, and mix with olive oil. Add a bit of lemon juice and one sheet of gelatin. Leave to cool, then fold in the cream.

2. Sweat the chopped shallots, parsley, and mushrooms and the pitted green olives in oil, cook a little further, and puree in the blender. Add half a pre-soaked sheet of gelatin. Spread the mixture on to a flat board or tray and chill. Once it has set, cut out four discs of 1¹/₄ in / 3 cm in diameter.

Artichokes and Crayfish

3. Fill four round forms up to a quarter full with the artichoke mousse, place a cut-out artichoke disc on top, and fill almost to the top with more mousse. Chop the remaining two small artichoke hearts, and sweat with the crushed garlic, a sprig of thyme, and rosemary, with the lid closed. Slice the large artichoke heart, drain, roll in flour, and deep-fry in olive oil.

4. Cook the crayfish in the broth. Prepare a vinaigrette with red wine vinegar, Madeira, and olive oil, add the peeled and chopped tomato and chopped black olives. Mix the vinaigrette with half a pre-soaked sheet of gelatin, stir well, then top up the round forms with this vinaigrette. To serve, place one round portion of Bavarian cream along with half an artichoke, three shrimps and a little deep-fried artichoke on each plate.

Carpaccio of John Dory and

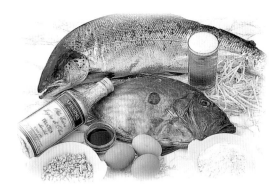

Preparation time: 45 minutes
Cooking time: 10 minutes
Sitting time: 1 hour
Difficulty: *

Serves four

1 salmon fillet, 1 lb / 500 g
1 John Dory fillet, 1¹/₂ lb / 800 g
¹/₈ lb / 50 g hop shoots (see below)
scant ¹/₄ cup / 100 g flour
1 bunch of tarragon
salt, pepper to taste

For the blini dough:
1 egg
1 egg white
¹/₂ tbsp / 15 g yeast
¹/₂ cup / 100 ml dark beer

For the balsamic vinaigrette:
(see basic recipes)

John Dory, so named not for any person but an English corruption of one of its French nicknames, *jean-doré*, is also called *saint-pierre* in France, as the spots on its sides are believed to be St. Peter's fingerprints, made when he picked up the fish to pay for his debt to the Romans. The flatfish is closely related to the plaice and, with its bony head and heavy skeleton, produces a lot of waste when it is prepared. But its subtle and soft flesh more than compensates: so well, in fact, that John Dory is often eaten raw, making it ideal for *carpaccio*.

Both the salmon and the John Dory should ideally be wild and as fresh as possible; the latter with red flesh and a corresponding tangy flavor. Since, however, John Dory is often hard to find outside of Europe, you may substitute a porgy for it instead. Before flattening the fillets with a dough roller, our

chefs, Jean and Jean-Yves Schillinger, recommend you grease the plastic wrap that covers the fish with a generous coating of oil.

The accompaniment is typical Alsatian, but probably not available anywhere else: the fresh hop shoots, consumed in the fall, are almost impossible to find in European markets, let alone American ones, so they may be replaced with basil sprouts (whose flavor, unfortunately, simply won't compare). If dark beer is not to your taste, you may use a light beer (light in color, not alcohol content) instead.

Finally, the blini are made with egg whites that have been whisked to near-stiffness, and the blini dough should be allowed to rest for one hour at room temperature.

1. Sift the flour and mix with salt, pepper, yeast, beer, and egg in a bowl. Beat the egg white until almost stiff and fold in. Leave to rest for 30 minutes.

2. Fillet the John Dory, remove the bones, and cut into thin slices (about an ¹/₈ in / 2 mm). Sandwich the salmon and John Dory fillets between two sheets of oiled plastic wrap and flatten; chill in the freezer for about 20 minutes, then cut into the desired shape.

Salmon with Hop Shoots and Blini

3. Bake the blini dough in a buttered frying pan for ten minutes over medium heat. Thoroughly wash and then blanch the hop shoots or sprouts. Prepare a classic vinaigrette with olive oil, balsamic vinegar, salt, and pepper.

4. To serve, arrange the salmon and John Dory carpaccio on the plates, salt and pepper, and sprinkle with the vinaigrette. Garnish with individual sprouts and tarragon leaves; serve the blini on the side.

Cucumber Ring with

Preparation time: 30 minutes
Marinating time: 10 minutes
Difficulty: ✶

Serves four

16 langoustines
1 cucumber
4 quail eggs
salt, pepper to taste

For the langoustine marinade:
2 ³/₄ oz / 80 g caviar (Ossetra or Sevruga)
2 egg yolks
1 bunch of chives
1 tbsp / 10 ml sherry vinegar
¹/₄ cup / 60 ml olive oil
1 tbsp / 10 ml soy sauce

Cucumber, a member of the pumpkin family, was first discovered three thousand years ago at the foot of the Himalayas. The local population called it *soukasa* and consumed it during summer festivities. The cucumber was also popular in antiquity, when it was seasoned with honey to render it less bitter. Today it is known for its fresh taste, and low-calorie nutritiousness. The perfect cucumber should be an even, deep green and very firm. The pale green pulp is crunchy and contains a great percentage of water. When thinly sliced, it becomes translucent.

Live langoustines are, of course, the freshest, though since they do not survive for long out of water, they are often sold very slightly cooked. Either way, they should be prepared straight away, as their flesh becomes tough when stored for too long.

The claws look threatening but are quite harmless, unlike, for instance, the claw of a lobster or crayfish.

To make an attractive ring of cucumbers, you will need two forms: one for the inside and one for the outside, and, if possible, a slicer. The ring can be made in advance and stored in the refrigerator wrapped in foil, but if this is the case, add the vinaigrette later. As the vinegar will start breaking down the cucumber's flavor if contact is prolonged, the dressing must always be added during the final stage.

To decorate this summer appetizer, choose either Sevruga or Ossetra caviar. Only a small amount is required, and since it is not an essential ingredient, there is no reason to splurge for the most expensive – Beluga – variety.

1. Slice the cucumber into thin and even rounds. Place a large round form on a plate, form the cucumber ring inside this form, and then place a second, smaller ring form in the center of the plate, using it to trim the inside edge of the cucumber ring to make it look neat. Remove any excess cucumber juice.

2. Shell the langoustines, remove the intestines, trim off the heads, and wash and cut the resulting tail pieces into thin strips. Transfer into a bowl.

Marinated Langoustines

3. Salt and pepper the langoustines. Add the egg yolks, olive oil, sherry vinegar, and soy sauce. Mix carefully.

4. Finally, chop the chives; stir into the langoustine mixture along with the caviar. Marinate for ten minutes. Fill the center of each cucumber ring with the langoustine mixture. Brush the cucumber slices with olive oil, and garnish the center with the yolk of a quail egg.

Exotic Fruit Basket

Preparation time: 15 minutes
Cooking time: 6 minutes
Difficulty: ✫

Serves four

1 pineapple
1 cantaloupe
2 papayas
2 egg yolks
1 cup red wine or port
2 cups / 500 ml whipping cream
1 tsp five-spice powder

Optional:
¹/₄ lb / 100 g raspberries
¹/₄ lb / 100 g strawberries

During their sea voyage across the oceans, Rudolf Sodamin and Jonathan Wicks, the two head chefs of the luxury cruise liner *QE II*, go on shore at every port of call to find the best local produce for their kitchen. Thus they create their own menus with an amazing array of exotic food, combining new methods with traditional ingredients. This fruit basket is one such creation – a souvenir of the Caribbean that is seasoned with a mixture of Asian spices. Five-spice powder, often available in Asian markets, is usually comprised of cloves, fennel seed, star anise, cinnamon, and hot (szechuan) peppercorns.

Given the luxury, our chefs prefer pineapples from Hawaii, but pineapples from the Antilles or Réunion are also excellent, if a bit smaller. The cantaloupe is extremely refreshing and contains a lot of fructose, minerals, and even beta-carotene. The papaya is related to the melon, and is sometimes called "tropical melon." If you want to use papaya for a spicy dish, use fruit that are still very green and firm as opposed to fruit that are ripening to their mature yellow color. The papaya we use here is more towards the latter stage, contains more fructose and thus more suitable for sweet dishes. If papayas are unavailable, you may substitute ripe avocados instead.

Of course, all the fruit should be chopped or cut at the last minute as, due to the oxidation that will occur the minute they come in contact with air, they will turn brown quickly and lose their flavor. The zabaglione sauce should also be made towards the end; whisk it constantly, especially when removing it from the bain-marie. This appetizer can be served all year round, as the ingredients are available throughout the year.

1. Cut the pineapple in half crossways. Slice, and cut out the center of each slice with a round cutter. Set aside.

2. Halve the melon and papaya and scoop out two dozen small fruit balls. Chill along with the pineapple.

with Asian Spices

3. Reduce the port to one-eighth of its volume. Stir in the egg yolks, five-spice powder and cream. Transfer the mixture to a bowl and place in a bain-marie, whisking constantly. Bring the bain-marie to a boil, cook from four to six minutes, and continue to whisk constantly until the zabaglione is nice and thick.

4. Trim the outer part of the cut-out pineapple slice to use for the decoration. Place a pour of zabaglione in the middle of each plate and a pineapple slice on top; heap the fruit balls on top of the pineapple slice. Pour a little more zabaglione on and around the fruit. Garnish with berries if you wish, and the outer part of the pineapple slice, laid over like an archway. Serve immediately.

Butterfly of Scottish

Preparation time: 10 minutes
Difficulty: ✫

Serves four

generous ³/₄ lb / 400 g Scottish smoked
    salmon
4 slices of bread (to toast)
1 lemon
¹/₈ lb / 50 g horseradish root
1 red onion
1 egg
¹/₂ cup / 100 ml soured milk
1 head of frisée
1 bunch of chives
1 bunch of flat-leafed parsley
salt, fresh-ground pepper to taste

This salmon recipe was created in honor of Queen Elizabeth II when she was attending a banquet with six hundred guests on the luxury cruise liner *QE II*. An international team of chefs was on hand to create a memorable meal for the queen's visit. One of the head chefs, of Malaysian origin, created this butterfly of smoked salmon. According to accounts of the feast, Her Majesty enjoyed both the Scottish and Norwegian salmon, though the Norwegian salmon, it was generally thought, was a bit on the lean side.

Pick a salmon with light-colored meat – the darker color is a result of its having been smoked a very long time. The consistency of the flesh should be firm, and the fish should still be raw: the smoking process should never be allowed to jump-start the cooking process. This ensures that the unique flavor of this fish will be unimpaired, provided that the salmon is not seasoned too much in later stages. After having rounded the edges against the direction of the grain, slice the salmon carefully with a sharp knife.

Horseradish has many benefits and an extremely strong aroma. It should, therefore, be used sparingly or it will dominate the salmon. If you wish, you can substitute horseradish root with a home-made chive cream.

For a little variety, the salmon could perhaps be marinated in salt and sugar, and finely chopped peppers, laced with ground pepper, might be served on the side.

1. Cut the smoked salmon fillet in half lengthwise. Trim the two halves of salmon, rounding off the edges.

2. Cut the fillets into very thin slices, so that the salmon will yield six slices per person (or two dozen slices). Grate the horseradish root. Mix the soured milk with a pinch of horseradish and season.

Smoked Salmon

3. For the garnish, hard-boil the egg. Finely chop the parsley, red onion, chives, and the egg. Wash the frisée and pluck into small flowers.

4. To serve, arrange six slices of salmon in the shape of a butterfly on each plate. Place a tablespoon of soured cream in the middle and mound the garnish on top. Arrange two chive tubes as abstracted antennae, and garnish with frisée leaves and a sprinkling of a few parsley leaves. Serve with hot toast and lemon slices.

Herb Fritters with

Preparation time: *1 hour*
Cooking time: *15 minutes*
Cooling time: *12 hours*
Difficulty: *✳*

Serves four
scant ¹/₄ cup / 100 g nettles
scant ¹/₄ cup / 100 g sugar
scant ¹/₄ cup / 100 g dextrose (see below)
2 cups / 500 ml water
juice of one lemon

For the batter:
1 cup / 250 g cornstarch
scant 1 cup / 200 ml water

1 egg (separated into yolk and white)

For the herbs and flowers:
8 baby carrots
4 sprigs of fennel
8 sprigs of carrot greens
1 dozen violets
4 tulips
4 sprigs of thyme
4 sprigs of red sage
4 sprigs of green sage
4 sprigs of lovage
4 sprigs of lemon balm
4 sprigs of flat-leafed parsley
¹/₂ cup / 125 ml sunflower oil

Our Belgian chef, Roger Souvereyns, would like to use this recipe to introduce the reader to the use of some unexpected plants. Most of these grow in ordinary gardens, but are generally (and mistakenly) regarded as inedible, though their therapeutic value is undisputed. Do take care in the selection of individual plants, though, and make sure you find out where they are from; some plants, particularly flowers, may have been treated with artificial colors and preservatives so they look more appealing to the uneducated buyer. Taste everything before preparing it, to make sure it does not have any undesired aftertaste – an indication of artificial additives.

There are many herbs suitable for making fritters, from the usual ones, such as basil and parsley, to the more unusual ones,

such as lemon balm and lovage – an herb originally from Persia that has blood-cleansing properties.

Wear gloves when you collect the nettles, then cook and drain them. The nettle is, incidentally, often used in European sauces and soups, and has many healing properties. Even the burning nettle sap, though it seriously irritates our skin at the slightest contact, is known to act as a circulation booster. If you are not partial to nettles, or if none are available, you can use tarragon or sage instead, using the same preparation methods.

1. Mix the water, sugar, dextrose, nettles, and lemon juice. Bring to a boil and take off the heat; set aside to cool and infuse for 12 hours. Strain and freeze. Once set, use a fork to loosen the mixture until crumbly, and then form into scoops with a spoon.

2. Separate the egg into yolk and white. Mix the egg yolk with the cornstarch, add water, and mix well. Whisk the egg white until stiff and carefully fold in with a spatula.

Nettle Dumplings

3. Wash and drain the herbs well. Heat the sunflower oil in a saucepan over medium heat. When it is hot, dip the herbs in the batter and deep-fry until slightly brown. Remove from the oil and leave to drain dry on absorbent paper towels.

4. Arrange the herbs and flowers as well as the nettle dumplings on the plate and serve immediately.

Smoked Monkfish with

Preparation time: 45 minutes
Cooking time: 15 minutes
Difficulty: ★

Serves four

4 monkfish tails, 5 oz / 150 g each
half a bunch each of flat-leafed parsley, basil
   (to yield 8 good leaves)
1 bunch each of tarragon (to yield 30 leaves),
   arugula leaves (to yield 20 leaves)
half a bunch each of lamb's lettuce, spinach
half an orange (for grated zest)
$^1/_2$ tbsp / 7 ml olive oil
salt, pepper to taste

For the sauce:
$^2/_3$ cup / 200 ml fresh-squeezed orange juice
$^1/_2$ cup / 100 ml clear chicken broth
$^1/_4$ cup / 50 ml olive oil
1 small clove of garlic
$^1/_8$ lb / 50 g fresh ginger root
2 bay leaves
4 crushed peppercorns
$^1/_4$ star anise

For the smoking pan:
$^7/_8$ cup / 200 g sawdust (see below)
2 bay leaves
4 crushed juniper berries
8 black peppercorns

Our chef, Roger Souvereyns, gets the inspiration for his recipes from his walks through the gardens of the Scholteshof restaurant, where he cultivates herbs, plants and vegetables for his kitchen. The herbs used in this recipe can all be easily grown in a windowbox or on a terrace, as they do not require much space at all.

The aromatic combination of basil, tarragon, spinach, and arugula constitute a veritable herbal bouquet. Arugula, with its strong, snappy flavor, is best picked before flowering. You can add more herbs if you wish, such as mint or chives.

Monkfish tails are tender, white and boneless; they should not contain any yellow veins. The tail flesh is particularly aromatic and delicious, particularly if smoked over sawdust from apple-tree wood with just the correct amount of spices. After it is smoked, monkfish can be stored in the refrigerator for several days.

The successful preparation of the sauce depends on the correct amount of herbs and orange zest, as well as reducing it correctly.

1. Put the sawdust and spices in the smoking pan. Heat over low heat. Season the monkfish with salt and pepper.

2. Place the monkfish on a grill in the smoking pan, close, and smoke for about 15 minutes, turning the fish once. Keep warm.

Herb Salad à l'Orange

3. Bring all the ingredients of the sauce, except for the olive oil, to a boil and reduce to one-fifth of its volume. Strain and stir in the olive oil over low heat. Wash the salad thoroughly, drain well, and add the orange zest, pepper, salt, and a teaspoon of olive oil. Stir well.

4. To serve, cut the smoked monkfish into thin slices, arrange on a plate, add the herb salad and season with the orange sauce.

Preparation time: 30 minutes
Cooking time: 20 minutes
Marinating time: 12 hours
Difficulty: ★★

Serves four

10 sea scallops (including coral)

For the scallop marinade:
$^1/_2$ / 100 ml cup olive oil
2 cloves of garlic
1 sprig of thyme, 1 bay leaf
1 tsp / 5 g black peppercorns

For the scallop puree:
coral from the ten scallops
1 onion

2 large button mushrooms
$^1/_4$ cup / 50 ml each white wine, cognac
$^1/_4$ cup / 50 ml cream
salt, pepper to taste

For the salad of winter vegetables:
2 wild artichokes ($^1/_4$ cup / 50 g diced)
1 baby pumpkin, 1 small red cabbage,
  1 small cauliflower (each $^1/_4$ cup / 50 g
  diced)
$^1/_8$ lb / 50 g beans
6 globe artichokes (to yield 6 hearts)
4 leeks ($^1/_4$ cup / 50 g diced)
1 shallot
half a bunch of chives
$^1/_2$ cup / 125 ml each milk, olive oil
$^1/_2$ cup / 125 g all-purpose unbleached flour
1 oz / 25 g raw duck or goose liver
$^1/_4$ cup / 50 ml sherry vinegar
salt, pepper to taste

For the yellow pepper vinaigrette:
(see basic recipes)

The scallop, symbol of the pilgrims of Santiago de Compostela (and see page 10 for more information), is highly rated in Spain, where it is prepared in an endless variety of ways. Our chef, Pedro Subijana, has always been partial to scallops, and for a long time was looking for a way to serve this delightful shellfish that was halfway between raw and cooked. Eventually, he arrived on the idea of preparing the shellfish and its delectable coral separately.

Unlike the traditional Galician method (the Galicia region in northwestern Spain is known for its shellfish) of serving scallops in their shell with tomato and bread crumbs, Chef Subijana proposes frying the scallop flesh on only one side very briefly, and then working the coral into a puree. Coral is produced before the mating season in summer, and its color depends on

the scallop's sex. It is vital that you buy scallops with coral for this recipe; ask the fishmonger for help if necessary.

Since scallops are ideally consumed during the cold season (when they are at their tastiest and are building up their coral), it is only fitting to combine them with winter vegetables. The wild artichoke is easier to clean if it is placed in the refrigerator with a few ice cubes before cooking. Admittedly a rarity in some markets, it may be substituted with a smaller, domestic variety, though its unique taste cannot be so easily replaced.

Cooking the vegetables separately is essential since they must retain their individual flavors and consistency: in their final form, one should be able to distinguish their different flavors.

1. Wash the scallops and marinate in olive oil mixed with sliced garlic, as well as thyme, lemon juice, and peppercorns for one day in the refrigerator. Remove the scallops from the marinade shortly before serving; drain, halve and pan-fry over very high heat on one side only, and only for a very brief amount of time.

2. For the scallop puree, chop the onion and brown, chop the mushrooms; add the chopped mushrooms and coral to the saucepan. Simmer, flambé with cognac and pour white wine over the mixture. Reduce, add a little cream, and cook for 20 minutes. Puree and adjust seasoning to taste.

Vegetables with Scallops

3. Cut the wild artichoke hearts into thin strips, dice the pumpkin, chop the red cabbage, and trim small florets off the cauliflower heat. Cook each separately in salted water and oil. Blanch the beans and extract from their pods. Clean the globe artichoke hearts, cook in water and milk, then quarter and chop. Dice the liver and chop the chives. Mix the vegetables with the shallots, liver, vinegar, oil, and chives in a salad bowl.

4. Fill four round forms (3 1/2 in / 9 cm in diameter) first with the scallop puree, then with the vegetables; press down so that everything mixes well. Remove the form and wrap the salad and puree with a leek strip. Chop the yellow pepper and prepare the yellow pepper vinaigrette; sprinkle over the four plates.

Smoked Salmon Cake with

Preparation time: 15 minutes
Cooking time: 3–4 minutes
Difficulty: ★

Serves four

5/8 lb / 300 g smoked salmon
scant 1/2 lb / 200 g green beans
2 large onions
1 tomato
juice of 1 lemon
1/4 cup / 50 g small capers
2 egg yolks

1/2 cup / 125 ml cream
1 tbsp / 10 ml olive oil
1 tbsp / 10 ml vodka
1 bunch of dill
1/4 lb / 40 g horseradish root (to yield 3 tbsp grated)
1/4 cup / 50 g pink peppercorns
salt, pepper to taste

Puff pastry:
(see basic recipes)

Here, the classic dish of smoked salmon on toast has been slightly modified: instead of toast, it is served on a cake made of puff pastry. This delicious appetizer is easily prepared, yet as our chef, Émile Tabourdiau attests, will meet the expectations of the most demanding gourmet.

The smoked salmon must be carefully selected, as there are so many species in the shops these days. The best option remains Scottish or Norwegian salmon, which are still superior to all other salmon varieties. If possible, smoke it yourself (see earlier smoking recipes for more information). Slice the fish very finely and carefully to yield pliant, wafer-like pieces.

Fry the onions very gently, as they should remain fairly crunchy but with a touch of brown.

Do not use too much horseradish, since its pungent flavor will overpower the salmon. Widely used throughout northern and eastern Europe, here the root is moderated by the cream, so that only a hint of its intense flavor remains to underscore the salmon's subtle flavor. The vodka complements this flavor as well.

The pink peppercorn is not really a variety of pepper at all, but a coral-colored berry, which is marinated, just like capers, in vinegar. Its tangy flavor, nuanced with an exotic note, further refines this appetizer.

To better organize your preparation time, Chef Tabourdiau suggests you decorate the plates in advance, and place the salmon on the puff pastry cakes on the plates at the very last moment.

1. Peel the onions, slice thinly, and fry in olive oil until brown but not until soft. Add the capers, dill sprigs, and a few drops of fresh lemon juice. Set aside to cool.

2. Mix the horseradish, cream, and vodka in a small bowl. Adjust seasoning to taste and add the pink peppercorns. Cook the green beans in salted water, rinse with cold water to arrest the cooking process, drain, and trim all of them to one uniform length.

Pink Peppercorns and Horseradish

3. Perforate the puff pastry cakes, place on a baking tray lined with greased paper, and bake in the oven for three to four minutes at 395 °F / 200 °C. Remove from the oven and set aside to cool at room temperature. Place the cakes on large plates, cover with the onion mixture, and arrange the folded salmon slices somewhat gathered in waves on top of the cakes.

4. Place the plates under the grill for five seconds. Place a ring of green beans (in a flower-petal outline) around the entire salmon cake and garnish the inside of the green bean petals with alternating arrangements of sauce, pink peppercorns and chopped egg yolk, and diced tomato and dill.

Chicken Salad with

Preparation time: 45 minutes
Cooking time: 20 minutes
Difficulty: ★★

Serves four

4 chicken breasts
16 langoustines (between $^1/_8$ and $^1/_4$ lb /
    80–100 g each)
1 tbsp / 10 g curry powder
4 cherry tomatoes
1 bunch of spinach (to yield 12 leaves)
1 bunch of lamb's lettuce (to yield 12 leaves)

4 button mushrooms
4 baby pumpkins
1 carrot
1 cucumber (to yield a scant $^1/_4$ lb / 100 g)
1 lemon
2 tbsp / 30 ml whipping cream
2 tbsp / 30 ml olive oil
2 sprigs of chervil
1 quart / 1 l broth
salt, fresh-ground pepper to taste

The combination of poultry and crustaceans lends this appetizers its unusual aspect. The fine-grained curry powder used to flavor it comes from India via the British, who first brought it to Europe. The exact composition of curry powder varies enormously: the basic spices usually found in all curry powders are cumin, nutmeg, and turmeric, but some also contain cloves, cayenne pepper, and ginger. Use curry quite sparingly, as too much curry will render the other ingredients bitter.

Our chef, Émile Tabourdiau, recommends you buy free-range chicken; their breast meat comes easily off the bone before it is steamed. The breasts contain less fat than the legs and are easier to prepare. To cook them without rendering them too tough, the breasts are wrapped in plastic wrap or cloth.

If you can find them, the relatively large Breton langoustines are ideal for the filling. They should be cooked in broth for only a very short time, otherwise their flesh disintegrates. You can use prawns or shrimps instead, but they are not quite so decorative as the langoustines.

Choose whole spinach leaves without tears or fissures; they are blanched in boiling water and immediately afterwards rinsed in cold water. Their flavor and color aptly complements the delicate aspect of the langoustine filling.

Cut the chicken breast open far enough for easy filling. To add a further visual feature, roll the spinach leaves into tiny balls and place them with the filling into the chicken breasts.

1. Cook the langoustines in a spicy broth, leave to cool and shell, but reserve four whole langoustines for the presentation. Blanch the spinach leaves, rinse with cold water, and drain on a kitchen cloth. Bend the four langoustines retained for decoration so they are arching backwards, and stick the front claws into the shell to hold the langoustine in position.

2. Skin the chicken breasts and cut each piece of meat open with a knife to make a pocket. Peel and hollow out the cherry tomatoes. Chop the peeled cucumber finely, season with cream and chervil; fill the cherry tomatoes with the cucumber.

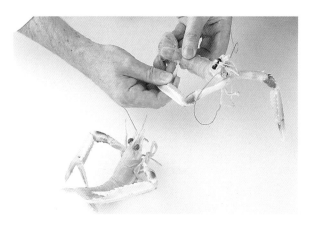

Curried Langoustines

3. Powder the langoustines with curry; season the chicken breasts, and fill with spinach and langoustines. Wrap in plastic wrap and steam for eight to twelve minutes. Once cooked, remove from the saucepan and set aside to cool in the plastic wrap.

4. Blanch the baby pumpkins, hollow them out, and fill with carrot balls and meat from the langoustines' claws. Slice the mushrooms thinly and sprinkle with olive oil and lemon juice. To serve, place a langoustine on each plate, surrounded by a fan-shaped arrangement of chicken medallions. Garnish with lamb's lettuce and the filled baby pumpkins and cherry tomatoes.

Preparation time: 15 minutes
Difficulty: ☆

Serves four

generous $^3/_4$ lb / 400 g rump steak
$^1/_8$ lb / 50 g aged Parmesan
2 oz / 50 g Périgord truffles

1 bunch of portulaca (see below)
1 bunch of arugula
1 lemon
$^1/_4$ cup / 50 ml sherry vinegar
$^3/_8$ cup / 75 ml walnut oil
$^3/_8$ cup / 75 ml peanut oil
salt, pepper to taste

Carpaccio is the Italian term for raw, wafer-thin slices of beef fillet. This delicious appetizer exists in many versions, as many fine ingredients are suitable for this kind of preparation. There are *carpaccios* of duck meat, salmon or sea bream (check the Table of Contents in this volume for many of these variations). Here, our Chef, Dominique Toulousy, presents a traditional *carpaccio*, but he has seasoned it in his own distinctive way.

The truffle season starts in January and ends in March. The black truffles from Périgord have slightly fissured skin and white marbled flesh, the density of which should be checked before purchase. You should also marinate the truffles in vinaigrette before preparation so they can lend their flavor to the vinaigrette.

It is difficult to find a harder and drier cheese than aged Parmesan, whose tangy flavor is incomparable. Parmigiano Reggiano is the most famous of all Parmesans; the *Grana padano* variety from the Po valley is also delicious. (Look for the name stamped on the rind to find out what kind of Parmesan it is.) To slice this very hard cheese wafer-thin in keeping with the carpaccio theme, it is recommended that you use a slicer or an extremely sharp knife.

Portulaca, extremely rare in American markets, is a type of purslane, a sturdy plant that originated in India. It is a rather fatty green, whose leaves are usually used in salads and soups. The best variety has large, slightly sticky leaves and is sometimes called gold portulaca, or gold purslane. The crunchy leaves of this plant form the ideal partner for the beef and Parmesan in this appetizer; if you can't find any, substitute a robust-flavored green of your choice.

1. Wash the salads thoroughly under running water. Slice one-half of the truffles thinly and cut the other half into fine strips.

2. Prepare the vinaigrette. Dissolve the spices in sherry vinegar, then stir in the walnut and peanut oils. Add all of the truffles. Leave to infuse for at least one hour.

Beef with Aged Parmesan

3. Cut the rump steak into paper-thin slices just before serving.

4. Lace the vinaigrette with lemon juice; salt and pepper the meat, sprinkle with vinaigrette. Dress the salads and arrange on the plates along with the meat slices. Garnish with the remaining truffle slices and strips and wafers of aged Parmesan.

Terrine of Porcini Mushrooms

Preparation time: 1 hour 30 minutes
Cooking time: 30 minutes
Difficulty: ★★

Serves four

20 small snails
generous ¾ lb / 400 g porcini mushrooms
2 eggplants
1 zucchini
2 tomatoes

For the broth:
1 carrot
1 onion

1 cup / 250 ml white wine
1 bunch of parsley

For the vinaigrette:
2 tbsp / 30 ml soy sauce
1 cup / 250 ml sherry vinegar
2 cloves of garlic
generous 1½ cups / 400 ml olive oil
1 bunch of thyme
2 bay leaves
salt, peppercorns to taste

To garnish:
chervil leaves

This cold appetizer is not only extremely delicious but also very striking visually. For the checkerboard pattern you will need firm, green medium-sized zucchini cut into even strips: the light strips are made of the zucchini without the skin; the dark ones of zucchini with the skin. Weaving is very easy, although it takes some time, so you may want to make the checkerboard the day before. Finally, the checkerboard is pressed onto the terrine and weighed down with a heavy object.

The eggplants should be very firm and fleshy. Though traditionally in season from April through May, nowadays one can safely buy them all year round. Since eggplants have a high water content, cook them long enough that there are no surprises later on, such as a runny terrine mixture.

After forming, the checkerboards are very fragile, and for easier handling they should be gently wrapped in plastic wrap. The same is true of the terrine squares. This appetizer is served warm, is not season-bound, and will keep for twenty-four hours.

1. Bake the eggplant in the oven for 20 minutes at 395 °F / 200 °C. Meanwhile, make a broth with white wine and vegetables, and cook the snails in it. After cooling down, scrape the flesh from the eggplants' skin.

2. Wash the porcini mushrooms, chop, and fry in olive oil. Chop garlic and parsley. Add the eggplant flesh. Cook this mixture well, adding a pinch of garlic and sprigs of parsley.

with Eggplant, Zucchini and Snails

3. Form four squares, a bit less than $^1/_2$ in / 1 cm thick, out of the eggplant and porcini mixture. Cut the zucchini in strips and weave into a checkerboard pattern. Prepare a vinaigrette with soy sauce, vinegar, garlic, salt, pepper, and olive oil.

4. Chop the tomatoes to make a pulpy consistency. Place a checkerboard on each square of terrine; season and brush with olive oil. Gently heat the terrines in the oven at a low setting. Arrange the snail meat and the terrines on the plates, sprinkle with vinaigrette and garnish with small dollops of chopped tomato and chervil leaves.

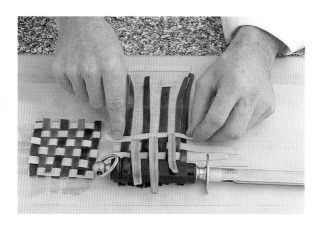

Goatfish with

Preparation time: 2 hours
Cooking time: 1 hour 30 minutes
Soaking time: 12 hours
Difficulty: ✷

Serves four

8 goatfish (scant $^1/_4$ lb / 100 g each)
$^5/_8$ lb / 300 g large white beans
1 small red pepper
1 allspice clove

3 cloves of garlic
1 small onion
1 carrot
1 bouquet garni
$^1/_4$ cup / 50 ml wine vinegar
$^1/_4$ cup / 50 ml soy sauce
$^5/_8$ cup / 50 ml olive oil
1 bunch of chives
half a bunch of thyme
1 bay leaf

In Toulouse, they love strong and hearty dishes such as *cassoulet*, which is customarily served with a small glass of vinegar to make it more digestible. Building on this tradition, our chef, Dominique Toulousy, has borrowed from Spanish tradition to created this delightful cold appetizer.

Preparing the beans is always time-consuming so we suggest you prepare them the day before. There are various theories on the origin of the large white bean but it was, in fact, Columbus who discovered this vegetable in Cuba, and Catherine of Medici who introduced it to France. The bean was only gradually incorporated into cooking, probably because it took so long to cook; before the soaking process was understood, it was considered indigestible. Among the best varieties of white beans available are the (American) Great Northern variety, which, once soaked, is extremely flavorful.

The Mediterranean goatfish (also known as red mullet) is available predominantly throughout September, and is deep red in color with flesh that is high in iodine. Unfortunately, it has many bones, so when filleting the fish (you also skin the fish completely) you should check the fillets for any remaining ones. Goatfish fillets are fried skin side down first for two minutes, and then a quick twenty seconds on the other side: this way, the fillets remain tender, and won't crumble apart.

Allspice corns, from the pimento tree, have an intense aroma and are not for the faint-hearted! You could, instead, make a sauce with a spice mix that is a little easier on the stomach, and also combines well with the goatfish. In any case, the dish is served with a just-warmed vinaigrette.

1. Soak the beans overnight; for the last two hours, add the onion, carrot, bouquet garni, and two cloves of garlic and then cook for 1 hour and 15 minutes. Transfer $^2/_3$ cup / 150 ml of the cooking liquid into a jar. Fillet the fish and remove any remaining bones with tweezers.

2. Chop a clove of garlic. Sweat the heads and bones of the goatfish in a little olive oil, then pour over vinegar, soy sauce and the $^2/_3$ cup / 150 ml of cooking liquid. Add thyme, bay leaf, and the garlic. Bring to a boil and then remove from the heat.

Vinaigrette and Beans

3. Cover this mixture and leave to infuse for ten minutes, adding the allspice, after five minutes. Meanwhile, roast the red pepper until the skin can be easily peeled off, then chop into small dice. Strain the goatfish-based sauce through a fine-meshed sieve, then stir in the $1/4$ cup / 50 ml of olive oil to make a vinaigrette.

4. Add the diced red pepper to the vinaigrette. Fry the goatfish in olive oil until brown, skin side down first, then very quickly, fry the other side. To serve, arrange a ring of strained white beans around the outer edge of the plate and place the goatfish fillets in the middle. Dress with the warm vinaigrette and sprinkle with chopped chives.

Brandade of Cod

Preparation time: 1 hour
Cooking time: 45 minutes
Difficulty: ★★

Serves four

2 lbs / 900 g fresh cod fillets
1 onion, 1 leek
$^1/_4$ cup / 50 ml cream
1 pint / 500 ml water

For the vinaigrette:
white of 1 egg
3 tbsp / 40 g mustard
1 tbsp / 15 ml red wine vinegar
1 tbsp / 16 ml custard
$^7/_8$ cup / 200 ml peanut oil
$^1/_2$ tbsp / 5 g salt and pepper

For the Basque sauce
2 lbs / 1 kg tomatoes
2 onions
1 green pepper
$^1/_4$ cup / 50 ml each white wine, stock

1 tbsp / 15 g concentrated tomato paste
2 tbsp / 30 ml olive oil
salt, pepper to taste

For the spicy sauce:
$^1/_2$ cup / 120 ml vinaigrette
generous 1 cup / 300 ml Basque sauce

For the purée:
scant $^1/_2$ lb / 200 g potatoes
2 cloves of garlic

For the brandade:
3 sheets of gelatin
$^5/_8$ cup / 150 ml cream
$^7/_8$ cup / 200 ml cooking liquid
$^3/_8$ cup / 30 ml olive oil
salt, pepper to taste

The traditional Provençal brandade is based on cod, cream, milk, garlic and olive; pounded together, it forms a delicious puree. This version, from Chef Gilles Tournadre, serves some of the same purpose, as it provides an ideal opportunity to use up the parts of the cod that are usually discarded: the underside, tail fillet, and other trimmings. In northern France, cod has many names, such as *doguette* or *moulou*; it is very popular in Normandy, where cod recipes abound. The ports of Dieppe and Fécamp are important cod suppliers.

Here, cod is enhanced in the traditional manner, with cream, and then cooked with leek like a soup. The resulting slightly sweet flavor provides a fitting contrast to the Basque sauce, which is stirred into the vinaigrette to lend an extra spicy note. Basque sauce can be served with other fish as well, such as

tuna, particularly the Bonito type. There are also chicken dishes, clear soups and some potato dishes that can carry the description *à la Basque*, having been prepared with tomatoes, peppers and raw Bayonne ham (from, naturally, Bayonne, France).

Chef Tournadre points out that combining the cod-potato mixture with the Basque sauce requires great care and attention, as you need to wind up with a smooth and even mixture. For this purpose, Tournadre prefers using French cream from Isigny, which carries the classification *appellation d'origine contrôlée* – a label of honor, meaning its production is carefully regulated by the French government – and which is high in pasteurized lactic fats.

1. For the Basque sauce, sweat the chopped onions and pepper in olive oil. Quarter the tomatoes. Pour over white wine and add the tomatoes, the tomato paste and the stock. After cooking, puree in the blender or food processor.

2. Prepare the vinaigrette. Cook the cod with a chopped onion, the bulb of the leek and the cream in water. Bring to a boil and then simmer with the lid closed for five minutes. Remove from the heat and leave the cod to cool in the cooking liquid.

with a Basque Sauce

3. For the spicy sauce, mix the vinaigrette with the Basque sauce. Prepare a potato puree with two cloves of garlic. Soak the gelatin.

4. Leave the cod to drain. To make the brandade, mix the gelatin with almost 1 cup / 250 ml of the cooking liquid. Blend everything with the puree and stir in olive oil. Leave to cool and fold in the cream. To serve, place two scoops of the brandade on each plate and decoratively surround with the spicy sauce.

Yellow Mackerels

Preparation time: 1 hour
Cooking time: 30 minute
Difficulty: ★

Serves four

16 yellow mackerels, or
8 common mackerels
10 spring onions
generous $^1/_4$ lb / 150 g small button
    mushrooms
$^5/_8$ lb / 300 g cauliflower
2 artichokes
1 clove of garlic
2 tomatoes
1 bouquet garni

$^3/_4$ cup / 200 ml olive oil
$^3/_4$ cup / 200 ml white wine
$^1/_2$ cup / 100 ml white vinegar
juice of 1 lemon
20 whole coriander seeds
2 juniper berries
$^1/_8$ lb / 5 g fresh ginger root (to yield $^1/_2$ tbsp
    grated)
1 bunch of cilantro
a pinch of sugar
salt, fresh-ground pepper to taste

To garnish:

half a bunch of green asparagus (optional)

Though rarely found outside the Haute-Normandie region where it is usually netted – since its tender, delicate flesh will not survive long transports – the yellow mackerel is worth consideration. It is a smaller sub-species of the common mackerel (about five inches / twelve centimeters long), and Chef Gilles Tournadre has a great fondness for it. This recipe has been passed down to Chef Tournadre by his grandmother and aunt, and carries a lot of childhood memories for him. However, given the yellow mackerel's rarity, the common mackerel will work as a worthy substitute.

The slightly acidic flavor of the coriander seeds lends this dish a particular note. Since the thin and very tender fillets have the tendency to contract during cooking, they must thus be cooked very gently and in stages. Before cooking, remove the backbone with a sharp knife, making sure you insert the knife at the right spot. As far as the remaining bones are concerned, our chef discourages the use of tweezers to extract them, as that might squash the delicate flesh and promote its disintegration during cooking.

The accompaniment of baby and young vegetables seasoned with ginger root emphasizes the original character of this appetizer and combines very well with the cilantro. And Tournadre's complex composition of two sauces can, if desired, be made even more spicy.

1. Slice the garlic and grate the ginger. Chop the bulbs of the spring onions, and sweat in olive oil, then add the garlic, sugar, ginger, lemon juice, cilantro, juniper berries, a tomato, the bouquet garni, a little white wine, and vinegar. As the sauce is being reduced by about a third, clean and strip the artichokes down to the hearts, slice, then incorporate into the mélange.

2. Blanch in salted water the green sprigs of the spring onions and, if using asparagus, the green asparagus; rinse with cold water and set aside.

with Baby Vegetables

3. Wash and fillet the mackerels, place in a pie dish with a bouquet garni and coriander seeds, and cover. Bake in the oven for seven minutes. Leave to cool in the cooking liquid.

4. To the reduced mélange, add the cauliflower, plucked into little florets, and the whole button mushrooms to the vegetables. Continue to cook for one or two minutes and then set aside. Arrange the fillets and vegetables on the plates; mix the two cooking liquids together, add a dash of olive oil, and stir well. Dress the fish and vegetables with this combined sauce. Serve garnished with asparagus tips or the green part of the spring onions.

Preparation time: 20 minutes
Cooking time: 1 hour 45 minutes
Difficulty: ☆

Serves four

2 breasts of duck
scant ¼ lb / 100 g Parmesan
salt, pepper to taste

For the dressing:
1 small can of truffle juice
2 limes
⅞ cup / 200 ml olive oil

For the garnish:
3 Belgian endives
1 bunch of lamb's lettuce
2 tbsp / 30 g mustard

In this recipe, beef – the classic ingredient for a *carpaccio* – is replaced with duck breasts. Served with the endive, this cold appetizer will please the diet-conscious as well as the discriminating palate.

Belgian endives were introduced in Brussels towards the end of the nineteenth century. The success of this vegetable with many names – called *witloof* in the Flemish part of Belgium, *chicon* in the French part, and *endive* in France – continues to this day. Low in calories and unique in texture as well as taste, Belgian endive combines well with most lettuces, even the more tangy varieties such as lamb's lettuce or watercress. Choose Belgian endives that are still firmly shut and very white, and avoid those whose leaves have frayed brown around the edges.

Before washing, the outer leaves should be discarded; before serving, the inner core should also be discarded as it tastes rather bitter. For this appetizer the endive is chopped finely and then dressed with truffle juice and prepared mustard. The dressing should be made with walnut oil, as it is an ideal partner for endives.

Regarding the duck breasts, these should come from very fresh and fleshy ducks with a thick layer of fat under their skin, which further enhances the meat. Before slicing the breasts wafer-thin, put the meat in the freezer for a while (about one hour and forty-five minutes) as this will make slicing them easier.

1. Place the duck breasts in the freezer for about 1 hour and 45 minutes to firm up, then cut into wafer-thin slices using a sharp knife or an electric carving knife.

2. Finely chop the endives and mix with mustard. Place a small mound of endives on every plate.

Duck Breast

3. Arrange the duck breast meat in a fan shape around the endive.

4. Prepare the dressing with truffle juice, olive oil, and lemon juice. Sprinkle the breasts with the dressing, place a ring of washed and drained lamb's lettuce leaves around the mound of endive, and garnish with grated Parmesan.

Preparation time: 30 minutes
Soaking time: 2 days
Cooking time: 15 minutes
Difficulty: ✶

Serves four

4 skate wings, ¹/₂ lb / 250 g each

For the broth:
1 onion
3 shallots
1 bouquet garni (of parsley, thyme, and bay
    leaf)
juice of one lemon
¹/₂ cup / 125 ml white vinegar
salt to taste

To garnish:
1 bunch of red frisée
1 bunch of green frisée
1 bunch of oak leaf

1 head of radicchio
4 cherry tomatoes
4 oz / 120 g salmon roe
2 eggs
half a bunch of chervil

For the remoulade:
1 cup / 250 g mayonnaise (see basic recipes)
1 tbsp / 15 g capers
¹/₂ cup / 125 g small gherkin pickles
1 can of anchovies
¹/₄ cup / 75 g prepared mustard
half a bunch each of parsley, chervil, tarragon

Skate, also called ray, is an instantly recognizable fish, with a beautiful wave-like swimming motion and streamlined, flat shape. Preparation is easy as the skate has only one central cartilage, from which the white flesh is simply and easily peeled off. Most often skate is sold in the form of whole wings. Our chef, José Tourneur, recommends marinating these in lightly salted water or in water laced with vinegar for two days, as this precaution prevents the release of the skate's natural ammonia aroma after cooking. The same procedure, incidentally, applies for shark meat.

Of the many varieties of skate, some with spikes, all are delicious. To check the wings for freshness, make sure their skin is shiny, and seems on the thin rather than the thick side.

The mixed lettuces will visually enhance this dish with their range of reds and greens. Frisée's subtle, hazelnut-hinted aftertaste will combine superbly with the slightly bitter tang of radicchio; its feathery leaves will visually complement the appearance of the brownish-green oak leaf lettuce.

If you prefer, use another white-fleshed fish instead of ray, such as white tuna or cod.

1. Prepare the skate wings and place them in a broth with chopped shallots, the bouquet garni, onion, and salt and pepper; cook for about 15 minutes.

2. Carefully take the skate wings out of the broth, drain, peel off the skin, and leave to cool in the refrigerator.

# of Skate

3. For the remoulade, stir the mustard, a few anchovies, gherkins, capers, chopped parsley, chervil, and tarragon into the mayonnaise. Hard-boil the eggs for the garnish, separate the yolk from the white, and chop separately.

4. To serve, arrange the skate wings next to the mixed lettuces on each plate, garnished with chervil leaves, parsley, and the separately chopped egg yolks and whites. Decorate with strips of cherry tomatoes. Serve the remoulade in a separate dish, decorated, if you prefer, with parsley and tomatoes.

Preparation time: 30 minutes
Marinating time: 48 hours
Cooking time: 8 minutes
Difficulty: ☆

Serves four

⁵/₈ lb / 300 g spaghetti
1 oz / 50 g dried porcini mushrooms
¹/₄ cup / 50 g black olives
3¹/₂ oz / 100 g can of tuna packed in oil
¹/₈ lb / 50 g marinated beef tongue

¹/₂ cup / 100 ml olive oil
zest of half an orange
¹/₄ bunch of basil (to yield 1 tsp chopped)
salt, pepper to taste

To garnish:
1 zucchini

All efforts by the French gastronomic establishment could not prevent Italy from remaining the chief exporter of pasta. With more than two hundred pasta varieties, the Italians have shown how the most traditional, hand-wrought processes can be successfully converted into a successful industry.

Spaghetti – the name is derived from the Italian word for string – is, of course, well-known the world over. Until recently it was indelibly associated with the classic Bolognese sauce, but there are other, more unusual methods of preparation, as this recipe helps to prove. Everyone should know by now, but for the benefit of Chef Luisa Valazza we'll mention it nonetheless: spaghetti should be cooked *molto al dente* in water laced with olive oil, and should only be cooked at the very last minute before serving.

Chef Valazza's spaghetti salad is served with chopped marinated porcini mushrooms and tuna in oil. The marinated beef tongue lends the dish that extra note, with an acidity that provides a sublime contrast to the tuna and pasta. For this Piedmontese specialty, the tongue must be marinated in a heady mixture of wine, herbs, garlic, and onions for two days; it should be turned seven times during this process. If you would prefer not to use tongue, you can use cooked ham instead; expect, of course, a slightly different, less hearty flavor.

Incidentally, Chef Valazza has created this appetizer to incorporate ingredients from all over Italy: oranges from Sicily, tongue from Piedmont, olives from Liguria and spaghetti, originally, from Naples.

1. Two days ahead of time, wash the beef tongue well; marinate in the herbed wine mixture described above. One day ahead of time, soak the dried porcini mushrooms in hot water to soften, then marinate overnight in vinegar. On cooking day, cut the marinated tongue of beef into fine strips. It must be stored in the refrigerator, and added to the salad only moments before serving.

2. Halve the olives, remove the pits; crumble the tuna and thinly slice the porcini mushrooms. Cut the orange zest into very fine strips and blanch.

Spaghetti Salad

3. Cook the spaghetti al dente; rinse immediately in cold running water, drain and toss with olive oil in a salad bowl.

4. Mix all ingredients, then add salt and pepper to taste. Arrange on the plates and garnish with zucchini strips and basil leaves.

A Ring of Potatoes with

Preparation time: 1 hour
Cooking time: 1 hour 30 minutes
Difficulty: ★★

Serves four

12 live sea scallops
12 flat oysters
5 potatoes
3 large shallots
1 bunch of flat-leafed parsley
$^1/_2$ cup / 125 ml olive oil

$^1/_2$ cup / 125 ml peanut oil
salt, pepper to taste

Perhaps our chef, Guy Van Cauteren of Belgium, was inspired by childhood memories of *tom-pouce*, the dainty Belgian pastry sandwich that is filled with cream, seasoned with hazelnuts and coffee powder, and sprinkled with grated coconut. Here, he has created a grown-up version of that childhood souvenir – a sort of savory *tom-pouce* appetizer of seafood and potatoes.

As is generally the rule, choose seafood that is absolutely fresh. Ideally, use flat oysters from Zeeland in the Netherlands, renowned for their superior quality, or, if they are unavailable, flat oysters from France or a French variety, such as Belon, that are now raised in the United States. Sea scallops are used for

their larger size, but, if you prefer, the seafood may be replaced with fresh salmon or monkfish medallions.

For this recipe use waxy potatoes with smooth and unblemished skin and no eyes or sprouts; ideally use a new potato. The potatoes are cut into cylinders before they are evenly sliced – this step in the preparation is crucial to this appetizer's presentation.

The shallots, fragrant members of the family of lilies and ideal for sauces, are also indispensable; here they are served oven-dried. Make sure they come out of the oven nice and crunchy and serve them instantly.

1. Cut the potatoes into cylinder shapes. Then cut into $^1/_4$ in / $^1/_2$ cm slices using either a slicer or a sharp knife. Steam, set aside to cool, then season with salt.

2. Peel the shallots and chop them very finely; place on an oven-proof plate and dry in the oven for 30 minutes. Deep-fry the parsley sprigs in peanut oil and leave to drain on paper towels; season with salt.

Scallops and Oysters

3. Open the scallops and extract the flesh. Rinse with water and then halve the scallops lengthwise. Open the oysters, extract the flesh, season with pepper and set aside. Sweat the seasoned scallops in a little olive oil for a few minutes.

4. To serve, place a potato slice on a chilled plate, with a scallop on top, and cap with another potato slice; repeat this process with the oysters. Sprinkle the ensemble with deep-fried parsley and the dried shallots. Season with a dash of olive oil.

Terrine of Calf's Foot Aspic

Preparation time: *1 hour*
Cooking time: *8 hours*
Cooling time: *12 hours*
Difficulty: ★★

Serves twelve

1 calf's foot
3 lbs / 1¹/₂ kg monkfish
1 bunch of spinach (to yield ¹/₄ lb / 100 g)
1 bunch of sorrel (to yield ¹/₄ lb / 100 g)
1 bunch each of balm, sage, tarragon, and
    flat-leafed parsley
5 shallots
1 lemon
¹/₂ lb / 250 g butter
¹/₄ cup / 50 ml olive oil

2¹/₂ cups / 750 ml Alsatian Riesling (white
    wine)
1 loaf country bread (for toast)
salt, fresh-ground pepper to taste

To cook the calf's foot:
1 leek
1 onion
1 clove of garlic
1 bunch of celery (for the
    greens only)
1 carrot
1 bunch of flat-leafed parsley
half a bunch of thyme
1 bay leaf
fresh-ground black pepper
coarse sea salt

The terrine presented here is a variation of the famous Belgian eel terrine, which is always generously seasoned with herbs. Here, the eel is replaced with monkfish, which has subtle white flesh and hardly any bones. Removing the monkfish's skin and central bone is easy. Cook the fish in aluminum foil, so that the juices are not lost and the flavor remains intense. To improve the flavor even further, add herbs and greens to the monkfish while it's cooking: sage is essential, and spinach is also very suitable for this purpose.

The breeding of veal in Belgium has been subject to increased and intensified controls, which is why the quality has much improved. There are two main breeds: a reddish-brown breed

from the eastern part of Belgium and a white-coated breed from around Namur in the southern part. Both breeds have very light-colored feet not covered by hide; these should be soaked in water overnight before preparation, which involves slow cooking in an oven at a low setting; this ensures an even distribution of heat. The result will be meat that is more tender. If Belgian veal is not available, substitute whichever high-quality veal your butcher recommends.

It is easier to remove the meat from the bone before it has cooled off completely. The natural gelatin content means the calf's foot releases a lovely and tasty aspic during cooking, which makes the preparation of the terrine far easier.

1. Gut, wash, and soak the monkfish. Flash-heat the calf's foot to drain the internal liquid and then bake in an oven with the listed ingredients for three to four hours.

2. Sweat the chopped shallots in butter. Add the salted and peppered monkfish and cook for a few minutes with the lid closed. Add the spinach, sorrel, balm, sage, tarragon, and parsley and continue cooking for 15 minutes. Remove the fish from the pan, reduce the cooking liquid, and then puree finely in the blender.

with Monkfish and Herbs

3. Leave the calf's foot to drain, remove the cartilage and chop the meat; strain the cooking liquid. Reduce to a jelly, skim off the fat and adjust seasoning to taste.

4. Fill the terrine dish alternately with fish, herb puree, meat and aspic until all the ingredients are used up. Chill for 12 hours. Invert the terrine and slice with a sharp knife. Garnish the plates with a ring of vinaigrette and arrange the terrine slices on the plates. Serve with toasted country bread.

Scallops of Salmon

Preparation time: 15 minutes
Cooking time: 10 minutes
Difficulty: ★

Serves four

1¹/₂ lbs / 800 g raw salmon
5 quail's eggs
16 asparagus stalks
1 bunch of lamb's lettuce
2 tsp / 10 g grated truffles
¹/₂ cup / 100 ml truffle juice

³/₄ cup / 200 ml walnut oil
1 tbsp / 20 ml wine vinegar
salt, pepper to taste

For the mayonnaise:
2 eggs
1 tbsp / 20 g mustard
3 tsp / 20 ml white vinegar
1³/₄ cups / 500 ml peanut oil

An avid traveler, the salmon has been a part of international cuisine for a very long time. Its provenance determines its quality, as it is influenced a great deal by its immediate environment. As an extremely nutritious fish it contains large amounts of vitamins and minerals, such as calcium, iron, zinc, and phosphorus.

Our chef, Freddy Van Decasserie, prefers Scottish salmon (as do many of the chefs in this volume) for its denser, darker flesh. He recommends you purchase a relatively large fish because it has a high natural fat content, which serves to retain the tenderness of the flesh after cooking. Reliable indicators of freshness are the salmon's flexibility (does it bend easily?) and the fat content of the meat; the color is not a reliable indication

of freshness as one might think since salmon, like many other fishes, will vary in its individual coloration. Choose a fillet from a six-pound (three-kilo salmon – whether you choose a wild or a farmed salmon is a personal matter. In Scotland, it must be said, there are many salmon farms, farming fresh as well as sea water types, that produce salmon of the highest quality. And, for a variation, the salmon could be substituted by a salmon trout or tuna fillet.

Our chef has conceived this recipe for the period leading up to Easter, which is symbolized by the quail's eggs. For the side vegetables, choose medium-sized green asparagus or snowpeas. Finally, this dish does not keep, which should not present a problem: your guests will eat it all.

1. Trim and peel the asparagus and boil it very briefly. Rinse immediately with cold water, and set aside. Boil the quail's eggs for six minutes and set aside as well.

2. Prepare a mayonnaise with the egg yolk, prepared mustard, and vinegar, folding in the olive oil bit by bit. Prepare a vinaigrette with truffle juice, grated truffles, 2 tbsp / 30 g of mayonnaise, and the wine vinegar. Mix well and stir in the walnut oil.

with Truffle Vinaigrette

3. Wash and fillet the salmon. Remove the bones and cut the fillet into four slices. Salt, pepper and place in a buttered dish; bake in the oven for just one minute at 395 °F / 200 °C. Hard-boil the quail eggs.

4. To serve, sprinkle the plates with vinaigrette. Place the salmon scallop on the plate, surrounded by a fan of asparagus spears, the lamb's lettuce, and half a quail's egg.

Bellevue Lobster with

Preparation time: 15 minutes
Cooking time: 20 minutes
Difficulty: ☆

Serves four

2 1 lb / 500 g lobsters
2 artichokes
1 head of broccoli
2 celery sticks
half an onion
$^1/_4$ cup / 50 ml peanut oil
juice of one lemon

$^1/_2$ tsp flour
8 sprigs of chives
half a bunch of chervil (to yield 1 tbsp / 15 g
    chopped)
salt, pepper to taste

For the mayonnaise:
2 egg yolks
1 tsp / 5 g mustard
4 tsp / 20 ml white vinegar
$^1/_4$ cup / 50 ml vegetable oil
salt, pepper to taste

Lobster is considered the king of the Brittany coast, but unfortunately, these days, it is rare in the region. One of the most famous lobster dishes is Bellevue lobster, which Madame de Pompadour is supposed to have served King Louis XV at his Bellevue residence near Meudon.

For this recipe, our chef, Freddy Van Decasserie, recommends putting in the effort to find female blue Brittany lobsters, as the females contain more meat than the males. Tie their claws with string and peg them, as they might still be active. Cook the lobster quickly in a broth refined with seaweed. The most humane method is to wait until the cooking stock has come to a rolling boil, and then plunge the lobsters in head first.

The mayonnaise should be made exactly to the instructions given by our chef; the olive oil, in particular, has to be added very slowly – dribbled in a continuous, thin line as you are stirring constantly. Otherwise, the sauce could curdle.

The visual impact of the lobster is emphasized by the various greens of the vegetables: chervil, watercress (if desired), artichoke hearts, and broccoli. The latter, a cousin of the cauliflower, not only looks good but also contains many nutrients. You can use the leaves as well as the flowers.

1. Prepare the broth for the lobster using half an onion and celery. Start cold, and immerse the lobster once the broth has come to a rolling boil. Cook for eight minutes over high heat. Then, leave the lobster in the broth to cool; the lobster will thus impart more flavor to the broth.

2. Halve the lobster lengthwise, beginning at the head. Roll up the tail so it will not be squashed during cutting. Extract the claw flesh and set two or three legs aside for decoration; cut the meat into medallions.

Chervil Vinaigrette

3. Prepare the mayonnaise with two egg yolks, a pinch of salt, pepper, mustard and vinegar. Add the olive oil in a very thin stream, stirring constantly. Put one tablespoon of mayonnaise, $1/4$ cup / 50 ml of water and the chervil leaves in a blender or food processor. Mix well and gradually stir in the peanut oil until it is fully blended.

4. Clean and trim the artichokes down to the hearts. Simmer the artichoke hearts for 15 minutes in water with the lemon juice and a pinch of flour; then quarter. Cook the broccoli al dente (you can steam it just as quickly) and rinse with cold water immediately after cooking. Arrange the ensemble on the plates in a decorative fashion, garnishing with sprigs of chives and lobster legs. Serve chilled.

Pigeon and Goose Liver

Preparation time: 1 hour 30 minutes
Cooking time: 1 hour 5 minutes
Difficulty: ★★★

Serves four

2 large Bresse pigeons (see below)
3¹/₂ oz / 100 g canned goose liver
4 lbs / 2 kg goose fat
4 carrots
4 turnips
8 radishes
¹/₄ lb / 50 g young peas
¹/₄ lb / 50 g green beans
1 1 oz / 20 g truffle
1 tbsp / 10 g spice mix
generous 1 cup / 300 ml truffle oil
1 cup / 250 ml olive oil

juice of half a lemon
sugar, salt, pepper to taste

For the aspic:
pigeon carcasses
1 carrot
1 onion
half a bunch of celery
1 bouquet garni
1¹/₂ tbsp / 20 g concentrated tomato paste
1 sheet of gelatin

For clarifying:
3 egg whites
1 carrot
1 leek (leaf only)
4 star anise

In France, breeding pigeons used to be the privilege of aristocratic judges, and during the *ancien régime* pigeons could only be found on the dinner tables of the rich. Today, breeding pigeons can be purchased all year round, unlike wild pigeons. The best time to buy fresh-killed pigeons is in June and July.

Our chef, Geert Van Hecke of Belgium, has devised this recipe around pigeons from Bresse in France, which measure in the neighborhood of a half a pound (two hundred and fifty grams) and have, according to Van Hecke, meat that is more dense and more tender than that of most other pigeons. This subtlety strikes a perfect balance with the marinated goose liver and the crunchy, young vegetables. Of course, markets differ consider-

ably in different countries, so in any event, look for succulent, mature pigeons, rather than the smaller squabs.

To lend the aspic the intense aroma it requires, star anise is added; the star anise flowers have healing properties. The herb got its name from its slightly aniseed flavor, although it is not related to the proper anise at all. It is also frequently an ingredient in the five-spice mix often used in Asian cooking, which also usually contains cloves, cassia (Chinese cinnamon bark), fennel, and fagara (or szechuan pepper).

1. Soak the gelatin ahead of time. Prepare a stock with the pigeon carcasses along with the bouquet garni, the tomato paste, and chopped carrot, onion, and celery stick. Cook for one hour, strain and add the pre-soaked gelatin. Clarify the stock with egg white, star anise, the green part of a leek and a chopped carrot.

2. Glaze the base of the four plates with this aspic. Season the goose liver with salt, pepper, and spice mix. Cook for a half an hour in goose fat at 155 °F / 80 °C, then set aside to cool for one hour.

on a Film of Aspic

3. Fry the pigeon meat rare; slice. Cut the goose liver and truffles into thin slices.

4. Clean and chop the vegetables and gently cook in olive oil with a pinch of sugar, salt, and pepper for a half an hour. Mix the cooked vegetables with the truffle oil and the juice of half a lemon. On the plates, arrange a row of alternating truffles and pigeon meat slices in the middle, with the goose liver slices on either side. Garnish with the vegetables.

Snail and Duck Stomachs Wrapped

Preparation time:	*30 minutes*
Cooking time:	*10 minutes*
Difficulty:	★★★

Serves four

36 small gray snails
4 duck stomachs
2 large potatoes (Bintje, if possible; see below)
2 shallots
1 clove of garlic

1 bunch each (to yield $^1/_4$ cup / 100 g total
   mixed): basil, chervil, parsley, sorrel,
   spinach and tarragon
$^1/_8$ lb / 50 g butter
1 tbsp / 25 ml cream
$^1/_4$ cup / 50 ml white wine
$^1/_4$ cup / 50 ml peanut oil
salt, pepper to taste

People have been eating snails for thousands of years. It inspires a variety of preparations. The Romans, in particular, were very fond of them, and were reportedly also the first to breed snails. In the French provinces, where snails are part of the staple diet, there are so many names for the snail that they could easily fill a whole dictionary. Snails are also very popular in Belgium, where the city of Namur has included the snail as a symbol in its coat of arms.

The small gray snails with the Latin description *helix aspersa* have fine and fruity flesh under a shell that is decorated with white and yellow spots. They should be washed under running cold water to remove the slime before they are placed in the frying pan while still alive. But if you can not stand the thought of killing the little creatures in this manner, rest assured: you can purchase shelled and prepared snails,

which will work quite satisfactorily for this appetizer from Chef Geert Van Hecke.

The duck stomachs should be marinated in coarse sea salt overnight and then cooked slowly in goose fat for two or three hours. This method serves to improve their flavor, which is then released in the potato wraps. In terms of the potatoes, Chef Van Hecke prefers the yellow-skinned Bintje potatoes, a French variety, though these may be hard to find in non-European markets. When choosing a substitute, bear in mind that Bintjes are fine-grained when young, and extremely flavorful. In order for the sauce to remain creamy it should not boil after the herbs have been added. The whole ensemble is served on a bed of crunchy lettuce, or, if you prefer, just a pool of sauce adorned with lettuce leaves and herbs.

1. Sweat the chopped shallots and garlic in 3 tbsp / 50 g butter. Stir in the snails and the previously diced duck stomachs. Fry over fast heat for one minute, then set aside. Chop the herbs.

2. Peel the potatoes and cut into thin, roughly rectangular slices. For the potato parcels, place four potato slices in a cross and fill with the meat mixture. Close the parcel; there should be three parcels per person.

in Potato Parcels with Herb Sauce

3. Season the parcels slightly and fry on each side in peanut oil for a couple of minutes. Leave to drain on paper towels.

4. Reduce the shallots with the white wine and snail juices, add cream and a little butter, and strain through a fine-meshed sieve. Distribute the sauce over the four plates, add the parcels, and a green salad.

Lukewarm Squid with

Preparation time:	*30 minutes*
Cooking time:	*20 minutes*
Infusing time:	*24 hours*
Difficulty:	✳✳

Serves four

2 lbs / 1 kg small squid
1 quart / 1 l chicken broth
2 tbsp / 30 g butter
1 sprig thyme

For the vegetables:
scant ³/₈ lb / 150 g parsnips
scant ³/₈ lb / 150 g heliantus tuberosus
  (a variety of tuberose)

scant ³/₈ lb / 150 g chervil (the bulbs only)
scant ³/₈ lb / 150 g parsley root
scant ³/₈ lb / 150 g fennel root

For the vinaigrette:
¹/₂ cup / 100 ml wine vinegar
¹/₂ cup / 100 ml balsamic vinegar
³/₄ cup / 200 ml olive oil
¹/₂ cup / 100 ml soy sauce
¹/₄ tsp chili sauce
¹/₄ tsp Tabasco
1 chopped anchovy
1 onion
1 clove of garlic
1 shallot
¹/₄ lb / 50 g fresh ginger root
1 bunch each of: mint, lemon balm, and thyme
salt, fresh-ground pepper to taste

Not far from the Versailles restaurant Trois Marches where Chef Gérard Vié holds court, the royal gardeners used to cultivate many fruit and vegetable varieties that are only rarely used today. Chef Vié's appetizer is dedicated to these rare vegetables.

Parsnips are members of the family of umbelliferous plants, and they are very similar to the carrot; thus the Romans gave both of them the same name: *pastinaca*. Parsnips, however, are white, and have a very intense aromatic flavor. There are many different parsnip varieties, from round ones to the longer types. Other root vegetables used here are the parsley root, similar in taste to celeriac, and the fennel root, which the Romans consumed both raw and cooked and, finally, the stunted chervil bulbs, with their white and sweet pulp.

The small squid are prepared in two stages, both of which require only very brief frying so the meat does not have a chance to dry out. The soy vinaigrette will finally be sprinkled onto the squid. Of the herbs, onion, ginger, and shallot for the vinaigrette, when all are chopped they should yield about one heaping cupful. You should prepare the vinaigrette the day before, as it will need twenty-four hours to infuse.

1. Prepare the vinaigrette and leave to infuse for 24 hours. Wash the squid, drain and cut into thin slices. Retain the ink.

2. Peel the vegetables, cut into sticks and cook each as a separate batch in chicken broth. Keep warm.

Vegetables and Herbs

3. Dress the vegetable sticks with part of the vinaigrette; strain the remaining vinaigrette and retain the oily liquid. Season the squid and briefly pan-fry half with part of the vinaigrette oil.

4. Fry the remaining squid with the remaining vinaigrette-oil, add the ink and gently cook for three to four minutes. Place a bed of vegetables in the middle of each plate, arrange the ink-stained squid in a ring around the vegetables; place the white squid on top of the vegetables. Decorate the rest of the plate with vegetable sticks in a radiating wheel, much like the spokes of wagons used at Versailles in the days of the royal gardens.

Glazed Terrine of

Preparation time: 2 hours
Cooking time: 24 hours
Difficulty: ☆

Serves ten

10 large cucumbers
3½ oz / 100 g prepared horseradish (from a
   jar)
7 oz / 200 g Beluga caviar
1 cup / 250 ml cream
generous ½ cup / 125 g cream mayonnaise
   (see basic recipes)
2 tbsp / 30 ml cream

juice of 1 lemon
1½ sheets of gelatin
2 lbs / 1 kg coarse sea salt
salt, pepper to taste
a small bunch of chives

Summer is the ideal season to try meat, fish or vegetable terrines. Whether you prefer to call them aspics, pies, or parfaits, terrines are visually striking and very delicious and can be served as an appetizer as well as a main course. This dish, with its elegant design and summery yet sumptuous ingredients, is ideal for a special occasion.

Cucumber has been popular since antiquity, when the Greeks and Romans consumed it in large numbers. This refreshing vegetable contains many healing substances, which is why it is frequently used in cosmetics. As a salad vegetable, it pops up in many regional specialties, such as the Greek tzatziki. Agriculturally, France's substantial cucumber cultivation, particularly in the Loire valley and in Provence is in fourth place behind Spain, Greece, and the export leader, the Netherlands.

Choose cucumbers with a dark green skin and very firm and crunchy pulp. Marinate the cucumber in coarse sea salt to draw out excess water and make it more digestible, though marinating it for too long will render it mushy and limp. After marinating, rinse the cucumber only casually, as the remaining salt will provide the necessary seasoning.

This dish needs to be prepared with a sense of moderation. Horseradish is a spicy and very hot root vegetable, which sailors used to eat when they suffered from malnutrition. Rich in vitamins and invigorating substances, horseradish can overpower other ingredients if it is not used sparingly. The cream should not be whipped too much before being folded in, as it may form lumps. Finally, this dish is completed with the addition of the sublime Beluga caviar, with its coarse grains and intense aroma.

1. Peel the cucumbers and retain half of the peel for lining the terrine. Use a slicer to slice the cucumber lengthwise into wafer-thin slices.

2. Leave the cucumber slices to infuse in coarse sea salt for 40 minutes. Rinse and drain on paper towels. Meanwhile, mix the cream mayonnaise into the cream, adding the juice of one lemon.

Cucumber with Horseradish

3. Line the terrine with plastic wrap and overlapping cucumber skin strips, letting them overlap the edges of the terrine by 1½–2 in / 4–5 cm. Soak the gelatin.

4. Mix the soaked gelatin with the horseradish and fold into the whipped cream. Prepare the cucumber slices so that you end up with three layers of ³⁄₈ in / 1 cm in thickness. Place one layer in the terrine, follow with a second layer of half of the cream filling, followed by a second cucumber layer and a final cream filling layer; finish with a layer of cucumber slices. Chill for 24 hours. Serve the terrine slices with the cream, a dollop of caviar, and the chive sprigs.

Marinated Scallops on

Preparation time: 15 minutes
Difficulty: ✮

Serves four

8 sea scallops
2 oz / 50 g salmon roe
1 cup / 200 g mixed lettuce (optional)
1 bunch of chives
salt, fresh-ground pepper to taste

For the marinade:
⅞ cup / 200 ml olive oil
juice of 1 lemon
salt, pepper to taste

For the chive sauce:
⅞ cup / 200 ml heavy cream
1 bunch of chives
1 bunch of chervil leaves
juice of 1 lemon
salt, pepper to taste

This recipe, by Chef Heinz Winkler, will win you over because it is so incredibly simple; apart from careful selection of the ingredients, preparation is very easy. European scallops are predominantly bred in Brittany, but our chef points out that the scallops from the northern German island of Sylt are also very good. In U.S. markets, there are many varieties, and if one prefers, substitute the smaller, more delicately flavored bay scallops from both the east and west coasts.

In this recipe, our chef abandons the usual method of frying the scallops and opts instead to simply slice them – similar to the preparation of *carpaccio* – and to marinate them in lemon juice and olive oil. The scallops should therefore be sliced very thinly, marinated for a short while only and consumed quickly,

as, if left out too long, they might oxidize and lose their characteristic iodine flavor.

The chive sauce underlines the scallops' flavor. Chives, part of the family of lilies, are quite popular, not least of all because of their high vitamin C content. Their freshness can be determined by the quality of the sprigs (they should be crisp and deep green); the bulb is used in the same way as onions.

The salmon roe provides the elegant note here. The large and crunchy grains are deep red; you could, in some cases, replace them with trout roe. You can, of course, also replace the salmon roe with proper Sevruga caviar if you wish to lend a note of extravagance to the dish.

1. Open the scallops, wash thoroughly, discard the bristles, extract the flesh from the shell, and slice very thinly.

2. For the marinade, mix olive oil, lemon juice, salt, and pepper in a shallow bowl. Marinate the scallops in this liquid for a while – about half an hour at the most.

a Bed of Chive Sauce

3. For the chive sauce, mix the heavy cream, chives, and chervil. Mix well, adjust seasoning to taste and add the juice of one lemon.

4. To serve, pour the sauce onto the plates and place the scallops on top, sprinkled with salmon roe. Garnish with chopped chives and, if desired, with mixed young lettuce such as mesclun as well.

Preparation time: 30 minutes
Difficulty: ☆

Serves four

16 large (sea) scallops
2 oz / 50 g Beluga caviar
2 oz / 50 g salmon roe
¼ cup / 60 g crème fraîche
1 bunch of chives
24 dandelion leaves (only the tips
   will be used)
juice of half a lemon
salt, fresh-ground pepper to taste

For the lemon marinade:
half a bunch of lemon balm
juice of half a lemon
juice of half a lime
⅝ cup / 150 ml olive oil
a pinch of sugar
1 tsp / 5 g sea salt

A real connoisseur of scallops, our chef, Harald Wohlfahrt, has them flown in from Ireland or Scotland to transform them into a *carpaccio* and tartare. The cold waters of the Irish Sea in particular provide the perfect breeding ground for many scallop varieties, which are caught from November through March.

The scallop has had many names, depending on period and region; the French call it large pelerine or Jacob's comb. Despite depictions dating from the Middle Ages, St. Jacob never carried the scallop that eventually became his symbol. Rather, it was the pilgrims of Santiago de Compostela who used the scallop as a plate, due to its shape; eventually it became the emblem of their union (see page 10 for more information and history).

You will need very fresh (that is, live) scallops that are still firmly shut. They always contain a little sea water and are quite difficult to open. Clean the inside of all unnecessary bits and begin preparation.

Lemon balm, originally from the Far East, has conquered Mediterranean cuisine. Here it is responsible for giving the marinade its strong flavor, combined with chives and dandelion, whose young leaves are slightly bitter. Lemon balm is often used instead of lemons because it has a similar taste but a less aggressive aroma. Finally, the caviar lends this dish an oily, salty, elegant note.

1. For the marinade, coarsely chop the lemon balm and mix with olive oil, lemon juice, and lime juice. Add sea salt and a pinch of sugar and leave to infuse for 24 hours.

2. Extract the flesh from the scallop shells, remove the exterior mucous, clean in ice water and drain on paper towels. Finely chop half of the scallops.

Tartare of Scallops

3. Season this tartare with half of the chives (finely chopped), a little marinade, salt, and pepper. Mix with half of the salmon roe. Mix the crème fraîche with the remaining salmon roe and a third of the caviar and season with lemon juice. Cut the remaining scallops into thin slices and distribute on the plates. Sprinkle with a little marinade.

4. Form the tartare into balls or dollops and place on top of the carpaccio; garnish with dandelion leaves and chives. Pour caviar sauce around the carpaccio and place the remaining caviar in the middle; garnish with chopped chives and marinade, and serve immediately.

Galantine of Goose Liver

Preparation time: 6–8 hours
Cooking time: 1 hour 15 minutes
Cooling time: 48 hours
Difficulty: ✳✳✳

Serves four

2 lb / 1 kg goose liver
6 pigeons (see below)
¹/₂ lb / 250 g pigeon meat
1 egg white
1 tbsp / 15 ml spinach stock
2 oz / 50 g chopped truffles
³/₄ cup / 200 ml old port
2¹/₂ tbsp / 40 ml cognac
³/₄ cup / 200 ml cream
³/₄ cup / 200 ml Madeira

2 tbsp / 30 g butter
1¹/₂ tbsp / 20 g terrine salt
¹/₂ tsp pickling salt
salt and pepper to taste

For the port aspic:
generous 1¹/₂ cups / 400 ml port
³/₄ cup / 200 ml each grape juice, pigeon stock
3 sheets of gelatin

To garnish:
1 bunch each of lollo rosso, lamb's lettuce, dandelion, chervil
1 head of frisée

For the vinaigrette:
¹/₂ cup / 100 ml each balsamic vinegar
¹/₂ cup / 100 ml grape seed oil
¹/₂ cup / 100 ml walnut oil
¹/₂ cup / 100 ml truffle oil
¹/₄ cup / 50 g pine nuts
salt, fresh-ground pepper to taste

Don't let the elaborate and long preparation for this appetizer put you off: the sublime quality of the galantine is extraordinary, and the effort will be well worth it.

For this combination of goose liver and pigeon, our chef, Harald Wohlfahrt, likes to use French foie gras, which he prefers to the imported produce from Hungary or Israel. Germany, unfortunately, hardly produces any foie gras. The pigeons should also be from France, preferably wild pigeons with soft feathers such as wood pigeons or ring doves; alternatively, you might substitute them with wild quail.

The truffle vinaigrette should be made with fresh truffles; they are, however, only available during the short truffle season in the autumn. You need medium-sized black truffles; they should not be too earthy.

It is a good idea to prepare the port aspic in advance. The bouquet of port, a concentrated Portuguese wine, is famous for its finesse and lends the aspic an elegant and complex character. The addition of grape juice (use natural grape juice) ensures this aroma will be maintained.

1. Skin and halve the goose liver and remove the tendons. Sprinkle with the salts and the pepper. Place the liver on a tray, pour over cognac and two tablespoons of port and chill for 24 hours. Remove the pigeon meat from the bone, cut into chunks of equal size, and marinate for two to three hours in terrine salt and half each of the port, Madeira, and cognac.

2. For the filling, cut half a pound of pigeon meat into strips, add the remaining terrine salt, and chill. Then mix, add the egg white and cream, and strain through a fine-meshed sieve. Sweat the truffles in butter, pour over the remaining port, Madeira and cognac, reduce, and chill. Prepare the vinaigrette. Roast the pine nuts for the vinaigrette; blend in.

and Pigeon with Port Aspic

3. Combine half of the chilled filling with the spinach stock, the other half with the truffle mixture; adjust seasoning to taste. For the aspic, reduce the port, grape juice, and sheets of gelatin at 100 °F / 50 °C to a syrup. Leave to chill and set, then chop the aspic into small dice. Wash the lettuces and soak the chervil.

4. Spread the spinach filling on the pigeon meat along with the truffle mixture. Roll in aluminum foil and close tightly. Steam at 155 °F / 80 °C for 15 minutes. Line the terrine form with aluminum foil, place a ³/₄ in / 2 cm layer of liver in the terrine followed by layer of galantine, and finishing with another layer of liver. Close with the foil. Steam for 25 minutes at 125 °F / 60 °C. Chill for 24 hours. Invert, slice with an electric carving knife. Serve with the jelly, lettuces, and vinaigrette.

Bavarian Cream

Preparation time: 1 hour
Cooking time: 45 minutes
Cooling time: 2 hours
Difficulty: ★★

Serves four

1 crab
⅝ cup / 150 ml cream
1 bunch of wild asparagus
1 large carrot
1 sheet of gelatin
half a bunch each of lemon balm, chervil

For the crab stock:
2 lb / 1 kg small crabs (blue or shore crabs)
1 bouquet garni (of bay leaf and sage)

7 oz / 200 g mixed vegetables (carrots,
    onions, celery)
2 cloves of garlic
4 tbsp / 50 g butter

1 tsp / 5 g fennel seeds
½ cup / 100 ml tomato sauce
1 tbsp / 15 g sugar, 1 tbsp / 15 ml Cognac
⅝ cup / 150 ml white wine and clear broth
2 tbsp / 20 g paprika, salt, and pepper mixture

For the parsley cream:
1 shallot, 3 eggs, 1 lemon
¼ cup / 50 ml cream
¼ cup / 50 ml olive oil
1 tsp / 5 ml parsley juice
1 tsp / 5 g mustard
⅛ lb / 50 g horseradish root, grated
⅜ cup / 80 g Béchamel sauce (see following
    recipe)
salt, pepper to taste

Our chef, Armando Zanetti of the Turin restaurant, Vecchia Lanterna, considers the crab to be the most important component of this appetizer. This type of crab, which inhabits the Atlantic and can grow to weigh around eleven or twelve pounds (five kilos), has enjoyed increased popularity over the past few decades, not least because of the delicious meat in its front claws. If you prefer, however, you could substitute a spider crab instead. Not very agile due to its long, inflexible legs, the spider crab is hardly capable of protecting itself against predators, so there is no reason to be afraid of handling a live spider crab – as opposed to its slightly more dangerous Atlantic cousin.

The same applies to the small crabs, whose rear legs are flat (which gives them a motion that has lent them the moniker "scuttling crabs") and have a pretty pattern. The crab stock, refined with aromatic fennel seeds, needs to cook for only a quarter of an hour. The cream is added after the cooking process, when the stock is still warm and thick. Our chef emphasizes the importance of adding the cream at the correct moment: if the stock is too hot the cream will curdle; if it is too cold you will not get an even emulsion.

This appetizer is subtle and elegant yet with strong flavors; at the same time it is light and balanced, so it is sure to be a hit with all your guests.

1. For the crab stock, fry the scant cupful of chopped vegetables with the garlic and the bouquet garni until brown. Add the crushed crabs, continue frying until brown and arrest the cooking process by pouring cognac and wine over the mixture. Add fennel, paprika, sugar, and tomato sauce. Reduce for 15 minutes, fill the saucepan with clear broth to the rim, and continue cooking 15 minutes. Strain through a fine-meshed sieve, chill, and then skim off the fat.

2. For the parsley cream, hard-boil the eggs, chop the shallot, grate the horseradish root and make the Béchamel sauce; mix the hard-boiled egg yolks with the mustard, shallot, horseradish and Béchamel sauce. Add lemon juice, cream, and olive oil; add salt, pepper, and parsley juice. Make the broth for the crabs with the listed ingredients, cook for ten minutes, and then cook the crabs in that broth for 15 minutes.

with Crustaceans

3. For the Bavarian cream, soak the gelatin in cold water. Add 1¼ cups / 300 ml of crab stock. Whip the cream and carefully fold into the broth; chill. Cook the asparagus in salted water, rinse in cold water, and chill as well. Prepare four fine carrot strips, blanch; set aside to cool and drain.

4. Line four ring forms with the blanched carrot strips. Fill the forms to three-fourths their volume with the Bavarian cream. Leave to cool, then add the crab meat that has been seasoned with lemon balm. Place a little parsley cream on every plate, place the Bavarian cream over this sauce, and arrange the asparagus in a fan shape next to the cream. Garnish with chervil.

Preparation time: 30 minutes
Cooking time: 20 minutes
Difficulty: ★

Serves four

8 baby carrots
4 baby turnips
4 small potatoes
4 spring onions
4 small artichokes
1 large leek
2 bunches of broccoli

For the horseradish sauce:
$^1/_4$ lb / 50 g horseradish root (to yield 1 tbsp grated)
1 shallot
3 eggs
juice of one lemon
1 tbsp / 15 g mustard
$^3/_4$ cup / 200 ml whipping cream
salt, pepper to taste

For the Béchamel sauce:
1 pint / 500 ml of milk
2 tbsp / 20 g butter
2 tbsp / 20 g all-purpose flour
a pinch of salt

This cold appetizer is meant to symbolize the variety of a vegetable garden – *alla giardiniera* simply means a dish that features chopped vegetables, usually ones fresh from the garden. Our chef, Armando Zanetti, a vegetable and garden lover, has enhanced this traditional recipe with a spicy horseradish sauce that replaces the usual mayonnaise.

Our chef uses hard-boiled egg yolk because it is more digestible than raw. Cream is also an important ingredient; it contains less fat than olive oil. And the fresh horseradish, laced with a dash of white wine, completes the picture. The horseradish root must only be grated at the last moment, otherwise it will become stale. Never use a horseradish root that is no longer fresh or has seedlings sprouting from it – these aging versions are so bitter they will destroy the sauce. It is best to cook the vegetables in stainless steel pots, as the neutral, clean metal helps to keep them fresh. You can compose the "vegetable garden" to your own taste with seasonal vegetables – in summer a mélange of raw and crunchy vegetables, in winter a mixture of heartier, cooked ones. Whatever vegetables you use, it is the sauce that will lend this dish its special character.

One last note: choose waxy potatoes for this dish, and do not over- or undercook them.

1. Wash the vegetables and chop decoratively. Divide the leek into four pieces and the broccoli into four florets. Peel the spring onions and trim, leaving 1 in / 2$^1/_2$ cm of green.

2. Cook each vegetable (except the potatoes) al dente, in its own batch of boiling salted water. The potatoes should be cooked normally.

Horseradish Sauce

3. For the Béchamel sauce, heat the butter and flour together. Leave to cool, then add the boiling milk. Bring to a boil and set aside. For the horseradish sauce, hard-boil the eggs, chop the shallot, and grate the horseradish root to yield one tablespoon. Mix three hard-boiled egg yolks with a tablespoon of mustard and then add the shallot, grated horseradish, and the Béchamel sauce.

4. Mix the horseradish sauce for two to three minutes, stirring in the lemon juice and cream. To serve, pool the sauce onto the plates, and decoratively arrange the vegetables.

Gazpacho with

Preparation time: 15 minutes
Cooking time: 30 minutes
Difficulty: ★

Serves four

1 spider crab (1½ to 2 lb / 700 g–1 kg)
2 lb / 1 kg tomatoes
2 red onions
1 clove of garlic
1 bunch of basil (to yield 7 good leaves)
¼ cup / 60 ml balsamic vinegar
2 tbsp / 30 ml extra virgin olive oil
salt, pepper to taste

For the broth:
1 onion stuck with cloves
1 carrot
1 bunch of parsley
half a bunch of thyme
1 bay leaf
salt, pepper to taste

Gazpacho is originally from Andalusia, but it is now popular all over Spain. A chilled, easy-to-prepare soup, it is made with tomatoes, cucumber, and peppers, plus bread crumbs (often from garlic bread), vinegar, and oil. Prepare the gazpacho the day before, so the flavors can blend well.

Fresh vegetables and crustaceans complement each other perfectly. Our chef, Alberto Zuluaga, out of concern for guests with weak stomachs, uses garlic and pepper sparingly; therefore the spider crab is presented here on a bed of onions and tomatoes. The spider crab should be of the *maja squinada*

variety, one of the largest and most common European types that lives on the Atlantic coast. Our chef, an avid fisherman himself, recommends weighing the crab in your hands: it should feel dense and heavy. After boiling the crab in the broth, extract the meat from the claws, legs, and the shell; and be forewarned that there is a great deal of cartilage underneath the shell.

Incidentally, a recipe for "white gazpacho," based on crushed almonds and ice water, was devised by Chef Alain Dutournier.

1. Cook the spider crab in the broth for 12 minutes, open the shell, and extract the meat. Make a broth with the claws, strain and set aside.

2. Slice the tomatoes and the garlic, and finely slice the onion. Sweat the onion in a casserole, but do not allow it to brown. Add the tomatoes and garlic and cook for ten minutes.

Spider Crab

3. Puree in the blender or food processor, adding vinegar, olive oil, and basil. Continue to blend for two minutes. Transfer into a bowl and add salt and pepper.

4. Mix the puree with the crab broth; strain and adjust seasoning to taste. Chill. To serve, form a pyramid of crab meat in the middle of the plates and pour the gazpacho around it. Garnish with basil leaves.

Basic Recipes

Balsamic vinaigrette

Recipe: Carpaccio of John Dory and Salmon with Hop Shoots and Blini by Jean & Jean-Yves Schillinger

Ingredients:
$7/8$ cup / 200 ml balsamic vinegar – $1^2/3$ cup / 400 ml olive oil – salt, pepper to taste

Preparation:
Mix the vinegar, salt and pepper in a salad bowl and gradually incorporate the olive oil.

Puff pastry

Recipe: Puff Pastry Tart with Tuna, Tomatoes and Basil by Dominique Le Stanc

Recipe: Smoked Salmon Cake with Pink Peppercorns and Horseradish by Émile Tabourdiau

Ingredients:
1 lb / 500 g flour – 1 tbsp / 15 g salt – 1 cup / 250 ml water – 1 lb / 250 g butter

Preparation:
Place the flour in a ring on a clean surface, depress the center, and add salt and water to it. Mix quickly and work into a dough ball. Leave to rest for 20 minutes, then roll out into a rectangle. Place the soft butter on the dough rectangle, flip the edges of the rectangle over the butter and roll out once more into a new rectangle. Repeat this process six times in 20-minute intervals.

Génoise

Recipe: Duck's Liver Tart with a Confit of Grapes by Dieter Kaufmann

Ingredients:
8 eggs – 1 cup / 250 g sugar – 1 cup / 250 g flour

Preparation:
Whisk eggs and sugar in a bowl in a bain-marie, heating all the while until room temperature. Remove from the heat, continue whisking rigorously at first, then whisk slower until the mixture has cooled. Fold in the flour carefully with a spoon. Fill into buttered and floured spring forms and bake for 30 minutes at 400 °F / 200 °C.

Chicken stock

Recipe: Velouté of Asparagus with Caviar Chantilly by Philippe Dorange

Ingredients:
2 lb / 1 kg chicken trimmings – 2 carrots – 1 large onion – 1 clove of garlic – 1 leek – 1 bunch of parsley – 1 sprig of thyme – half a bay leaf – 1 clove – a pinch of coarse sea salt

Preparation:
Chop the chicken trimmings, place in a casserole, cover with cold water, bring to a boil and blanch for two to three minutes. Rinse under running cold water and drain. Transfer the trimmings back to the casserole along with all the vegetables. Add the salt. Cover with water, bring to a boil and simmer for two hours. Strain through a fine-meshed sieve.

Lobster soup

Recipe: Lobster Gazpacho by Michel Haquin

Ingredients:
2 lobsters, 1 lb / 500 g each – 1 carrot – 1 onion – $1/2$ cup / 100 ml dry white wine – 2 tbsp / 30 ml cognac – 1 bouquet garni with extra parsley – 1 sprig of thyme – half a bay leaf – pepper and salt – $1/4$ cup / 50 ml vegetable oil – $1^1/4$ cup / 300 ml veal or fish broth – 1 tbsp / 15 g concentrated tomato paste – $1/2$ cup / 20 ml cream – $1/2$ cup / 20 g rice

Preparation:
Separate lobster heads and tails, split the heads lengthwise. Remove sand and place coral in a bowl. Chop carrot and onion and sweat in olive oil. Add lobster meat and cook until the meat has been cooked well and the shell has turned red. Add tomato paste, cognac and white wine and reduce. Cover with broth, bring to a boil and simmer for ten minutes. Remove the lobster. Crush the lobster heads with a mortar and pestle, transfer to the cooking liquid and mix with the cream, the rice (which has been soaked in $1/2$ cup / 125 ml of cold broth) and the coral. Cook for ten minutes, strain through a fine-meshed sieve and adjust seasoning to taste.

Garlic sauce

Recipe: Terrine of Beans and Duck's Liver by Jean Bardet

Ingredients:
2 cloves of garlic – 1 cup / 250 ml cream – 1 cup / 250 ml milk – 2 oz / 50 g butter – 1 tbsp / 15 g confectioners' sugar – 2 tbsp / 30 ml aged red wine vinegar – salt and pepper

Preparation:
Blanch garlic cloves in water twice, rinsing under cold running water after each blanching process. Heat butter in a small frying pan. Add garlic cloves and a tablespoon of sugar and brown slightly. Pour in the vinegar and then the cream and milk. Add salt and pepper and cook for 20 minutes. Strain through a fine-meshed sieve.

Mayonnaise

Recipe: Terrine of Lentils and Langoustines with Caviar Cream by Michel Blanchet

Recipe: Langoustine Tartare in a Delicate Oyster Aspic by Richard Contanceau

Ingredients (to yield $1^1/2$ cups / 300 g mayonnaise):
2 egg yolks – 1 cup / 250 ml peanut oil – 1 tbsp / 15 ml white vinegar – $1/2$ tbsp / 5 g salt – ground white pepper – 1 tsp / 5 g mustard

Preparation:
Mix egg yolks, mustard, salt, and pepper in a bowl. Whisking constantly, add oil in a very thin stream. Stir in the vinegar and season to taste.

Mayonnaise with horseradish and caviar

Recipe: Carpaccio of Langoustines with Caviar Cream by Jean-Pierre Bruneau

Ingredients:
2 egg yolks – 1 cup / 250 ml peanut oil – 1 tbsp / 15 ml white vinegar – ½ tbsp / 5 g salt – ground white pepper – 1 tsp / 5 g mustard – 1 tbsp / 12 g grated horseradish – ¾ cup / 185 g spicy broth – 3½ oz / 100 g caviar

Preparation:
Mix egg yolks, mustard, salt, and pepper in a bowl. Whisking constantly, add oil in a very thin stream. Stir in the vinegar, grated horseradish, spicy broth, and, at the end, the caviar.

Paprika vinaigrette

Recipe: Salad of Winter Vegetables with Scallops by Pedro Subijana

Ingredients:
1 yellow pepper – 1 cup / 250 ml olive oil – 1 egg yolk – 2 tbsp / 40 ml sherry vinegar – salt, pepper

Preparation:
Wash, halve, seed, and cut the pepper into chunks, chop in the food processor and season with salt and pepper. Add egg yolk and sherry vinegar, continue blending while adding the oil in a very fine stream until the vinaigrette has the consistency of a light mayonnaise. Strain through a fine-meshed sieve and season to taste.

Cream mayonnaise

Recipe: Glazed Terrine of Cucumber with Horseradish by Jean-Pierre Vigato

Ingredients (to yield 1½ cups / 300 g mayonnaise):
2 egg yolks – 1 cup / 250 ml peanut oil – 1 tbsp / 15 ml white vinegar – ½ tbsp / 5 g salt – ground white pepper – 1 tsp / 5 g mustard – 1¼ cup / 300 ml cream – juice of 1 lemon

Preparation:
Mix egg yolks, mustard, salt, and pepper in a bowl. Whisking constantly, add oil in a very thin stream, stir in the vinegar at the end. Mix the mayonnaise with cream and lemon juice and season to taste.

Hot mustard mayonnaise

Recipe: Turbot and Lobster Pâté with a Delicate Sauce by Michel Bourdin

Ingredients:
2 egg yolks – 1 cup / 250 ml peanut oil – 1 tbsp / 15 ml white vinegar – ½ tbsp / 5 g salt – ground white pepper – 1 tsp / 5 g mustard – ¼ cup / 50 ml cream, lightly whipped – ½ cup / 100 ml tomato juice – juice of 1 lemon

Preparation:
Mix egg yolks, mustard, salt, pepper and vinegar in a bowl. Whisking constantly, add oil in a very thin stream. Add the tomato juice, carefully fold in the slightly whipped cream. Season with lemon juice.

Vinaigrette

Recipe: Terrine of Foie Gras by Horst Petermann

Ingredients:
2 tbsp / 20 ml walnut oil – 2 tbsp / 20 ml olive oil – 1 tsp / 5 ml sherry vinegar – 1 tsp / 5 ml balsamic vinegar – 1 tbsp / 15 ml mustard – ½ cup / 100 ml oxtail cooking liquid – salt and pepper – 1 bunch of tarragon

Preparation:
Mix all ingredients in a bowl with a whisk, then add the room-temperature oxtail cooking liquid. Add the vegetables listed in the recipe, leave to infuse, and add the chopped tarragon leaves at the end.

The Participating Chefs

Fernando Adría

born May 14, 1962

Restaurant: **El Bulli**
Address: 30, Apartado de Correos Cala
Montjoi 17480 Rosas, Spain
Tel. (9)72 15 04 57; Fax (9)72 15 07 17

As a young, talented 21-year-old back in 1983, Fernando Adrìa received two Michelin stars for his culinary achievements in El Bulli, his restaurant on the Costa Brava whose kitchens had previously been run by his friend Jean-Louis Neichel. Awarded 19 points and four red chef's hats by Gault-Millau, Adrìa has also fared well with the Spanish restaurant guides: four stars in Campsa and 9.5/10 in Gourmetour. A winner of the "Spanish national gastronomy award", Fernando Adrìa also received the "European culinary grand prix" in 1994. When his work leaves him time, this chef is a great supporter of the Barcelona soccer team.

Hilario Arbelaitz

born May 27, 1951

Restaurant: **Zuberoa**
Address: Barrio Iturrioz, 8
20180 Oyarzun, Spain
Tel. (9)43 49 12 28; Fax (9)43 49 26 79

Born in the heart of the Spanish Basque Country, whose gourmet traditions form the emphasis of his cooking, Hilario Arbelaitz began his career in 1970 at Zuberoa, where he became chef in 1982. Since then, he has received numerous French and Spanish awards: two Michelin stars and three red chef's hats and 17 points in Gault-Millau, as well as four Campsa stars. In 1993 he was named "Best Chef in Euzkadi" (the Basque Country), after being named "Best Chef in Spain" in 1991. He brings equal measures of enthusiasm to the Basque game of pelota and family life, and is very interested in the history and future of his profession.

Firmin Arrambide

born September 16, 1946

Restaurant: **Les Pyrénées**
Address: 19, place du Général de Gaulle
64220 Saint-Jean-Pied-de-Port, France
Tel. (0)5 59 37 01 01; Fax (0)5 59 37 18 97

Firmin Arrambide has been at the helm of this restaurant not far from his place of birth since 1986, garnering two Michelin stars and three red chef's hats and 18 points in Gault-Millau for Les Pyrénées. His regionally inspired cuisine won him second place in the 1978 Taittinger awards and carried him to the finals of the Meilleur Ouvrier de France competition in 1982. True to his Basque origins, Arrambide hunts woodpigeon and woodsnipe in the fall, and also loves mountain climbing; occasionally, though, he enjoys simply soaking up the sun by the side of the swimming pool.

Jean Bardet

born September 27, 1941

Restaurant: **Jean Bardet**
Address: 57, rue Groison
37000 Tours, France
Tel. (0)3 47 41 41 11; Fax (0)3 47 51 68 72

Before opening a restaurant in Tours under his own name in 1987, Jean Bardet traversed the whole of Europe, working mainly as a sauce chef at the Savoy in London. A member of Relais et Châteaux, Relais Gourmands and the Auguste Escoffier Foundation, he was awarded four red chef's hats in Gault-Millau (19.5) and two Michelin stars. In 1982 he had the honor of preparing dinner for the heads of state at the Versailles Summit. Jean Bardet is an enthusiastic cigar smoker (American Express awarded him the title of "Greatest Smoker in the World" in 1984) and in the fall indulges his passion for hunting together with friends.

Giuseppina Beglia

born May 16, 1938

Restaurant: **Balzi Rossi**
Address: 2, Via Balzi Rossi
18039 Ventimiglia, Italy
Tel. (0)18 43 81 32; Fax (0)18 43 85 32

Since 1983 her restaurant has towered over this famous vantage point and the caves of the Balzi Rossi ("red cliffs"), but Giuseppina Beglia herself is just as well known in Italy for the television cookery programs broadcast under her direction between 1985–90. A member of Le Soste, the prestigious Italian restaurant chain, she holds two Michelin stars, three red chef's hats in Gault-Millau (18) and 82/100 in the Italian Gambero Rosso guide. In 1992 she won the first "Golden Key of Gastronomy" to be awarded by Gault-Millau to chefs outside of France. Giuseppina Beglia is very interested the flower arrangements in her restaurant, and loves skiing in the nearby Alps.

Michel Blanchet

June 16, 1949

Restaurant: **Le Tastevin**
Address: 9, avenue Eglé
78600 Maisons-Laffitte, France
Tel. (0)139 62 11 67; Fax (0)1 39 62 73 09

After a top-notch training from 1967–71 at *Maxim's*, *Lutétia* and *Ledoyen*, Michel Blanchet took over the reins at *Tastevin* in 1972; today, the restaurant boasts two Michelin stars. Blanchet's talents have more than once carried him through to the final rounds of prestigious awards: the Prosper Montagné prize (1970 and 1972); the Taittinger prize (1974); and the Meilleur Ouvrier de France competition in 1979. Michel Blanchet is a Maître Cuisinier de France and a member of the "Culinary Academy of France". A great lover of nature, he enjoys rambles through the woods – during which he sometimes also collects mushrooms – as well as cycling and hiking.

Michel Bourdin

born June 6, 1942

Restaurant: **The Connaught**
Address: Carlos Place, Mayfair
London W1Y 6AL, England
Tel. (0)171 491-0668; Fax (0)171 495-3262

One of the old and distinguished line of French chefs in Great Britain, Michel Bourdin has been delighting London diners at the *Connaught* since 1975. The recipient of numerous prizes (Prosper Montagné, Taittinger) since training at *Ledoyen* and under Alex Humbert at *Maxim's*, he has been Chairman of the British branch of the "Culinary Academy of France" since 1980. In addition, he is a member of the "100 Club", and like Paul Haeberlin is also an honorary member of the Chefs des Chefs association. His pastry-chef colleagues, the twins Carolyn and Deborah Power, have made the *Connaught* famous for its desserts.

Michel Bruneau

born February 11, 1949

Restaurant: **La Bourride**
Address: 15-17, rue du Vaugueux
14000 Caen, France
Tel. (0)2 31 93 50 76; Fax (0)2 31 93 29 63

"Normandy is proud of herself" – this is the motto of Michel Bruneau, who never tires of enumerating the sumptuous produce of the Calvados region on his exhaustive, tempting menu. Starting off his career in the midst of the plantations in Ecrécy, on the banks of the Guigne (1972–82), he then moved to *La Bourride* in Caen, where he has been since 1982. Here he continues to delight gourmets with his inventive cooking, steeped in regional traditions, which has also impressed the critics: two Michelin stars, three red chef's hats in Gault-Millau (18). In his spare time, Michel Bruneau enjoys cooking for friends and playing soccer.

Carlo Brovelli

born May 23, 1938

Restaurant: **Il Sole di Ranco**
Address: 5, Piazza Venezia
21020 Ranco, Italy
Tel. (0)3 31 97 65 07; Fax (0)3 31 97 66 20

One "sun" – it was only fitting that the Italian restaurant guide Veronelli should pay tribute to this restaurant with the sun in its name by awarding it this distinction. Looking back on a 120-year-old family tradition, *Il Sole di Ranco* is run in a masterly fashion by Carlo Brovelli, who took over the reins in 1968 after training at the college of hotel management in La Stresa. A member of the Le Soste, Relais et Châteaux and Relais Gourmands chains, Brovelli has received many accolades: two Michelin stars, three chef's hats in Gault-Millau (18), 84/100 in the Italian Gambero Rosso. Carlo Brovelli loves cycling and soccer, as well as his favorite sport, hunting.

Jean-Pierre Bruneau

born September 18, 1943

Restaurant: **Bruneau**
Address: 73-75, avenue Broustin
1080 Brussels, Belgium
Tel. (0)24 27 69 78; Fax (0)24 25 97 26

For a good 20 years now, Jean-Pierre Bruneau has run the restaurant bearing his name which stands in the shadow of the important Koekelberg Basilica in the center of Brussels. The sophisticated creations of this Belgian "Maître Cuisinier" have won him many distinctions: three Michelin stars, four red chef's hats in Gault-Millau, three stars in Bottin Gourmand and 94/100 in the Belgian restaurant guide Henri Lemaire. He is also a member of Traditions et Qualité. Outside of the kitchen, he enjoys hunting and car racing (first hand); in addition, he collects old cars.

Alain Burnel

born January 26, 1949

Restaurant: **Oustau de Baumanière**
Address: Val d'Enfer
13520 Les Baux-de-Provence, France
Tel. (0)4 90 54 33 07; Fax (0)4 90 54 40 46

Alain Burnel served his apprenticeship in Beaulieu at *La réserve de Beaulieu* (1969–73), in Nantes at *Frantel* under Roger Jaloux, in Marseilles at *Sofitel* and in Saint-Romain de Lerps at the *Château du Besset*, where he served as chef from 1978-82 before taking over the reins from the famous Raymond Thuillier in Baux, whose restaurant is now owned by the Charial family. Alain Burnel has earned two Michelin stars, three white chef's hats in Gault-Millau (18) and is a member of Traditions et Qualité, Relais et Châteaux and Relais Gourmands. In his free time this chef is a keen cyclist, and was even once a participant in the Tour de France.

Jan Buytaert

born October 16, 1946

Restaurant: **De Bellefleur**
Address: 253 Chaussée d'Anvers
2950 Kapellen, Belgium
Tel. (0)3 664 6719; Fax (0)3 665 0201

Despite being a dyed-in-the-wool Belgian who has spent a large part of his career in his native country (first at the *Villa Lorraine* in Brussels from 1973–4), Jan Buytaert worked for two years in the kitchens of *Prés et Sources d'Eugénie* in Eugénie-les-Bains under Michel Guérard (1974–5). In 1975, after this French interlude, he opened his current restaurant, which has earned him two Michelin stars and is one of the best in the region. This Belgian Maître Cuisinier loves gentle activities such as hiking and riding, and also enjoys working in the garden.

Jacques Cagna

born August 24, 1942

Restaurant: **Jacques Cagna**
Address: 14, rue des Grands Augustins
75006 Paris, France
Tel. (0)1 43 26 49 39; Fax (0)1 43 54 54 48

This distinguished chef has worked the most famous restaurants of the French capital (1960 at *Lucas Carton*, 1961 at *Maxim's*, 1964 at *La Ficelle*), and was even Chef to the French National Assembly (1961–62) before opening his own restaurant under his own name in 1975, for which he has received high honors: two Michelin stars, two red chef's hats in Gault-Millau (18) and three stars in Bottin Gourmand. Jacques Cagna is a Knight of the "Mérite nationale des Arts et des Lettres". He knows his way around Asia very well, speaks fluent Japanese and is keen on classical music, opera and jazz.

Stewart Cameron

born September 16, 1945

Restaurant: **Turnberry Hotel & Golf Courses**
Turnberry KA26 9LT, Scotland
Tel. (0)1655 331 000; Fax (0)1655 331 706

Since 1981, the kitchens of the *Turnberry* Hotel – one of only two 5-star Scottish restaurants – have had a real Scot at the helm: Stewart Cameron, who previously worked at *Malmaison*, the restaurant of the *Central Hotel* in Glasgow. This chef is also a member of the "Taste of Scotland" and of the British Branch of the "Culinary Academy of France". In 1986 and 1994 he was privileged to play host in his restaurant to the participants of the British Golf Open. When he gets the chance, Stewart Cameron goes hunting or fishing. A rugby fan (of course!), he is one of the Scottish Fifteen's most faithful supporters.

Mario Cavallucci

born May 20, 1959

Restaurant: **La Frasca**
Address: 38, Via Matteoti
47011 Castrocaro Terme, Italy
Tel. (0)543 76 74 71; Fax (0)543 76 66 25

Two Michelin stars, 4 chef's hats in Gault-Millau (19), one sun in Veronelli, 89/100 in Gambero Rosso: what more could Mario Cavallucci want? Working in perfect harmony with the restaurant's proprietor and cellarman, Gianfranco Bolognesi, this young, energetic chef has already received many accolades. A member of the Le Soste restaurant chain, he has vigorously supported Italy's great culinary tradition since 1978. This extraordinarily busy chef nevertheless manages to find a little spare time for fishing, reading, seeing the occasional movie, and playing cards, soccer and billiards.

Bernard & Jean Cousseau

born September 15, 1917 born May 6, 1949

Restaurant: **Relais de la Poste**
Address: 40140 Magescq, France
Tel. (0)5 58 47 70 25; Fax: (0)5 58 47 76 17

Bernard Cousseau embodies the regional gastronomy of Landes. Honorary president of the Maîtres Cuisiniers de France, he serves a fine regional cuisine to his guests at the Relais de la Poste, which openend in 1954 and has been holding two Michelin stars since 1969. On the height of his extraordinary career, the Chef is now an officer of the Mérite Agricole and a Knight of both the Légion d'Honneur and the Palmes académiques. His son Jean has been working with him at the Relais de la Poste since 1970, after an examplary Franco-Hispanic career at the Café de Paris in Biaritz, the Plaza-Athénée in Paris and the Ritz in Madrid.

Francis Chauveau

born: September 15, 1947

Restaurant: **La Belle Otéro**
Address: Hôtel Carlton (7th floor)
58, La Croisette
06400 Cannes, France
Tel. (0)4 93 69 39 39; Fax (0)4 93 39 09 06

Although born in Berry in the northwest of France, Francis Chauveau's encounter with Provencal cooking has led to outstanding results, which visitors to the legendary Palace-Hotel in Cannes – holder of two Michelin stars – have been enjoying since 1989. Francis Chauveau gained his first experience as a chef in the Hôtel d'Espagne in Valencay, continuing his career at the Auberge de Noves in 1965. Later, he worked in prestigious restaurants such as the Auberge du Père Bise, the Réserve de Beaulieu, the Terrasse in the Hotel Juana in Juan-les Pins, and in the famous restaurant L'Amandier in Mougins from 1980–89.

Richard Coutanceau

born: February 25, 1949

Restaurant: **Richard Coutanceau**
Address: Place de la Concurrence
17000 La Rochelle, France
Tel. (0)5 46 41 48 19; Fax (0)5 46 41 99 45

Richard Coutanceau, whose restaurant boasts a marvelous location in "green Venice" between Marais Poitevin and the Côte Sauvage, started out his career in Paris at L'Orée du bois in 1968. He then moved to La Rochelle and the Hôtel de France et d'Angleterre, where he worked from 1968-82. This native of Charentais has received many distinctions: two stars in Michelin, three stars in Bottin Gourmand and three red chef's hats and 17 points in Gault-Millau. His restaurant belongs to the Relais Gourmands chain, and he is also a member of the "Young Restauranteurs of Europe". Richard Coutanceau is an avid tennis player and a keen fisherman.

Jacques Chibois

born: July 22, 1952

Restaurant: **La Bastide St-Antoine**
Address: 45, avenue Henri Dunant
06130 Grasse, France
Tel. (0)4 92 42 04 42; Fax (0)4 92 42 03 42

During the course of a career involving many moves, Jacques Chibois has met many famous names in French gastronomy: Jean Delaveyne in Bougival, Louis Outhier in La Napoule, Roger Vergé in Mougins, and the famous pastry chef Gaston Lenôtre. Since 1980 he has repeatedly worked under Michel Guérard, and was awarded two Michelin stars during his time at Gray d'Albion in Cannes (1981–95). He opened La Bastide Saint-Antoine in Grasse in 1995. In his spare time, Jacques Chibois is an enthusiastic cyclist and nature-lover, as well as a keen hunter and angler.

Jean Crotet

born: January 26, 1943

Restaurant: **Hostellerie de Levernois**
Address: Route de Combertault
21200 Levernois, France
Tel. (0)3 80 24 73 68; Fax (0)3 80 22 78 00

Amidst a splendid park of Louisiana cedar, willow and ash, through which a small river flows, Jean Crotet offers discerning diners a sophisticated cuisine which has been awarded two Michelin stars and three stars in Bottin Gourmand. He is a Maître Cuisinier de France, as well as a member of Relais et Châteaux and Relais Gourmands chains. In 1988, after working for 15 years at the Côte d'Or in Nuits-Saint Georges, he settled down in Levernois, near Beaune. In his spare time Jean Crotet enjoys fishing, flying a helicopter, playing tennis, hunting and gardening.

Serge Courville

born: December 9, 1935

Restaurant: **La Cote 108**
Address: Rue Colonel Vergezac
02190 Berry-au-Bac, France
Tel. (0)3 23 79 95 04; Fax (03) 23 79 83 50

Serge Courville names his three teachers – Roger Petit, Robert Morizot and Jean-Louis Lelaurain – with warmth. Although not much interested in accolades, he has nevertheless reached the final of numerous culinary competitions (Prosper Montagné prize, 1971; Trophée national de l'Académie Culinaire, 1972; Taitinger prize, 1973). Since 1972, he and his wife have together run La Cote 108, which in 1982 received one Michelin star. When not working, Serge Courville enjoys cooking for friends; he is also a passionate reader and cyclist and spends a lot of time in the wilds, fishing or hunting for mushrooms.

Michel Del Burgo

born: June 21, 1962

Restaurant: **La Barbacane**
Address: Place de l'Église
11000 Carcassonne-La Cité, France
Tel. (0)4 68 25 03 34; Fax (0)4 68 71 50 15

This young man from the northern province of Picardy has worked in the kitchens of Alain Ducasse in Courchevel, Raymond Thuillier in Baux-de-Provence and Michel Guérard in Eugénie-les-Bains, all in the south of France. After a short stay in the Rhône valley and Avignon (1987-90), Michel Del Burgo was in 1991 appointed chef of La Barbacane in the center of Carcassonne by Jean-Michel Signoles. In 1995 he was awarded his second Michelin star, the "Lily of the restaurant trade" and the Gault-Millau "golden key", as well as three red chef's hats and 18 points in the latter guide. Michel Del Burgo rates the cooking of his fellow chefs in the "Land of the Cathars", but is also fond of music, motor sport and hiking.

Joseph Delphin

born: September 4, 1932

Restaurant: **La Châtaigneraie**
Address: 156, route de Carquefou
44240 Sucé-sur-Erdre, France
Tel. (0)2 40 77 90 95; Fax (0)2 40 77 90 08

A Maître Cuisinier de France and member of the "Culinary Academy of France", Joseph Delphin delights gourmets from the Nantes area with his culinary skills. A knight of the Mérite agricole, this chef has also received the Vase de Sèvres award from the French President. His restaurant, *La Châtaigneraie* (one Michelin star), sits right on the banks of the Erdre, and can be reached by road, river or helicopter...You are sure to be won over by the warmth of the welcome from the Delphin family, as Jean-Louis, a member of the "Young Restauranteurs of Europe", works here together with his father.

Philippe Dorange

born: May 27, 1963

Restaurant: **Fouquet's**
Address: 99, avenue des Champs Élysées
75008 Paris, France
Tel (0)1 47 23 70 60; Fax (0)1 47 20 08 69

Does one actually need to to introduce the legendary *Fouquet's* in these pages? Surely not, nor the prestigious restaurants in which Philippe Dorange has worked in the past: Roger Vergé's *Le Moulin de Mougins* (1977–81), Jacques Maximin's *Negresco* in Nice (1981–88), and lastly *Ledoyen* in Paris, where he was chef from 1988–92. All in all, a fine career path for a young chef whose Mediterranean origins are reflected in his culinary preferences, a fact which is particularly esteemed by his Champs-Élysées clientele. When not in the kitchen, Philippe Dorange likes to box, drive sports cars or play soccer.

Claude and Eric Dupont

born June 7, 1938; April 16, 1966

Restaurant: **Claude Dupont**
46, Avenue Vital Riethuisen
Brussels 1080, Belgium
Tel. (0)2 426 0000; (0)2 426 6540

The Belgian and French gourmet restaurants have positively showered awards on Claude Dupont's cooking: two Michelin stars since 1976, three white chef's hats in Gault-Millau (17). and 92/100 points in the Belgian Henri Lemaire guide. In 1967 he was awarded the Prosper Montagne prize, and in 1973 the Oscar of Gastronomy. In addition, this chef ran the Belgian pavilion at the 1970 World Fair in Osaka. His son was taught by the Brussels master chefs Freddy Van Decasserie, Pierre Wynants, and Willy Vermeulen. Today he works with his father.

Lothar Eiermann

born: March 2, 1945

Restaurant: **Wald- & Schloßhotel Friedrichsruhe**
Address: 74639 Friedrichsruhe, Germany
Tel (0)7941 60870; Fax (0)7941 61468

For over 20 years now Lothar Eiermann has worked at Friedrichsruhe, the summer residence of the Prince von Hohenlohe-Öhringen which belongs to the Relais et Châteaux chain. Before this, he traveled throughout the whole of Europe, working as a chef in Switzerland between 1964-72 in the *Grappe d'Or* in Lausanne and in the Hotel *Victoria* in Glion. He then worked in the *Gleneagles* Hotel in Scotland, traveled south to England, and returned to Scotland, where he managed a hotel from 1972-3. This Bordeaux-wine enthusiast also has a degree in Economics from the University of Heidelberg, and depending on the season, enjoys skiing, cycling or playing tennis.

Constant Fonk

born: September 1, 1947

Restaurant: **De Oude Rosmolen**
Address: Duinsteeg 1
1621 Hoorn, the Netherlands
Tel (0)229 014752; Fax (0)229 014938

Thanks to Constant Fonk, the town of Hoorn in North Holland has had a two-Michelin-starred restaurant since 1990. After his first highly promising steps in the Amsterdam *Hilton* (1965–6), and the *Amstel Hotel* (1966–7), our chef returned to his home town, where in 1967 he began work in *De Oude Rosmolen*, finally taking over the reins of the kitchen in 1976. A lover of fine cuisine and good wines, he especially enjoys partaking of both with like-minded people. As far as sport is concerned, golf is his favorite form of exercise, and makes a change from the kitchen.

Louis Grondard

born: September 20, 1948

Restaurant: **Drouant**
Address: 16-18, rue Gaillon
75002 Paris, France
Tel (0)1 42 65 15 16; Fax (0)1 49 24 02 15

It is no easy task to have catered for the members of the jury of the prestigious Goncourt literary prize every year since 1990; rather, it requires someone with the skills of this chef, who was named Meilleur Ouvrier de France in 1979. Louis Grondard served his apprenticeship at *Taillevent* and at *Maxim's*, first in Orly, then in Roissy. He then achieved his first successes in the Eiffel Tower restaurant and in the famous *Jules Vernes*, which opened in the Tower in 1983. To quote Michel Tournier, "The stars [two in Michelin] fall as his due from heaven." Louis Grondard has also received three white chef's hats and 17 points in Gault-Millau. He loves literature, music and opera.

Philippe Groult

born: November 17, 1953

Restaurant: **Amphyclès**
Address: 78, avenue des Ternes
75017 Paris, France
Tel (0)1 40 68 01 01; Fax (0)1 40 68 91 88

A devoted pupil and colleague of Joïl Robuchon at *Jamin* from1974–85, this native Norman now runs his own restaurant, to the satisfaction of diners and critics alike. Named Meilleur Ouvrier de France in 1982, today Philippe Groult has two Michelin stars and three red chef's hats (18) in Gault-Millau. In 1988 he was a contender in the "Culinary Olympics" in Tokyo, and one year later took over the reins in the kitchen at *Amphyclès*. He has been a member of Devoirs Unis since 1978. Philippe Groult is a keen traveler, a connoisseur of the Far East and an enthusiastic martial arts practitioner.

Marc Haeberlin

born: November 28, 1954

Restaurant: **Auberge de L'Ill**
Address: 2, rue de Collonges-au-Mont-d'Or
68970 Illhaeusern, France
Tel. (0)3 89 71 89 00; Fax (0)3 89 71 82 83

This worthy heir to the Haeberlin dynasty will on no account disappoint the gourmets who, once lured by the success of his father Paul, return to this temple of Alsatian cuisine. Three Michelin stars, four red chef's hats (19.5!) in Gault-Millau and four stars in Bottin Gourmand are the impressive distinctions garnered by this former student at the college of hotel management in Illkirch. Completing his training with Paul Bocuse and the Troisgros brothers, he proved his skills in Paris at the *Lasserre* back in 1976. When time allows, Mark Haeberlin occupies himself with painting and cars. In winter he goes downhill-skiing on the slopes of the Vosges.

Santi Santamaria

born July 26, 1957

Restaurant: **El Racó de Can Fabes**
Address: Carrer Sant Joan, 6
08470 San Celoni, Spain
Tel. (9)3 867 2851; Fax (9)3 867 3861

Since 1981, Santi Santamaria has taken great pleasure in serving specialties from his native Catalonia to his discerning clientele. His restaurant, which is just a stone's throw away from Barcelona, at the foot of Montseny national park, has been awarded three Michelin stars and 8/10 in Gourmetour. In addition, Santi Santamaria is a member of Relais Gourmands and Traditions et Qualité. Our chef also organizes gastronomic seminars, on herbs in the spring and on mushrooms in the fall. These gourmet workshops are always a great success. In his free time, Santi Santamaria enjoys reading.

Ezio Santin

born May 17, 1937

Restaurant: **Antica Osteria del Ponte**
Address: 9, Piazza G. Negri
20080 Cassinetta di Lugagnano, Italy
Tel. (0)2 942 0034; Fax (0)2 942 0610

Ezio Santin's culinary talents have been common knowledge since 1974, when he became chef at the *Antica Osteria del Ponte*. Three Michelin stars, four red chef's hats in Gault-Millau (19.5), one sun in Veronelli and 92/100 in Gambero Rosso: these honors justify the high regard in which he is held by his fellow Italian chefs, who have elected him chairman of Le Soste, an association of the best restaurants in Italy. Ezio Santin enjoys reading in his spare time. An enthusiastic fan of Inter Milan soccer club, he is also interested in modern dance.

Nadia Santini

born July 19, 1954

Restaurant: **Dal Pescatore**
Address: 46013 Runate Canneto sull'Oglio, Italy
Tel. (0)376 72 30 01; Fax (0)376 70304

Since 1974 Nadia Santini has presided over the kitchens of *Dal Pescatore*, which was opened in 1920 by her husband's grandfather. The outstanding reputation of this restaurant is impressively documented in both Italian and French restaurant guides: two Michelin stars, four red chef's hats in L'Espresso/Gault-Millau (19), one sun in Veronelli and 94/100 in Gambero Rosso. A member of Le Soste, Relais Gourmands and Traditions et Qualité, she was awarded the prize for the "Best Wine Cellar of the Year" by L'Espresso/Gault-Millau in 1993. Nadia Santini is interested in history, especially the history of the culinary arts, from which she draws inspiration.

Maria Santos Gomes

born August 10, 1962

Restaurant: **Conventual**
Address: Praça das Flores, 45
1200 Lisbon, Portugal
Tel. (0)1 60 91 96; Fax (0)1 387 5132

The *Conventual* is located in the historic Old Town of Lisbon, right by the Parliament. There, in 1982, Dina Marquez engaged the young chef Maria Santos Gomes – to the great delight of Lisbon politicians, who dine there regularly. Much of the restaurant's decor comes from the former cloister of Igreja (hence the restaurant's name). Maria Santos Gomes' inventive cuisine has already earned her one Michelin star; in 1993, she won first prize in the "Portuguese Gastronomy Competition", which always takes place in Lisbon. In addition to cooking, she loves literature, going on walks and traveling.

Nikolaos Sarantos

born December 5, 1945

Restaurant: **Hôtel Athenaeum Inter-Continental**
Address: 89-93, Syngrou Avenue
117 45 Athens, Greece
Tel. (0)1 902 3666; Fax (0)1 924 3000

From 1971–88, Nikolaos Sarantos traveled around the Mediterranean and the Middle East, honing his culinary skills in the various *Hilton* Hotels in Teheran, Athens, Corfu, Kuwait City and Cairo before finally settling down at the *Athenaeum Inter-Continental* in 1988. Nikolaos Sarantos is a member of the jury at international cooking competitions in San Francisco, Copenhagen and Bordeaux. Chairman of the "Chef's Association of Greece", he is also a great sports fan, and a keen tennis, soccer and basketball player.

Fritz Schilling

born June 8, 1951

Restaurant: **Schweizer Stuben**
Address: Geiselbrunnweg 11,
97877 Wertheim, Germany
Tel. (0)9342 30 70; Fax (0)9342 30 71 55

A chef since 1972, Fritz Schilling opened his restaurant in the Main valley near the romantic little town of Wertheim in 1990. His refined and versatile cuisine, which cultivates the best German gastronomic traditions, has already earned him two Michelin stars and four red chef's hats in Gault-Millau (19.5). A member of Relais et Châteaux and Relais Gourmands, his restaurant is one of the best in Germany. In his spare time, Fritz Schilling loves listening to pop music. A passionate driver, he enjoys playing golf and likes most beach sports.

Jean and Jean-Yves Schillinger

born January 31, 1934   born March 23, 1963
died December 27, 1995

Jean Schillinger was Chairman of Maître Cuisiniers de France and a symbol of Alsatian gastronomy; his restaurant in Colmar (1957–95) boasted two Michelin stars, three red stars in Gault-Millau (17), and three stars in Bottin Gourmand. A Knight of the Ordre de Mérite, he raised the profile of French cuisine throughout the world, from Japan to Brazil and Australia.

His son Jean-Yves belongs to the fourth generation of the restaurant family and has worked all his life in famous restaurants: the Crillon and Jamin in Paris, and La Côte Basque in New York. From 1988 to 1995 he worked in the family-owned restaurant in Colmar.

Rudolf Sodamin and Jonathan Wicks

born April 6, 1958; June 14, 1958

Restaurant: Passenger Ship *Queen Elizabeth II* Home port: Southampton, Great Britain

These two chefs work for the shipping company Cunard Line, which owns several liners apart from the *Queen Elizabeth II*. The Austrian Rudolf Sodamin is chef de cuisine and chief pastry chef. He has attracted the notice of many restaurants in Austria, France, Switzerland, and the United States. In New York he worked in the famous Waldorf Astoria.

Jonathan Wicks has worked in several London restaurants, among them the Mayfair Intercontinental, Grosvenor House in Park Lane, and the *Méridien* in Piccadilly. In 1987 he was appointed chef de cuisine of the *Queen Elizabeth II*.

Roger Souvereyns

born December 2, 1938

Restaurant: **Scholteshof**
Address: Kermstraat, 130
3512 Stevoort-Hasselt, Belgium
Tel. (0)11 25 02 02; Fax (0)11 25 43 28

Since 1983, Roger Souvereyns has presided over the *Scholteshof*. This 18th-century farmstead has a large vegetable garden which used to be tended by his friend and gardener Clément, and which is the source of the wonderful fresh fruit and vegetables used in his cooking. Roger Souvereyns has two Michelin stars, four red chef's hats in Gault-Millau (19.5), and 95/100 in the Belgian restaurant guide Henri Lemaire. A member of Relais et Châteaux, Relais Gourmands and Traditions et Qualité, he is a collector of antiques and old pictures. He also loves opera, and enjoys swimming and cycling.

Pedro Subijana

born November 5, 1948

Restaurant: **Akelaré**
Address: 56, Paseo del Padre Orcolaga
20008 San Sebastian, Spain
Tel. (9)43 21 20 52; Fax (9)43 21 92 68

Since 1981, Pedro Subijana has had his own restaurant overlooking the Bay of Biscay. Awarded two stars in Michelin and 9/10 in Gourmetour, he was named "Best Cook in Spain" in 1982. Subijana underwent a traditional training at the college of hotel management in Madrid and at Euromar college in Zarauz, and became a cooking teacher in 1970. In 1986 he became Commissioner General of the European Association of Chefs, whose headquarters is in Brussels. He presents food programs on Basque Television and on Tele-Madrid. Pedro Subijana loves music and the movies.

Émile Tabourdiau

born November 25, 1943

Restaurant **Le Bristol**
Address: 112, rue du Faubourg Saint-Honoré
75008 Paris, France
Tel. (0)1 53 43 43 00; Fax (0)1 53 43 43 01

Since 1964, Émile Tabourdiau has worked only in the most famous of restaurants: First at *Ledoyen*, then at *La Grande Cascade*, and finally, since 1980, at *Le Bristol*, located in the immediate vicinity of the Élysée Palace and boasting magnificent large gardens. A former pupil of Auguste Escoffier, Émile Tabourdiau is a member of the "Culinary Academy of France", and was the winner of the Prosper Montagné prize in 1970 as well as Meilleur Ouvrier de France in 1976. He restaurant has one Michelin star. In his spare time he loves painting, and enjoys playing tennis and spending time in his garden.

Dominique Toulousy

born August 19, 1952

Restaurant: **Les Jardins de l'Opéra**
Address: 1, place du Capitole
31000 Toulouse, France
Tel. (0)5 61 23 07 76; Fax (0)5 61 23 63 00

Dominique Toulousy has only been resident in Toulouse since 1984. Hanging out his shingle on the Place du Capitole, he reaped accolades by the dozen: "Golden Key of Gastronomy" (1986), three red chef's hats in Gault-Millau (18) and two Michelin stars, as well as the title of Meilleur Ouvrier de France (1993). Before this, he had his first successes in Gers, a region known for its generous cuisine. Dominique Toulousy is a member of the "Young Restauranteurs of Europe", the Prosper Montagné association, Eurotoques, and Traditions et Qualité. He enjoys poring over old cookbooks and loves gardening, tennis and swimming.

Gilles Tournadre

born June 29, 1955

Restaurant: **Gill**
Address: 8 & 9, quai de la Bourse
76000 Rouen, France
Tel. (0)2 35 71 16 14; Fax (0)2 35 71 96 91

Even a Norman can occasionally be persuaded to leave his native region in order to learn his craft: Gilles Tournadre started out his career at *Lucas Carton*, followed by the *Auberge des Templiers* of the Bézards and *Taillevent*, before finally winding up – on his own two feet – in Bayeux, and lastly in 1984, back in his home town. His career successes have justified all these changes: the young gastronome can boast two Michelin stars and three red chef's hats (17 points) for his restaurant right near Rouen cathedral. A member of the "Young Restauranteurs of Europe", this enthusiastic sportsman loves judo, golf and motor sports, and is also a passionate conservationist.

José Tourneur

born January 4, 1940

Restaurant: **Des 3 Couleurs**
Address: 453, avenue de Tervuren
1150 Brussels, Belgium
Tel. (0)2 770 3321; Fax (0)2 770 8045

The three colors which José Tourneur chose in 1979 as the logo and name of his restaurant are those of the Belgian national flag. The restaurant, which is wholly dedicated to Belgian cuisine, has one Michelin star and was awarded 88/100 in the Belgian restaurant guide Henri Lemaire. A self-taught cook, Tourneur gained further experience in Brussels and Nice, won the Prosper Montagné prize in 1969, and was chef de cuisine at the Brussels *Carlton* from 1969–79. He is also a member of the "Order of the 33 Masterchefs of Belgium", the "Culinary Academy of France", and the "Vatel Club". His other interests all revolve around the sea: he loves ships, and enjoys fishing and waterskiing.

Luisa Valazza

born December 20, 1950

Restaurant: **Al Sorriso**
Address: Via Roma, 18
28018 Soriso, Italy
Tel. (0)322 98 32 28; Fax (0)322 98 33 28

Taking their cue from the name of the restaurant which she and her husband Angelo have run since 1981 in their home town in the Piedmont region, the food critics have all "smiled" on Luisa Valazza, awarding Al Sorriso two Michelin stars, four chef's hats in Espresso/Gault-Millau (19.2), one sun in Veronelli and 90/100 in Gambero Rosso. Our chef, who is also a member of the Le Soste chain, remains modest in the midst of this avalanche of praise, carefully cooking the recipes she has amassed since 1971 in the *Europa* in Borgomanero. Luisa Valazza is passionately interested in art, especially painting and literature. A keen museum-goer, she is also an enthusiastic practitioner of winter sports.

Guy Van Cauteren

born May 8, 1950

Restaurant: **T'Laurierblad**
Address: Dorp, 4
9290 Berlare, Belgium
Tel. (0)52 42 48 01; Fax (0)52 42 59 97

Before opening his restaurant *T'Laurierblad* ("The Bay leaf") in 1979, Guy Van Cauteren was taught by some of France's most outstanding chefs: Alain Senderens at *Archestrate* in Paris, and the Allégriers at *Lucas Carton* (1972–4). He then spent several years cooking at the French Embassy in Brussels (1974–9). Since then, he has acquired two Michelin stars, three red chef's hats in Gault-Millau (17) and 89/100 in the Belgian restaurant guide Henri Lemaire. In addition, he was the fortunate recipient of the bronze Bocuse in 1993, and holds the title of Maître Cuisinier de Belgique. Guy Van Cauteren collects old books and enjoys traveling. In his spare time, he relaxes by cycling.

Freddy Van Decasserie

born October 10, 1943

Restaurant: **La Villa Lorraine**
Address: 75, avenue du Vivier d'Oie
1180 Brussels, Belgium
Tel. (0)2 374 3163; Fax (0)2 372 0195

Freddy Van Decasserie started off at *La Villa Lorraine* in 1963 as a kitchen boy and worked his way up the hierarchy until finally becoming head chef and the recipient of numerous awards: two Michelin stars, three red chef's hats in Gault-Millau (18), three stars in Bottin Gourmand and 92/100 in Henri Lemaire. He is a Maître Cuisinier de Belgique and a member of the "Culinary Academy of France" and Traditions et Qualité. In his spare time, he stays fit by being a "training partner" to the racing cyclist Eddy Merckx . He also swims and goes to the occasional soccer match.

Geert Van Hecke

born July 20, 1956

Restaurant: **De Karmeliet**
Address: Langestraat, 19
8000 Bruges, Belgium
Tel. (0)50 33 82 59; Fax (0)50 33 10 11

Geert Van Hecke was introduced to his craft by Freddy Van Decasserie at the *Villa Lorraine* in 1977, then served a stint with Alain Chapel at the famous *Cravache d'Or* in Brussels, finally opening his own restaurant in a renowned historic house in the heart of Bruges, the "Venice of the North". To date, his cooking has earned him two Michelin stars, three stars in the Bottin Gourmand, three red chef's hats in Gault-Millau (18) and 92/100 in Henri Lemaire. A winner of the "Best Chef in Belgium" award, he is also a member of Traditions et Qualité. It was not sheer coincidence which led him to settle in Bruges, a well preserved medieval town and popular tourist destination, as he is interested in art and enjoys visiting museums.

Gérard Vié

born April 11, 1943

Restaurant: **Les Trois Marches (Trianon Palace)**
Address: 1 boulevard de la Reine
78000 Versailles, France
Tel. (0)1 39 50 13 21; Fax (0)1 30 21 01 25

The incomparable chef of the *Trois Marches* (since 1970) started his career at the tender age of 13 at *Lapérouse*. Then followed stints at *Lucas Carton* and the *Plaza-Athénée* in Paris and *Crillon Tower's* in London, as well as three years with the *Compagnie des Wagons-Lits* (1967–70). Today, Gérard Vié can boast two Michelin stars and three red chef's hats (18). Recipient of the "Silver Table" award from Gault-Millau in 1984, he was presented with the "Golden Key of Gastronomy" in 1993. An enthusiastic fan of the theater, opera and movies, he collects paintings and is a Chevalier des Arts et Lettres. He also loves hiking and swimming.

Jean-Pierre Vigato

born March 20, 1952

Restaurant: **Apicius**
Address: 122, avenue de Villiers
75017 Paris, France
Tel. (0)1 43 80 19 66; Fax (0)1 44 40 09 57

Jean Pierre Vigato started off as a cellarman and served an apprenticeship in various restaurants before his first major successes at *Grandgousier* in Paris from 1980–3. In 1984 he set up on his own, opening *Apicius* in his native Paris. The restaurant, named after a famous Roman epicure, was awarded its first Michelin star in 1985, and its second two years later. It also boasts three red chef's hats in Gault-Millau (18). A member of Relais Gourmands, Jean-Pierre Vigato was Gault-Millau "Best Chef of the Year" in 1988, and chef at the French Pavillion at the 1992 World's Fair in Seville, Spain.

Heinz Winkler

born July 17, 1949

Restaurant: **Residenz Heinz Winkler**
Address: Kirchplatz 1,
83229 Aschau im Chiemgau, Germany
Tel. (0)8052 17990; Fax (0)8052 179 966

At only 31 years of age, Heinz Winkler already boasted three Michelin stars: how on earth did he do it? Perhaps by training at the *Victoria* in Interlaken, under Paul Bocuse, and at *Tantris* in Munich, before opening the *Residenz Heinz Winkler* in 1991. To crown it all, this gastronome has three white chef's hats (18) and was "Chef of the Year" in 1979 as well as "Restauranteur of the Year" in 1994 in Gault-Millau. Heinz Winkler is a member of Relais et Châteaux, Relais Gourmands, Traditions et Qualité, and the Italian chain Le Soste. He enjoys poring over old cookbooks, playing golf and skiing.

Harald Wohlfahrt

born November 7, 1955

Restaurant: **Schwarzwaldstube**
Address: Tonbachstrasse 237,
72270 Baiersbronn, Germany
Tel. (0)7442 49 26 65; Fax (0)7442 49 26 92

Harald Wohlfahrt started work at the *Schwarzwaldstube*, the restaurant of the Hotel *Trauben-Tonbach* in the heart of the Black Forest, in 1976, and has been chef there since 1980. He learned his trade at *Stahlbad* in Baden-Baden and *Tantris* in Munich. Voted "Chef of the Year" in 1991 by Gault-Millau, he currently boasts three Michelin stars and four red chef's hats (19.5). He is also a member of Relais Gourmands and Traditions et Qualité. While his main interests, unsurprisingly, are eating- and cooking traditions, Harald Wohlfahrt is also an outstanding athlete, with swimming, soccer and cycling being his favorite sports.

Armando Zanetti

born December 11, 1926

Restaurant: **Vecchia Lanterna**
Address: Corso Re Umberto, 21
10128 Turin, Italy
Tel. (0)11 53 70 47; Fax (0)11 53 03 91

A native Venetian, Armando Zanetti ran the *Rosa d'Oro* in Turin from 1955–69 before opening the evocatively named *Vecchia Lanterna* ("Old Lantern") restaurant in the same city in 1970. Today, our chef, who devotes himself chiefly to the traditional cuisine of his native country, proudly boasts two Michelin stars and four chef's hats in Espresso/Gault-Millau (19.2/20). In his spare time, Armando Zanetti tirelessly researches European cuisine of bygone eras. He derives special pleasure from trying new dishes, both his own and those of his fellow chefs.

Alberto Zuluaga

born March 31, 1960

Restaurant: **Lopez de Haro y Club Nautico**
Address: Obispo Orueta, 2
48009 Bilbao, Spain
Tel. (9)4 423 5500; Fax (9)4 423 4500

As a Basque from the Spanish province of Vizcaya on the Bay of Biscay, Alberto Zuluaga is especially proud to be able to exercise his profession in the true capital of his native province. He has been chef of the five-star luxury restaurant *Club Nautico* in the banking district of Bilbao since 1991. Before this, from 1987–91, he cultivated his love of Basque cuisine and culinary traditions at the *Bermeo* in the same city, earning the title of "Best Cook in Euzkadi" (the Basque Country) in 1988. It goes without saying that our chef enjoys playing Basque boules in his spare time, but he also likes car racing. He is also an enthusiastic mushroom hunter when time allows.

Glossary

ADD LIQUID: adding liquid such as wine or broth to the contents in the frying pan to loosen them from the base of the pan.

ADJUST SEASONING TO TASTE: seasoning a dish towards the end of preparation, or seasoning its components as you complete their preparation, with salt, pepper, spices, or herbs according to taste rather than measurement.

AÏOLI: a Provençal garlic mayonnaise (in French, *ail* meants garlic) traditionally served with steamed fish, hard-boiled eggs, or vegetables, such as crudités.

AL DENTE: to keep pasta or vegetables from being overcooked, and thus render them too soft to resist slightly a diner's bite, Italians instruct they be cooked "to the tooth."

AMERICAN SAUCE: a sauce made with roasted root vegetables and crushed lobster shells; the sauce is flambéd with brandy, white wine is added, and it is finally whisked with butter. It is traditionally served with fish and shellfish.

ASPIC: a flavored jelly, often made from clarified meat juices (but also from vegetables or fish) that sets to form a clear or semi-clear elastic mixture, prepared with pectin or gelatin. Used as a base for molded dishes as well as a garnish – served, for example, as a cubed accompaniment next to a terrine that is based on the same aspic.

BAIN-MARIE: an extremely delicate method of cooking ingredients, such as custards or sauces, that will turn if subjected to a sudden change in temperature. A pot, bowl, or pan of food is placed in a larger pot that is filled with warm water (sometimes boiling, sometimes at a lower temperature); the combination is then cooked in an oven or on the stove.

BAKE AU GRATIN: to sprinkle cooked dishes with bread crumbs, cheese, or pats of butter and bake at high heat, allowing a crust to form.

BASTE: to moisten roast meat (such as roast beef, roast duck, suckling pig, roast turkey, etc.) with the meat's own juices to prevent the meat from drying out while in the oven. Basting is also done to encourage skin to become crispy or a crust to build up.

BÉCHAMEL SAUCE: one of the French "mother sauces," made with flour, butter, and milk (the proportions determine its consistency, which may vary), blended into a creamy sauce and served hot.

BIND IN A ROUX: to bind (or thicken) sauces or bind vegetables together in a heated mixture of equal amounts of flour and butter.

BLANCH: a technique with two purposes: the first is to cook ingredients, particularly vegetables, in boiling water for just a moment to either soften a harsh flavor or scent, or kill germs or enzymes. The second is to pour boiling water over fruit, vegetables, or nuts to facilitate peeling or shelling; alternately, they may be dipped in the boiling water for a moment (as in blanching tomatoes).

BLINI: the traditional small Russian pancakes made with buckwheat flour, usually served with soured cream, caviar or smoked salmon.

BOUQUET GARNI: a bunch of herbs that are tied together and used for seasoning soups, casseroles, etc. The traditional bundle consists principally of thyme, bay leaf, and parsley, but rosemary, marjoram, lovage, fennel, leek, or celery might also be used, depending on the recipe and the region.

BRAISE: a technique (in the oven or on the stove) of cooking vegetables or meat, although it may also be used with certain kinds of fruit. The ingredients are first browned in butter, oil, or lard, then a small amount of liquid (such as water, broth, stock, or wine) is added, the pan is tightly covered, and the ingredients are slowly cooked. The ingredients thus cook in fat, liquid and vapor, with tender, flavorful results.

BREAD: to roll meat, poultry, vegetables, or fish in a mixture of flour, eggs, and bread crumbs, for subsequently frying or deep-frying.

BRIEFLY FRY: to fry meat or other ingredients in a little hot fat, just until brown.

BROTH: a spiced cooking broth, which is the result of having cooked meat, fish, or vegetables in water; the cooking ingredients impart their flavor into the water and turn it into stock that can then be used for cooking other ingredients.

BROWN: to cook briefly over a high or medium-high heat, usually in a buttered or oiled frying pan on top of the stove. Often used to cook a tender piece of meat or a slice of bacon, or thin slices of vegetables such as potatoes; the method browns the exterior but enables the interior to remain moist.

BRUNOISE: a mélange or mixture of vegetables that have been either shredded, grated, or diced finely, and are then slowly cooked in butter, to be used primarily to flavor sauces or soups.

CARPACCIO: a classic Italian dish with a legendary history (see *carpaccio* recipes throughout this volume), in which extremely thin slices of filleted, raw meat (usually beef) are dressed with oil and lemon juice, a mayonnaise or mustard dressing, or with an olive oil vinaigrette, and served as an appetizer. The term has also come to include types of fish and shellfish.

CARVE: to slice meat, poultry or fish, or to cut these for presentation, traditionally in front of the dining guests. A large and very sharp knife and a chopping board are required for carving.

CHANTILLY: part of the French culinary vocabulary, meaning dishes (*à la chantilly*), from sweet puddings to savory appetizers, that are served with or mixed with whipped cream. The dessert Chantilly cream is a sweetened whipped cream, often flavored with a liqueur or vanilla extract.

CHARLOTTE: A charlotte is multi-layered; a form begins with spongecake, finger biscuits (ladyfingers), waffle, or buttered bread base, topped with layers of either a pudding of pureed fruit, or whipped cream or custard.

CHARTREUSE: a pie made with chopped meat, vegetables and bacon, cooked in a bain-marie, and served cold. There is also a liqueur of the same name, that comes in green or yellow varieties and was originally developed by the monks of La Grance Chartreuse in France.

CLARIFY: to make a cloudy liquid, such as a soup or sauce, clear by stirring in slightly whisked egg white, carefully heating, cooling, and, finally, straining through a seive or cheesecloth; the egg whites attract the sediment.

CLARIFIED BUTTER: butter that is slowly melted, causing it to divide into milky solids at the bottom of the pan and clear liquid on the surface. The top is skimmed of any foam, and the clear liquid is poured off to be used in cooking.

COCKLES: molluscs of the family *cardium*, who have striped and ribbed brown-and-white (to varying degrees) shells. Cockles are at home in the flat coastal waters of the Atlantic and the Mediterranean. Wash thoroughly to clean them of substantial amounts of sand, and serve raw with lemon juice, fried, or steamed.

CONSOMMÉ: a meat or vegetable broth, cooked and reduced for a long time and finally clarified until it is translucent. Served cold or hot, and often used as the base for a stock or soup.

CORAL: the roe of crustaceans, from lobsters to scallops, so named because, when cooked, it turns a salmon-pink color that resembles the color of some ocean coral; regarded by gourmets as a particular delicacy.

CROUTONS: roasted or toasted diced bread, used to garnish soups, baked dishes or salads; often browned in garlic, herbs, or spices.

CRUDITÉS: a French term for raw vegetables, usually cut into strips, served as an appetizer with dips, a cold dressing, or sauce.

CUSTARD: sauce for puddings made with confectioners' sugar, an egg yolk, milk, and a pinch of salt, rounded off with cream. Often cooked in a bain-marie.

DEEP-FRY: to cook (usually until crisp and brown) ingredients, usually vegetables, fish, or meat, by immersing them in extremely hot oil or other fat. The exterior crust formed seals in the food's flavors and moisture.

DIJONNAISE: French term for dishes prepared with light Dijon mustard, a special, creamy kind of mustard made with mustard grains soaked in sour, fermented juice of unripe grapes, and hailing originally from Dijon, France. A mayonnaise with mustard flavor, served with cold meat, is also called a Dijonnaise.

FLAMBÉ: though often a technique of presentation intended to impart a sense of drama to a dish – the word is French for "flaming" – it may also be a step during the cooking process. Either way, it involves pouring liquor on top of foods still cooking and lighting the alcohol to better render the food's aroma.

FOLD IN: to carefully mix ingredients without vigorous stirring, as in folding roe into a cream sauce, or a warm ingredient into a cool one.

GALANTINE: a classic French layered dish, often consisting of a spicy pie that is cooked rolled in cloth or thin strips of meat, or in an appropriate form.

TO GARNISH: an art that completes the plate; to arrange accompaniments decoratively around the main part of a dish, often referring back to the dish's ingredients or flavorings.

GAZPACHO: a cold vegetable soup of Spanish origin traditionally made with ripe tomatoes, red peppers, cucumber, olive oil, garlic and bread crust.

GLAZE: to glaze dishes with their own juices, aspic, or sugar.

GRILL: a method of cooking that retains a certain freshness in the food, either on wood or charcoal over a grill.

HOISIN SAUCE: a spicy reddish-brown sauce from China made from fermented soy beans, flour, salt, sugar, and raw rice. Its natural coloring lends visual depth to many Chinese dishes.

JELLY: (also see aspic) clear or semi-clear elastic mixture, prepared with pectin or gelatin; also: meat juices set to form a jelly.

JULIENNE: to cut vegetables (often raw) into thin strips often about matchstick size; some chefs prefer to julienne by hand, some use a slicer.

LANGOUSTINE: a French term for a crustacean that is wholly different from either a prawn, a crayfish, or a shrimp. Langoustines have pink or pale-red bodies and elongated, but pronounced front claws; their flavor is both sweet and subtle, and lends them well to dishes such as terrines. Unfortunately, langoustines can not survive for too long out of water, and so are often sold cooked in regions far from the coast.

LARD: to lace or wrap lean meat with strips of bacon, truffle slices, or cloves of garlic to prevent it from drying out, and to impart additional flavors.

MARINATE: a technique known in virtually every cuisine in which fish, meat, poultry, vegetables, or even fruit are coated with a mixture of, usually, oil, vinegar, and lemon juice flavored with herbs and spices. As the food absorbs the flavors of the marinade, it also tenderizes, thus reducing cooking time, and in some cases even replacing the cooking process.

MOUSSE: a French word for foam. A mousse is an airy yet substantial sweet or savory dish that owes its soft, delicate and fluffy structure to egg whites that have been whisked until stiff, or whipped cream. To further bind a mousse, gelatin may be added as well.

PARFAIT: in French, the word means perfect or complete; a cold dish made with a delicate stuffing, bound with gelatin or egg white, filled into forms and inverted after chilling. A sweet parfait is a chilled pudding, usually composed of ice cream, jelly, egg cream, a lacing of syrup or liqueur, and cream, served in a special high glass.

PERSILLADE: from the French word for parsley; a mixture of finely chopped parsley and garlic or of thin strips of cold beef and vinegar, oil, and plenty of parsley.

PHYLLO DOUGH: a dough made with sticky flour (wheat), water, and oil (fat) that is rolled out paper-thin, cut into slices, brushed with oil, and stacked, often between layers of wax paper. Used frequently in the Near East, Turkey, Greece, Austria, and Hungary. It is similar to puff pastry, which may be used instead.

POACH: to cook ingredients by immersing them in a small amount of liquid over low heat, often used for fish or dumplings.

PRAWN: an often-confusing term, sometimes used to describe any large shrimp, or to refer to langoustines (see langoustines), or to refer to freshwater shrimps. However, prawns in the strictest sense of the word are both salt and fresh water dwellers, migrating from one to the other to spawn. They are larger than shrimps and have longer legs and narrower bodies. King prawns may also be marketed as jumbo shrimps, particularly in the United States.

PUREE: to work soft ingredients into a smooth and even mixture, usually using either a blender or a food processor.

REDUCE: to cook a sauce or gravy for so long that its liquid content evaporates, resulting in a distilled, thick, and more intensely aromatic sauce.

RÉMOULADE: a sauce; essentially an herb mayonnaise and mustard blend seasoned with chopped tarragon, chervil, parsley, gherkin pickles, and capers. It is available in some shops as a ready-made product, and often accompanies cold meat, fish, and crustaceans.

RINSE WITH COLD WATER: a technique used to arrest the cooking process immediately, rather than let a just-cooked ingredient keep cooking in its absorbed heat. Invaluable for keeping vegetables crisp and green, and pasta al dente.

ROAST: often a misunderstood term, to roast something simply means to cook it in the oven uncovered, that is to say in dry heat, until brown and crisp. Nuts and kernels become more aromatic through roasting; tender pieces of meat or vegetables benefit from it as well.

SAFFRON: spice harvested from the stamen of the saffron flower (a kind of purple crocus). As the tiny dust threads containing the saffron powder can only be picked by hand it is the world's most expensive spice. Fortunately, only extremely small amounts are required to add its pungent flavoring or unique yellow color to, for instance, fish and rice dishes, curries and puddings.

SAUTÉ: to fry ingredients briefly over direct heat in a little butter or oil until slightly brown.

SCALLOPS: a mollusc with a characteristic flat shell. It moves about with the shell open, using a large muscle; that muscle is the part that is consumed, along with the orange coral. Scallops are usually prepared and served in their shell, and come in two basic types: the small, delicately flavored bay scallop, and the larger, slightly stronger-flavored sea scallop.

SCOOP: a technique of scooping out dumplings, balls and similar shapes with a specially fashioned scoop or a spoon, sometimes for further blanching.

SCORE: to make incision on both sides of a piece of meat or fish for decorative reasons, also useful for preventing food from splitting and achieving even cooking on all surfaces.

SHRIMP: the most popular crustacean in the United States is actually a grouping of hundreds of sub-species. Essentially, a shrimp is a small crustacean without claws or shears, with slim legs and a large, plump body. The color varies according to species, but most turn orange-red when cooked. Shrimp exist in cold and warm waters and in fresh water as well as in sea water. They form the basis for a variety of dishes in many countries, and range in size from colossal to miniature.

SIMMER: to cook ingredients in liquid over a low heat to prevent the liquid from boiling, or to reduce the heat from ingredients that have reached a boil to a slower rate of cooking.

SKIM: to remove the fat floating on the surface of a liquid (usually soups or sauces) with a skimming spoon or by straining the liquid; sometimes also used when clarifying sauces or butter.

SOUFFLÉ: a light, airy dish based on eggs from the French term for inflating. Can be sweet or savory, served hot (which may require some delicate handling) or cold. The airy and fluffy structure is achieved by folding whisked egg whites that are very stiff into a warm sauce or puree. Often cooked in a special round and straight-sided soufflé dish.

STEAM: a technique that has gained in popularity in the past decade or two. To steam food is to cook it over vapor rising from boiling stock or liquid, using a steamer equipped with a rack, or in multi-layered metal or bamboo steam pots. Also used to describe the process of cooking ingredients in their own juices, with perhaps a very small amount of liquid or fat added.

STOCK: the juices produced by meat, poultry, vegetables, or fish during cooking, used to form the base of sauces. Can be purchased ready-made, or made far in advance and kept chilled or frozen until ready to use.

STRAIN: to pass ingredients (mostly liquid) through a sieve; a technique often used for clarifying sauces and stocks.

STUFFING: a mixture of chopped meat or fish with herbs and spices for filling pies or poultry. Rice, vegetables, rice, bread crumbs, or eggs mixed with meat or entrails are also used for stuffing.

SWEAT: to cook vegetables, in particular onions, or flour, over a low heat in fat without allowing them to turn brown, but only until they soften and begin to glisten, as if sweating.

TARTARE: traditionally, a dish comprised of raw ground beef prepared with finely chopped onions, gherkins, capers or parsley, pepper and salt; increasingly, chefs are discovering other ingredients to present as tartares, such as fish.

TERRINE: a dish made with finely chopped meat, poultry, game, fish, or vegetables (or a combination of any of these), cooked in a deep dish or form with straight walls (also called a terrine, or a terrine form). Terrines are usually served cold, and are often bound in aspic.

GARNISH: the decoration of a dish, considered a crucial aspect in many cuisines; also used to refer to ingredients added to a soup or sauce, such as cream or chopped onions in soup, or chopped herbs in a sauce.

THICKEN: to thicken or bind simmering sauces by stirring in egg yolk and cream, milk, or butter.

TRUFFLES: this delicacy actually includes quite a few varieties, the most famous of which is the black truffle. Essentially, a truffle is a large wild edible mushroom with a bulbous stem and a fleshy red-brown cap, but its sublime flavor and the effort involved in harvesting it have helped to make it one of the most luxurious ingredients used in cooking. It is found by truffle dogs or pigs in the fall, under oak and chestnut trees.

VELOUTÉ: another of the "mother sauces" from French cuisine, so named for its velvety consistency (in French, velours means velvet). This thick, white sauce is made with butter, flour, veal or chicken stock, and seasoned with salt and pepper. Available ready-made.

VINAIGRETTE: a salad dressing based on the perennial combination of vinegar and oil, often laced with herbs, deepened with mustard, and finally seasoned with salt and pepper.

ZABAGLIONE: this light, airy, foamy sauce is made with egg yolk, sugar and white wine or Champagne. Served hot or cold with puddings, and also called sabayon in France.

Index